"A God of Justice?"

# "A God of Justice?"

*The Problem of Evil in*
*Twentieth-Century Black Literature*

Qiana J. Whitted

University of Virginia Press
*Charlottesville and London*

University of Virginia Press
© 2009 by the Rector and Visitors of the University of Virginia
All rights reserved
Printed in the United States of America on acid-free paper

*First published 2009*

9 8 7 6 5 4 3 2 1

Library of Congress Cataloging-in-Publication Data

Whitted, Qiana J., 1974–
 "A god of justice?" : the problem of evil in twentieth-century Black literature /
Qiana J. Whitted.
  p.  cm.
 Includes bibliographical references (p. ) and index.
 ISBN 978-0-8139-2796-1 (alk. paper) — ISBN 978-0-8139-2797-8 (pbk. : alk. paper)
 1. American literature—African American authors—History and criticism. 2. American
literature—20th century—History and criticism. 3. Religion in literature. 4. Justice in
literature. 5. Evil in literature. 6. African Americans—Intellectual life—20th century.
7. Literature and society—United States—History—20th century. I. Title.
 PS153.N5W455 2009
 820.9′382—dc22

                                                                              2008038361

For Naima,

*My Love Supreme*

You wouldn't think that a person who was born with God in the house would ever have any questions to ask on the subject. But as early as I can remember, I was questing and seeking.

—ZORA NEALE HURSTON, *Dust Tracks on a Road*

# CONTENTS

# PREFACE

IN JANUARY 2003, the U.S. Senate released the full transcript of Langston Hughes's 1953 closed-door testimony before Senator Joseph McCarthy's Permanent Subcommittee on Investigations, giving the public the opportunity to become reacquainted with Hughes's most politically radical verse.[1] The African American poet was interrogated about his writings from the 1930s and 1940s that openly supported the ideology of the Left—among them, the poems "Good Morning, Revolution," "Ballad to Lenin," and "One More 'S' in the U.S.A.," the play *Scottsboro, Limited,* and Hughes's columns from the *Chicago Defender*. One work, however, that subjected Hughes to particularly intense and prolonged questioning from the committee was the lyric poem "Goodbye, Christ." It begins:

> Listen, Christ,
> You did alright in your day, I reckon—
> But that day's gone now.
> They ghosted you up a swell story, too,
> Called it Bible—
> But it's dead now,
> The popes and the preachers've
> Made too much money from it.

(lines 1–8)

It was inevitable that this protest poem would be summoned forth during Hughes's interrogation before the Senate. "Goodbye, Christ" had haunted its creator since the poem first appeared in the international publication *Negro Worker* in 1932.[2] To be sure, Hughes's writings were known to generate controversy throughout his career, especially among black elites who felt that his creative engagements with folk culture and politics were inappropriate avenues of black representation. And while many of his poems, fictional works, and plays feature favorable images of religious worship, Hughes proudly published others that denounced the duplicitous Christian faith of a society hampered by race and class inequality. Prior to the publication of "Goodbye, Christ," for example, he responded to the conviction of

xi

the Scottsboro Nine with the poem "Christ in Alabama" (1931) and nimbly deflected criticisms about the poem's opening declaration that "Christ is a nigger,/Beaten and black" (lines 1–2).[3]

But it was Hughes's farewell to Christ that would be called upon again and again by outraged readers to malign his moral character and artistic ability. In the 1930s, black preachers and intellectuals debated its provocative sentiments on the editorial pages of the *Pittsburgh Courier,* while pressure from protesters who redistributed the poem in the 1940s would lead civic groups, churches, and universities to ban Hughes from speaking to their organizations.[4] Did the verses fictionalize Hughes's own religious views, they wanted to know? Had months spent touring the Soviet Union in the 1930s transformed the poet who wrote "Feet o' Jesus" into an atheist and a Marxist?

These kinds of concerns generally made Hughes uneasy in spite of the support he received from friends and fellow writers like Arna Bontemps and Melvin B. Tolson. He attempted to resolve the matter in a 1941 essay in which he bluntly stated: "'Goodbye, Christ' does not represent my personal viewpoint" ("Concerning," 209). But by directing the poem's complaints specifically against living persons—most notably, the evangelist Aimee McPherson—Hughes found his reputation and his finances easily targeted by picket signs denouncing the poet as an "atheistic Red" ("Social Poet," 211). In his two-volume biography of Hughes, Arnold Rampersad uses the furor over the poem to mark critical moments of disappointment and hardship, revealing, with each crisis, a poet besieged by "'lots of wires,' a 'Mountain of mail,' and newspaper 'Clippings by [the] ton'" on the subject (*Hughes,* 2: 4). Six years after writing "Concerning 'Goodbye, Christ,'" Hughes offered a wry account of his protesters' antics in "My Adventures as a Social Poet" (1947). Often in these public responses as well as in his private correspondence, Hughes implores his critics to reflect upon his entire body of work and to consider how his experience as a black man in America shapes his social, political, and religious outlook. In other instances, a more guarded Hughes insists on his right to privacy by shifting conversation away from his personal opinions and reframing the debate around his creative process and technique as a writer.

All of these approaches proved to be rather frustrating for people like Senator Everett Dirksen of Illinois, who demanded simple, clear explanations that would confirm their suspicions. Consider the following exchange from the 1953 hearings:

*Senator Dirksen:* Do you know whether this poem was reprinted in quantities
  and used as propaganda leaflets by the Communist party?
*Mr. Hughes:* No, sir, it was not. It was reprinted in quantities as far as I know,
  and used as a propaganda leaflet by the organizations of Gerald L. K. Smith
  and the organization of extreme anti-Negro forces in our country, and I
  have attempted to recall that poem. I have denied permission for its publication over the years. I have explained the poem for twenty-two years,
  I believe, or twenty years, in my writings in the press, and my talks as
  being a satirical poem, which I think a great pity that anyone should think
  of the Christian religion in those terms, and great pity that sometimes
  we have permitted the church to be disgraced by people who have used it
  as a racketeering force. The poem is merely the story of racketeering in
  religion and misuse of religion as might have been seen through the eyes
  at that time of a young Soviet citizen who felt very cocky and said to the
  whole world, "See what people do for religion. We don't do that." I write
  a character piece sometimes as in a play. I sometimes have in a play a villain. I do not believe in that villain myself.
*Senator Dirksen:* Do you think that any twelve-year-old boy could misunder-
  stand that language, "Goodbye Christ, beat it away from here now"?
*Mr. Hughes:* You cannot take one line.
*Senator Dirksen:* We will read all of it.
*Mr. Hughes:* If you read the twelve-year-old the whole poem, I hope he would
  be shocked into thinking about the real things of religion, because with
  some of my poems that is what I have tried to do, to shock people into
  thinking and finding the real meaning themselves. Certainly I have written many religious poems, many poems about Christ, and prayers and
  my own feeling is not what I believe you seem to think that poem as
  meaning.
*Senator Dirksen:* I do not want to be captious about it, and I want to be entirely
  fair, but it seems to me that this could mean only one thing to the person
  who read it.
*Mr. Hughes:* I am sorry. There [are] a thousand interpretations of Shakespeare's
  Sonata. (U.S. Senate, *Testimony*, 981–82)

What emerges from the debate over Hughes's own sonata are invigorating conversations about interpretive freedom and the consequences of dissent in communities of faith. Critical questions surface, in particular, about
how religious ideas, symbols, and language are read and regulated in black
creative expression. Is there room for a work such as "Goodbye, Christ"
in the controlling narrative of the religious life and literary imagination
of African American people? And should Hughes's own ambivalence over

legitimizing the grievances of the "villain" compel us—as readers, teachers, and academic scholars—to reconsider how deep-rooted cultural assumptions about spiritual belief can sometimes hinder more dynamic and multidimensional articulations of black experience?

The transcribed exchange between Hughes and the Senate subcommittee offers an instructive, if not cautionary, vantage point from which to address these questions. Consider, for instance, how Hughes reminds the subcommittee in his prepared statement that, "in my book of poems, *Shakespeare in Harlem*, there is a poem called "Ku Klux" in which a Klansman speaks. But I am not a Klansman. In *The Weary Blues* there is a poem called "Mother to Son" in which an aged mother speaks. But I am not an aged mother" (Rampersad, *Hughes*, 2: 214). With the "I" of "Goodbye, Christ," Hughes begins to move away from the black cultural nationalism of the New Negro Renaissance (with which he did self-identify) and instead, as Anthony Dawahare argues, he foregrounds class inequalities shared by poor blacks and whites (*Nationalism*, 92–110). When discussing the poem in 1941, Hughes explains: "The *I* which I pictured was the newly liberated peasant of the state collectives I had seen in Russia merged with those American Negro workers of the depression period who believed in the Soviet dream and the hope it held out for a solution of their racial and economic difficulties" ("Concerning," 208).

Despite the poet's attempts to provide his readers with a primer in the fundamentals of literary analysis and contextualization, Senator Dirksen continued to probe the connection between Hughes's work and his personal politics in the 1953 hearing.

> *Senator Dirksen:* May I say, sir, from my familiarity with the Negro people for a long time that they are innately a very devout and religious people—this is the first paragraph of the poem [recites the first stanza from "Goodbye, Christ"]. Do you think that Book is dead?"
>
> *Mr. Hughes:* No, sir, I do not. That poem, like that handbill, is an ironical and satirical poem.
>
> *Senator Dirksen:* It was not so accepted, I fancy, by the American people.
>
> *Mr. Hughes:* It was accepted by a large portion of them and some ministers and bishops understood the poem and defended it.
>
> *Senator Dirksen:* I know many who accepted the words for what they seem to convey.
>
> *Mr. Hughes:* That is exactly what I meant to say in answer to the other gentleman's question, that poetry may mean many things to many people. (980–81)

This dialogue offers a glimpse into the way Hughes's verse seems to con-
found familiar cultural scripts and pose unclassifiable dangers when placed
alongside the senator's purported familiarity with African Americans as
"innately a very devout and religious people." In his testimony, Hughes
attempts to challenge the assumptions of this line of questioning by returning to the poem and stressing the text's capacity to defy expectations
through multiple meanings and multiple readers. Recall, too, his aforementioned reference to the "thousand interpretations of Shakespeare's
Sonata." This strategic emphasis on matters of interpretation urges those
who would engage the poet on the basis of preconceived notions about
his racial and religious identity to regard Hughes, instead, as an individual
who embodies ever-changing dimensions and degrees of difference, even
within cultural constructs that are presumably fixed.

On occasion, Hughes also employs cunning and self-reflexive religious
references to argue his defense. When asked by Chief Counsel Roy Cohn
if he had ever attended a Communist Party meeting, for instance, Hughes
states: "I would like a definition of what you mean by communism, and also
what you would call a Communist party meeting. As you know, one may
go to a Baptist church and not be a Baptist" (977). Later, when asked how
it might be possible for him to "desire the Soviet form of government and
not believe in communism," Hughes includes, as part of his reply, "One can
desire a Christian world and not be a Baptist or a Catholic" (995). With
this strategic indirection (guided, no doubt, by the advice of his attorney),
Hughes strives to highlight his own irreducible subjectivity by unhooking
inner belief from outward affiliation with a single dogma or institution. He
goes on to admit: "I have believed in the entire philosophies of the left at
one period in my life, including socialism, communism, Trotskyism. All
'isms' have influenced me one way or another" (976). And so, in cautioning his questioners not to judge a book by its cover—or a poem by its
title—Hughes invites a more careful investigation of his career, relationships, and life experiences.

As persuasive as Hughes's argument may seem, he nevertheless went
though great pains to distance himself from "Goodbye, Christ." To those
who insisted on using select verses from the 1930s and 1940s to characterize his body of work, Hughes reiterated that such poems were simply
not representative of his writing career. Hughes treated "Goodbye, Christ"
as "a regrettable error of his immature youth," to borrow Rampersad's
phrase, and for decades, he struggled to prevent his critics from reprinting
the text (Rampersad, *Hughes*, 2: 4). As a result, the poem is absent from

his collections of poetry and overlooked in most modern anthologies, with two of the rare exceptions being the posthumously published *Good Morning, Revolution: Uncollected Writings of Social Protest*, edited by Faith Berry (1973), and *The Collected Poems of Langston Hughes*, edited by Arnold Rampersad (1995).

Of course, Langston Hughes is not the only African American writer to invoke images of spiritual crisis and critique in order to, as he explains, "shock people into thinking and finding the real meaning [of religion] themselves." Yet I offer the controversy surrounding "Goodbye, Christ" as a signpost for what is at stake when African American writers defy charges of blasphemy and the comforts of inherited tradition to reexamine the faith of their fathers and mothers, expose religious hypocrisy, and demand reasoned explanations for the persistence of evil and human suffering in black life. In evaluating these subversive literary utterances in the chapters ahead, I hope to move beyond the kind of narrow cross-examinations and unchecked assumptions made notorious by Senator McCarthy's subcommittee, but I do not seek to glibly romanticize the "shock" of religious heterodoxy. My aim is always to think carefully and critically about the literary structure and philosophical resonance of the spiritual struggles embodied by the skeptics, backsliders, and blasphemers of African American fiction. More specifically, to make the case for how questions about divine justice and the problem of evil function as the inscrutable crux of black literary engagements with religion after 1900, I have chosen texts that offer a critically diverse range of representations from Countée Cullen, Richard Wright, Alice Walker, James Baldwin, Ernest Gaines, Toni Morrison, and others.

Today readers continue to wonder if a black voice that accuses God of "getting in the way of things" is a fitting subject for any American poet, much less the poet laureate of Harlem ("Goodbye, Christ," line 25).[5] Yet even as Hughes maintained that the relationship that he shared with God was hidden in an envelope marked "personal" (Hughes, "Personal"), his body of work took risks in expressing a variety of views about the nature of God, the meaning of suffering, and the value of worship. The poet joins the community of twentieth-century black writers under investigation in this study, creative thinkers from every major literary era whose fictional works offer strident reevaluations of divine justice and black Christian traditions in modern America.

# ACKNOWLEDGMENTS

THERE ARE many people who helped to make this book possible and guide me to its completion. The support of my professors at Hampton University and my mentor, Margaret Dismond Martin, remain a proud and lasting positive influence in my life and work. At Yale University, where this project began as my dissertation with the assistance of a Ford Foundation Fellowship, I am grateful for the direction of Robert Stepto, John Blassingame, Hazel Carby, Gilbert Bond, and Glenda Gilmore.

I would like to acknowledge the generous departmental support I received from the University of South Carolina, and to thank my colleagues who so kindly offered feedback on portions of the manuscript: Kwame Dawes, Greg Forter, John Muckelbauer, Stephanie Mitchem, Todd Shaw, David Crockett, Rheeda Walker, Terry Weik, Danielle Holley-Walker, and Melissa Pearson. Thanks and appreciations are due Thadious Davis, Cheryl Wall, Edward J. Blum, Maurice Wallace, Trudier Harris, and Herman Beavers for their support. For his meticulous eye and good cheer, I owe special thanks to my research assistant, Jeremey Cagle. I also gratefully acknowledge the generous feedback of two anonymous readers, the copyediting acuity of Susan Murray, and the guidance of Cathie Brettschneider and Ellen Satrom at University of Virginia Press.

I am thankful for the support of my wonderful husband, Kenny, the unconditional love of my parents, Patricia Nottingham Dzandu and Waide Robinson, and the words of encouragement from my family, Thena Robinson, Jaimé Dzandu, Lafayette Robinson, Janice Fitzgerald Robinson, Thomas Nottingham, Ellen Bolling, Pearl Bailey, Willetta Whitted, and Kenneth Whitted. I am privileged to have, in Danielle Elliott and Heather Williams, two best friends whose optimism and tough love I have treasured since graduate school. I would also like to thank my fellow "Mocha Moms," Elise Ahyi and Tracey Weldon, for keeping me grounded during this process.

Not a day goes by that I do not remember my grandmother Jessie Nottingham, who passed away shortly after I began this project. I will forever appreciate her compassionate and adventurous spirit, her audacious love of books, and the courage with which she faced the difficult, unanswerable questions. I dedicate this book to her great-granddaughter, Naima Jessie Whitted, born just before the last chapter was complete.

A SHORTER version of chapter 1 appeared as "'In My Flesh Shall I See God': Ritual Violence, Racial Redemption, and Countée Cullen's 'The Black Christ,'" *African American Review* 38, no. 3 (2004): 379–93. The excerpt from "slaveships" by Lucille Clifton is taken from *The Terrible Stories*, copyright 1996 by Lucille Clifton and used with permission of BOA Editions, Ltd., www.boaeditions.org. The excerpt from "The Reason" by Bill Lavender is used with permission of the author. The excerpt from "Hymn to a Hurricane" by Rachel Eliza Griffiths is used with permission of the author. The excerpts from "JESUS WAS CRUCIFIED, or It Must Be Deep" and "and when the revolution came" by Carolyn Rodgers are used with the permission of the author.

# "A God of Justice?"

# INTRODUCTION

# "Would He Be to Us *a God of Justice?*"

loaded like spoons
into the belly of Jesus
where we lay for weeks for months
in the sweat and stink of our own
breathing
Jesus
why do you not protect us
——Lucille Clifton, "slaveships"

Tʜᴇ "problem of evil" begins in the midst of inexplicable suffering. Its dimensions are commonly phrased as the question: How can an all-powerful, benevolent, and just God allow pain and undeserved suffering to occur? To persist for generations unabated? While the dilemma is not, by any means, unique to the American descendants of African slaves, the continuing struggle to reconcile a Christian logic of love with the experiential reality of enslavement and racial oppression makes the problem of evil paramount to understanding how religion lives among African American people. In recent years, the subject has received considerable attention from black theologians and religious philosophers. Yet this book puts forth the work of African American creative writers as a wide and invigorating lens through which to examine religious crisis and critique. If we allow that "the problem of evil is really not just one problem, but a cluster of interrelated arguments and issues," as the religious philosopher Michael L. Peterson has stated (*Evil*, 2), then it follows that literature, with its labyrinthine narrative processes and innovative explorations of human development, is a form of cultural expression that is especially well-suited to challenge, reaffirm, and elaborate upon philosophical speculations. This is one of the major premises upon which *"A God of Justice?": The Problem of Evil in Twentieth-Century Black Literature* is based.

Consider how the religious and existential problem, as it is understood by Western theistic traditions, haunts the poet Lucille Clifton in the 1996 poem "slaveships," which opens this introduction. She brings to her historical journey the rare observations of Middle Passage survivors, the recovered logs of ship surgeons, and illustrated diagrams that disfigure black humanity for fiscal gain. But can the knowledge that "we lay for weeks for months/in the sweat and stink of our own/breathing" (lines 3–5) offer insight into the *spiritual meaning* of black suffering? With enslaved souls trapped inside the "belly" of a God that appears to be as cold and unsympathetic as a ship's cargo hold, the poem's collective voice divulges a small, but insistent uncertainty about the assurances of divine justice. Clifton's verse collapses into an unanswerable question, one that is both prayer and accusation: *Why do you not protect us?*

It is my contention that African American literary engagements with religion are driven by endless reverberations of the plea sounded in "slaveships." Such representations, particularly after 1900, have been too long overlooked and explained away by platitudinous narratives of black spiritual endurance and communal redemption. "You wouldn't think that a person who was born with God in the house would ever have any questions to ask on the subject," admits Zora Neale Hurston in her 1942 autobiography, *Dust Tracks on a Road*. Nevertheless, modern black literature abounds with seekers like Hurston who, in grappling with life's elusive mysteries, remain unsatisfied with the preacher's "simple, clear-cut explanation" (216). While some struggle with personal crises of faith, others express concern over atrocities such as the Middle Passage and the arbitrary and disproportionate hardship of black people worldwide. Here are angry mourners, blasphemous church mothers, skeptical youth, revolutionary atheists, and backsliders who refuse to kneel before a "white man's God." The profound spiritual struggle so often articulated through their cry for divine justice is *central* to understanding black literary representations of religion and spirituality in the twentieth century.

THE THEOLOGIAN, educator, and social activist Benjamin E. Mays was among the first to observe this literary trend in his 1938 study *The Negro's God, as Reflected in His Literature*. This prescient theological and sociohistorical excavation of black autobiography, fiction, essays, sermons, and spirituals from 1760 to 1937 by "the intellectual forerunner of the contemporary black theology movement" provides a useful point of departure for my literary analysis (Matthews, *Ancestors*, 7). From the verses of enslaved

Christian poets to Depression-era Sunday school quarterlies, Mays unveils in his book the diverse manifestations of African American ideas of God to an audience that he believed was overexposed to religious caricatures of blacks in popular culture. He notes among the ecclesiastical discourse of the "Negro masses," the enduring presence of a "traditional, compensatory pattern" of belief and an unquestioned faith in God's benevolence (*Negro's God*, 96). On the other hand, Mays surmises that the image of God in "classical" black literature—secular discourses of narrative, public address, and academic writing—tends to focus less on otherworldly concerns and emphasizes, instead, the role of religion in "social rehabilitation" and earthly deliverance (96).

Mays contends, however, that a curious shift occurs after World War I. His examination of selected works by writers such as Nella Larsen, Walter White, Countée Cullen, Langston Hughes, and Georgia Douglas Johnson leads him to remark upon an unusual manifestation of "spiritual depression and skepticism" in the fiction of this younger generation (7). Although he never explicitly uses the phrase "the problem of evil" in his explications, Mays's conclusions in *The Negro's God* point to an increasing desire on the part of creative writers to explore the philosophical dilemma in literary representations of black life.

> There is a tendency on the part of recent Negro writers to consider the idea of God as useless in any effort to reconstruct the world socially. Many of these ideas are not flat denials of the existence of God, but they show incredulity, frustration, and pessimism which make the idea of God of little value in social crises. . . . [T]he traditional views of God as exemplified in the Negro masses and in the white man's conceptions of God are abandoned as useless in the social struggle. They run the entire gamut from mere protest against traditional ideas and abandonment of the same to a complete denial of the existence of God. (251)

With this in mind, Mays regards the proliferation of religious skepticism in literature as an aberrant symptom of post–World War I disillusionment, a spiritual disease awaiting political and economic remedy. He advises his readers that unless social situations improve, black communities that have been sustained for so long by their "firm faith in God" will run the risk of becoming as "irreligious" as Larsen's Helga Crane or as "militant" and "communistic" as the speaker in Hughes's "Goodbye, Christ" (244). It is, perhaps, an awareness of the seismic implications of this developing literary trend that causes Mays to begin his analysis of modern black writing with the cautionary statement: "we move now into new territory" (218).

My work is galvanized by Mays's efforts to envision a black cultural tradition that is comprehensive enough to sustain a range of religious representations and takes seriously the intrepid questions of seekers and skeptics.
Yet the issues he raised so perceptively seven decades ago in *The Negro's God*
await fresh modes of textual analysis and systematic critical inquiry. Since
1938, black American writers have continued to explore the inexplicable
nature of God and human suffering in astonishingly provocative ways.
Unlike Mays, whose sociological agenda emphasizes how artistic works
can be used prescriptively as evidence of historical realities, I scrutinize in
this study the aesthetic, thematic, and narrative structures of black spiritual
inquiry that coalesce around what Susan Neiman asserts is "the guiding
force of modern thought"—the problem of evil (*Evil in Modern Thought*,
2). I investigate how the texts of writers such as Countée Cullen, Nella
Larsen, Richard Wright, Alice Walker, James Baldwin, Ernest Gaines,
and Toni Morrison challenge sacred belief systems and institutions that
sanction racial subjugation, misogyny, and unquestioned acceptance of the
status quo. To this end, the first half of my study examines three specific
concepts that formulate questions about the meaning of suffering in relation to black experience: the crucified black Christ, the mourner's bench,
and spiritual infidelity. The two remaining chapters analyze texts that go
beyond defining spiritual crisis and advocate more systematic responses to
evil, specifically through improvisational blues structures and experimental
renderings of a black utopia.

To be sure, we can find "solutions" to the problem of evil embedded
in the spirituals, sermonic traditions, and other ritualistic elements of traditional black churches. Christian faith has a long and rewarding legacy
among African Americans, beginning in earnest during the Second Great
Awakening of the late eighteenth century. Cornel West thoughtfully
reminds us that "the intellectual life of the African slaves in the United
States—like that of all oppressed peoples—consisted primarily of reckon-
ing with the dominant form of evil in their lives. The Christian emphasis
on against-the-evidence hope for triumph over evil struck deep among
many of them" ("American Africans," 85). This same hope formed the
foundation for American abolition movements as orators, politicians,
and autobiographers centered their harshest judgments on the contradictions of proslavery religion. Yet after Emancipation, with so many of the
promises of liberation unfulfilled and fresh forms of oppression being sys-
tematized after Reconstruction, African Americans voiced more strident
reevaluations of the liberating God portrayed in Exodus. The concern, as

posed in an 1865 issue of the *Christian Recorder*, suggests a persistent sense of unrest at the race's wilderness wanderings: "Has Providence so little care for human lives as to permit the sacrifice of over a million of them for the purpose of overthrowing the system of slavery, only that its victims may be treated worse than slaves after they are free?"[1]

Creative works further instantiate these agonizing moments of doubt and frustration throughout the twentieth century to the extent that readers who peruse the fiction of modern black writers for "reflections of a Negro's God" are routinely confronted with a host of characters wrestling, ironically enough, with his absence. The bewildered voice in W. E. B. Du Bois's 1906 poem "A Litany of Atlanta" cries out, "*What meaneth this?* Tell us the Plan; give us the Sign!" (92). His protest against God's neglectful silence is only one example of the spiritual pleas that flourished in the wake of renewed racial terror. Ultimately such texts "theorize" about God and evil in the sense that Barbara Christian uses the verb—through narrative forms, stories, riddles, and "the play with language" ("Race," 281). So while prior studies have made significant claims about black religious discourse by relying on eighteenth- and nineteenth-century writing,[2] this book establishes the chilling relevance of Du Bois's query in fictional renderings of religious crisis during the years of the Depression, segregation, civil rights activism, Black Nationalism, and womanist advocacy movements. Such struggles effectively demonstrate, in the words of Celie from *The Color Purple* (1982): "It ain't easy, trying to do without God. Even if you know he ain't there, trying to do without him is a strain" (Walker, 176).

## "Whence Then Is Evil?" Defining the Problem

> Every time we make the judgment *this ought not to have happened*, we are stepping onto a path that leads straight to the problem of evil.
>
> —SUSAN NEIMAN, *Evil in Modern Thought*

The critical approach of this study is informed, in part, by arguments that circulate through the philosophy of religion, a branch of academic inquiry that differs from theology in its critical examination of fundamental religious beliefs and experiences.[3] In addition to raising questions about the nature and existence of God, scholarship in this area evaluates the degree to which monotheistic conceptions of God's sovereignty and benevolence are reasonable given the presence of evil. As a result, philosophical formulations of the problem of evil generally fall under two broad categories that Michael L. Peterson identifies as "theoretical" and "existential" (*Evil*, 3).

The former tends to scrutinize the logical consistency and evidential probability of theistic arguments from evil, while the latter is less abstract and "has been conceived to have a kind of 'real life' dimension" (7). Peterson goes on to explain:

> The existential problem involves how the experience of evil conditions one's attitude toward God and perhaps the world. The problem cannot simply be reduced to an emotional or psychological one or divorced from the structure of one's beliefs and values. Rather it arises when the experience of evil, which is conditioned by moral convictions as well as a variety of theoretical commitments, can make it impossible to embrace religious faith. (7)

The subjective nature of the existential problem, as arising from the "experience of evil," yields the most imaginative returns for the authors in this study, although both dimensions clearly inform and influence one another. Between the two expansive formulations of the theoretical and the existential problem, philosophical arguments have been used to make cases for and against atheism, to advocate religious pluralism as well as fundamentalist readings of scripture, and to reflect upon horrors beyond human understanding. In devising these arguments, scholars typically separate *natural evil*, or the kind of suffering attributed to physical causes such as illness, birth defects, and natural disasters, from acts of *moral evil* for which human beings are responsible. John G. Stackhouse Jr. also notes distinctions between moral evils that are intentional and involuntary, committed against others and against the self, and evils that occur only in particular instances versus systemic structures that cause pain and suffering (*Can God Be Trusted?* 36–38).

As an intellectual field of study, philosophers often attribute the origins of the problem of evil to ancient wisdom literatures and Greek thinkers such as Epicurus, whose riddle is restated by David Hume as: "Is God willing to prevent evil, but not able? Then he is impotent. Is he able, but not willing? Then he is malevolent. Is he both able and willing? Whence then is evil?" (*Dialogues*, 243). Unraveling this problem demands careful scrutiny of the cultural meanings inscribed in terms such as "God" or "evil." Among theistic religious traditions in Africa, Central America, and India, for instance, the power of divine being(s) can vary, as does the way in which suffering is understood in relation to human agents. The Yoruba people of Nigeria are "ever aware of the presence of evil," notes E. O. Oyelade: "Instead of running away, they simply live with it, seeking whatever solutions are possible and accepting with little or no complaints whatever cannot be overcome, as their lot in life" ("Yoruba Religion," 157). Stackhouse also remarks upon the way in which traditional Native American religions perceive good and evil subjectively as indicators of personal desire, a kind of illusion that does not necessarily constitute "a meaningful judgment about the actual nature of things" (*Can God Be Trusted?* 25). In this context, "'evil' is just what *we* do not enjoy, what diminishes *our* health or happiness or security. Nature is what is" (31). So the problem posed by the classic question, "Whence then is evil?" is not impervious to change; for some, it is not even a genuine problem.

Black writers, as we shall see, explore the terms of the debate in these and other distinct ways by raising questions, most specifically, about the moral evils that the theologian Anthony Pinn identifies as "oppression, injustice, inequality, and the resulting psychological and physical damage" (*Why Lord?* 13). In explicating how literary texts grapple with the issues, my readings draw frequently on the pertinent claims of theistic and nontheistic humanism and existentialism to theorize these literary representations. West African religious beliefs and practices also warrant particular attention for their explicit and implicit influences on black American communities of faith. Yet it must be made clear from the outset that the questions raised among Christian studies scholars serve as the foundation for my analysis of African American literature since it is with (and against) this belief system that the narratives often struggle.

Traditionally, black Christian communities understand God as self-existent and infinite in power, wisdom, and goodness in keeping with the teachings of the Bible. The evolution of this faith among enslaved blacks and their descendants has been fraught with difficulty to be sure, yet many came to envision the sacred history of their experience in scriptural accounts—most notably, Moses and the Exodus, and Jesus Christ's sacrifice for humanity. Like the children of Israel, black communities commonly believe that they, too, have "drunken the dregs of the cup of trembling" and long for the moment when God might pass the burden into the hands of their oppressors (Isa. 51:17).[4] The Book of Job also serves as a biblical resource, reassuring blacks that become more deeply committed to God's righteousness in the midst of suffering that their faithfulness will be rewarded. As a result, my understanding of the culture is guided by the intellectual community of theologians, religious historians, and philosophers from 1969 to the present—the period West refers to as the "Golden Age of African-American

Religious Studies."⁵ Likewise, contemporary discussions of the problem of evil in white European and American scholarship often overlook the specific experience of black suffering (focusing almost exclusively on the horrors of the Holocaust), and so this study is attentive to African American religious thinkers who examine how the question of God's justice contributes to the varieties of black religious experience in particular.

The theologian James Cone has argued, for instance, that the articulation of black liberation theology began as "prophetic self-criticism" within small midcentury church communities as increasingly, black Christians put forth scriptural interpretations that bolstered more assertive programs for social and political equality (*For My People*, 102). By the 1960s, Cone, Gayraud S. Wilmore, Preston Williams, J. Deotis Robert, Albert Cleage, and others were publicly advocating readings of the gospel that rejected white images of black inferiority and, using black culture and history as the primary frame of reference, located their hope within the struggle for justice among the poor and oppressed. In the National Committee of Negro Churchmen's "Black Power Statement," released in 1966, black clergy responded to the nation's social and economic disparities, urban riots, white Christian hypocrisy, and the rise of Black Nationalist ideology following the assassination of Malcolm X. A year later, when black ministers separated from the National Council of Churches, they issued a similar statement asserting their identity as Christians who embraced the Black Power movement. They also admitted to their own past mistakes, acknowledging that the black church has often "fallen prey to the dominance of white society" and, in doing so, "has unwittingly become a tool for our oppression, providing an easy vehicle for escape from the harsh realities of our own existence" (Cone, *For My People*, 16). Black theology, according to Cone, originates from this kind of introspection, from an ability to recognize the church's weaknesses and mistakes with the specific intention of redirecting these energies toward change. Importantly, he points out that, in the beginning, black theology "was simply the black church criticizing itself in order to become a more effective participant in the black liberation struggle" (102).

So when William R. Jones published his study *Is God a White Racist?: A Preamble to Black Theology* in 1973, the title question was not intended simply to startle his readers, but to generate a dialogue with colleagues like Cone who, he argues, were taking the omni-benevolence of God for granted in their work (*White Racist?* x).⁶ He claims that their assumptions foster a belief system that treats acts of unmerited oppression and pain as part of a "suffering-servant" ethos, relegating true liberation for black sufferers to the afterlife (16). Believers are, therefore, disinclined to resist on their own behalf or in the interest of their communities when suffering is justified as part of a larger divine plan. Jones goes on to insist that, to awaken the church's spiritual quietism, no ideas should be out of bounds; he further refuses to assign "positive value" to sacred claims simply because they have been traditionally associated with black Christian faith.[7] Ultimately, however, Jones refutes his title's accusation of divine racism by suggesting a modified understanding of God's power as persuasive, rather than coercive and absolute. Humanity exists as a "co-responsible" and "co-determining power" with the free will to bring about good or evil (188). This system, described by Jones as "humanocentric theism," underscores the obligations of men and women to fight against oppression, while theorizing that God maintains his sovereignty in allowing such substantial human freedom.

Significantly, Jones employs the term "theodicy" to characterize the nature of his response to the problem of evil in black life. Theodicy is generally understood as a systematic affirmation of God's goodness and power in light of the reality of evil and suffering. Unlike a *defense* that critiques particular logical and evidential arguments against theism (such as the "free will defense"), scholars observe that *theodicy* goes a step further by formulating "positive, plausible reasons for the existence of evil in a theistic universe" (M. Peterson, *Evil*, 8). The "Augustinian Theodicy" formulated by St. Augustine of Hippo classifies evil as the corruption of goodness that originates not with God, but with the fall of man. The "Irenaean Theodicy," based on the writings on St. Irenaeus, maintains that the presence of evil in the world is intended to prepare humanity for a spiritual maturation that brings men and women closer to God. Yet, as Susan Neiman explains, there are also broader and more secular ways to conceive of theodicy, particularly in the modern post-Enlightenment consciousness, as "any way of giving meaning to evil that helps us face despair. Theodicies place evils within structures that allow us to go on in the world" (*Evil in Modern Thought*, 239).

Jones adopts a comparable attitude with his claim that every person possesses a "functional theodicy" that shapes his/her approach to suffering. "Each individual makes a fundamental judgment about the character of specific sufferings," he explains, "whether each is good (positive), bad (negative), or neutral; whether he must endure the suffering he encounters or should annihilate it; whether suffering can be eliminated or whether it is an inevitable part of the human condition" (xxiv). Each text under investigation in this book elaborates upon Jones's hypothesis and, in the process, mounts a similar "cross-examination of black Christianity and the black church" (xv). Convinced that the misery her family and her race has suffered holds a spiritually redemptive purpose, for instance, the elderly mother in Cullen's poem "The Black Christ" (1929) relies on her faith to endure southern racial violence. On the other hand, after being unjustly forced to work on a chain gang for seven years, the former church deacon Herald Loomis from August Wilson's play *Joe Turner's Come and Gone* (1988) flashes his knife at heaven and refuses to be enslaved by the onerous sacrifices of "Mr. Jesus Christ." For Loomis, there is nothing "positive" about suffering: "I don't need nobody to bleed for me! I can bleed for myself!" (92). Literary sources such as these provide dynamic illustrations of how functional theodicies materialize and evolve through the individual choices, collective circumstances, and interpersonal relations of everyday life.

Exploring the evils faced, in particular, by African American women is central to the creative methodologies of womanist theology. Religious scholars such as Renita Weems, Jacquelyn Grant, Delores Williams, M. Shawn Copeland, Emilie M. Townes, and Stephanie Mitchem call attention to the way race, class, and gender operate as "tridimensional oppressions" for black women throughout history, giving rise to questions about the relationship between suffering and salvation (Mitchem, *Womanist Theology*, 106). What is especially useful about the critical reflections that emerge from this academic community is their willingness not only to name social and spiritual wrongs, but to demonstrate the processes through which black women confront moral evils and shape their own functional theodicies. Womanist theologians further complicate generalizations about the otherworldly and survivalist nature of black women's belief by offering a nuanced reconsideration of suffering. As Mitchem argues: "Suffering in itself is not salvific. It is redemptive only in that it may lead to critical rethinking of meaning or purpose, as might any life crisis. Such reexamination is part of the process of human maturation. However, suffering is a distinctive starting place for thinking about salvation as it brings into sharp focus human experience in relation to God" (109). For African American writers like Zora Neale Hurston, Nella Larsen, James Baldwin, Alice Walker, Toni Morrison, and others who depict the inner lives of black women in their fiction, suffering does indeed serve as a "starting place" for the kind of maturation that Mitchem describes and can be extended to include female characters who do not ultimately reaffirm faith in the Christian God.

The prevalence of black atheists, agnostics, and humanists in twentieth-century black literature also makes the work of Anthony Pinn valuable for understanding how African Americans respond to the moral evils that are of primary concern to their communities. Since the 1995 publication of *Why Lord?: Suffering and Evil in Black Theology*, Pinn has explored the problem of evil in black religious histories and in studies devoted to demystifying the principles of African American humanism.[8] He has argued that when confronted with inexplicable pain and suffering of moral evil, believers typically seek to resolve the dilemma in one of four ways: "(1) rethinking the nature of evil; (2) rethinking the power of God (humans become God's coworkers); (3) questioning of God's goodness/righteousness; (4) questioning/denial of God's existence" (*Why Lord?* 111). To be sure, the lines of demarcation between the four responses frequently intersect and overlap as seekers in African American literature often contemplate any and all of them at once. The narrator of Cullen's "The Black Christ" suffers a crisis of faith and "questions God's goodness" in the wake of his brother's murder. But once he is reminded of the miracle of Jesus Christ's resurrection, he "rethinks the nature of evil" and, as in many early twentieth-century texts, concludes by speaking somewhat appreciatively of a God who will "try me when I doubt his love" (137). Conversely, we find frequent appeals in black writing to the "silent," "mute," and "sleeping" God, who—if he *does* exist—remains indifferent or unconcerned with the sufferings of the oppressed (Clifton's poem "slaveships" provides an example of this). More common in recent years, however, are the texts that uphold some idea of divine goodness, but allege that God's authority is limited by design. Narratives that "rethink the power of God" in this manner typically seek to spur human activity by emphasizing the earthly obligations of humanity to work against individuals and systemic structures that cause evil. I agree, then, with Pinn's assessment that "Black folklore and modern Black literature often bring into question the theistic beliefs held dear by Christian black religion," and I frequently employ his classifications as a reference point for analyzing the various philosophical methods at work in the literature (*Why Lord?* 157).[9]

## From Walker's *Appeal* to *The Green Pastures:* Black Religion and Literature in Context

> Imagine that you are creating a fabric of human destiny with the object
> of making men happy in the end, giving them peace and rest at last,
> but that it was essential and inevitable to torture to death only one tiny
> creature—that baby beating its breast with its fist, for instance—and to
> found that edifice on its unavenged tears, would you consent to be the
> architect on those conditions? Tell me, and tell the truth.
>
> —FYODOR DOSTOEVSKY, *The Brothers Karamazov*

The well-known conversation in a Russian tavern between Alyosha and
Ivan Karamazov is often cited as a fictional archetype for the debate over
"the eternal questions, of the existence of God and immortality" in Western culture (*Brothers Karamazov*, 217). Yet Fyodor Dostoevsky's 1880 serial
novel *The Brothers Karamazov* refuses simply to pit Alyosha's strong Christian devotion against Ivan's intellectual reasoning in bitter rivalry; instead,
the exchange reveals two deeply compassionate siblings, each longing to
decipher the inscrutable purpose of human suffering in a place where their
faith and logic might entwine. Ivan claims to accept God's existence, but he
argues that "it's the world created by Him I don't and cannot accept" (218).
The older Karamazov makes his case, not by seeking justice for the corporate suffering of mankind, but by focusing on the occurrence of suffering in
innocent children. He states: "I want to forgive. I want to embrace. I don't
want more suffering. And if the sufferings of children go to swell the sum
of sufferings which was necessary to pay for truth, then I protest that the
truth is not worth such a price" (227).

Ivan recounts for Alyosha examples of children murdered under horrifying circumstances not of their own doing. And afterward, he confronts
his younger brother with the aforementioned scenario in which Alyosha is
asked to imagine himself as the Creator. Would he allow a child to be tortured to death to assure the perfect happiness of all of humanity? Alyosha,
a novice at the town monastery, freely confesses that he would not create
such a world. But he also refuses to compare his own human weakness and
infallibility to Jesus Christ, declaring: "But there is a Being and He can
forgive everything, all and for all, because He gave His innocent blood
for all and everything. You have forgotten Him, and on Him is built the
edifice, and it is to Him they cry aloud, 'Thou art just, O Lord, for Thy
ways are revealed!'" (227). Both viewpoints are taken seriously in the novel,
although Alyosha remains the only one of the Karamazov brothers who

escapes madness, banishment, or death. He, too, is faced with moments of spiritual crisis, but rather than concede to Ivan's rationalism, Alyosha clings to a favored elder's message of "active love" as a way to manage suffering and use pain as a springboard for redemption (60).

The passionate debate serves as a useful literary model that has direct influence on the writers in this study. One can easily see the impact of *The Brothers Karamazov* in the works of Richard Wright, James Baldwin, and Toni Morrison, or in stories such as "The Sky Is Gray" by Ernest Gaines—an acknowledged admirer of Dostoevsky. In Gaines's story, which takes place in a segregated southern town, the purpose of an innocent child's suffering is debated among the black patients in a dentist's office waiting room. The fact that the subject of their conversation—a young boy howling with a toothache—is *also* black and poor makes him a paradigmatic example of "unavenged" racial oppression and class inequalities as well: "Look like it's the poor who suffers the most," an elderly black woman reflects, "I don't understand it" (95). As I discuss in chapter 4, Gaines's parable goes on to imagine an exchange between the woman, a black preacher, and a college student that places the sentiments expressed by Ivan and Alyosha in concert with the way white power structures and religious institutions have distorted interpretations of God's justice to control black spiritual and material freedom.

Placing a story like "The Sky Is Gray" in historical context, however, reminds us that fifty years *before* Dostoevsky's meditations on suffering, the black abolitionist David Walker posed a similar question:

> I ask every man who has a heart, and is blessed with the privilege of believing— Is not God a God of justice to all his creatures? Do you say he is? Then if he gives peace and tranquility to tyrants, and permits them to keep our fathers, our mothers, ourselves and our children in eternal ignorance and wretchedness to support them and their families, would he be to us a God of *justice*? I ask, O ye *Christians!!!* Who hold us and our children in the most abject ignorance and degradation, that ever a people were afflicted with since the world began—I say, if God gives you peace and tranquility, and suffers you thus to go on afflicting us, and our children, who have never given you the least provocation—would he be to us *a God of justice*? (*Appeal*, 7–8)

In his stirring *Appeal to the Colored Citizens of the World*, published in 1829, Walker expresses the strength of his convictions by drawing on an unshakable belief in God's judgment in the afterlife, a belief that is shared by his audience of Christians, black and white. The argument of the free black writer from Wilmington, North Carolina, is premised on the idea that

"God is just and I know it" (24). Nevertheless, the four articles of Walker's *Appeal* take the time to elaborate upon a defense that insists that the misery of the enslaved will be expiated through God's wrath on the souls of their enslavers. To those who believe that African slavery is divinely sanctioned and behave as if "God is asleep," he also cites evidence from the Bible and world history to demonstrate how the sin of slavery has been alleviated in the past. Walker's insistent query—"would he be to us *a God of justice?*"—can be understood, of course, as part of a larger rhetorical strategy to expose the hypocrisy of proslavery religious ideology. Yet anyone who examines the social and cultural contexts of black spiritual struggle during the twentieth century must remain attentive to the questions that Walker raised a century earlier. One must also be alert to the possibility that not all African Americans are convinced that the kind of divine justice so vividly described in the *Appeal* is adequate to redress their suffering.

Truly, as Yolanda Pierce explains, the notion of Christianity as a "contradictory faith" is intensified by the reality of human enslavement. Her recent analysis of nineteenth-century autobiographies in *Hell without Fires: Slavery, Christianity, and the Antebellum Spiritual Narrative* further elaborates the social and linguistic processes that early black Americans went through to establish meaningful spiritual identities. The ways in which biblical rhetoric "has consistently been used to exploit, denigrate, and discriminate" (3) against black men and women are well-known, from the mark of Cain and Noah's curse to the scriptural admonitions for servants to "obey their masters" in verses such as Ephesians 6:5. She also notes that in the "institutional promotion of pro-slavery religious rhetoric," the ministers and political leaders who used Old and New Testament scriptures in this manner "not only attempted to justify slavery's existence, but also tried to reinforce the commonplace notion that slavery was *good* for slaves and masters" (130). According to Pierce, the narratives of former slaves such as George White and John Jea, and Zilpha Elaw, a free black preacher, implicitly refute these claims and demonstrate alternative ways of engaging religious discourse. For these writers, "it was not enough to be taught that the elevation of masters and the degradation of slaves was a legitimate and divinely sanctioned hierarchy. It was not enough merely to listen to the word of God, without being allowed to read and interpret for oneself" (132).

For example, John Jea, a Nigerian-born man who was enslaved in New York, speaks of a spiritual kinship between himself and Lazarus, the New Testament figure who is reborn through Christ's words. Pierce also illustrates how, after his conversion, Jea actively blends his narrative voice with the "language of Canaan—Canaan, the promised land, reserved by God for the nation of Israel after their deliverance from slavery in Egypt" (45). Particularly interesting, however, is how this same act of religious appropriation can be applied to early black Christian understandings of hell. Pierce's assessment of hell as a metaphor for earthly suffering offers a perceptive glimpse into how enslaved blacks responded to classic considerations of the problem of evil. Despite widespread claims that slaves freely embraced an "unqualified faith,"[10] she maintains that African Americans during this time did, indeed, wonder: "Why is hell on earth reserved for some people and not for others? How does one cope with the daily realities of living in hell?" (7). In response, the theodicy that issues forth from nineteenth-century spiritual narratives strives to reconsider evil's nature—or, as Pierce states, to "transform the concept of hell"—by interpreting earthly suffering as a "purifying process" (7) or a "rite of passage" (9) to spiritual salvation. While Pierce notes that this approach does not preclude the possibility of liberation in one's lifetime, there are echoes of David Walker's rhetoric in her insistence that, "the slave convert to religion must believe that hell exists; his or her sense of justice rests on the notion of spiritual retribution" (8).

The examination of five lesser-known black spiritual autobiographies in *Hell without Fires* supplements our understanding of how popular figures like Frederick Douglass, Harriet Jacobs, and Henry Bibb labored in their narratives to differentiate their faith from "the corrupt, slaveholding, women-whipping, cradle-plundering, partial and hypocritical Christianity of this land" (Douglass, *Narrative*, 93). Characters in novels such as William Wells Brown's *Clotel* (1853) and Harriet E. Wilson's *Our Nig* (1859) also contest the morality of white Christian readers, but are careful *not* to question theism itself, or the deeply held beliefs of their brothers and sisters in bondage. One noteworthy exception to this trend appears in Martin Delany's novel *Blake; or, The Huts of America*, which first appeared in serial form in the early 1860s. In the narrative, a runaway slave named Henry upsets his elders when he disavows their belief in the "oppressor's religion." He states: "Religion! . . . That's always the cry with black people. Tell me nothing about religion when the very man who hands you the bread at communion has sold your daughter away from you!" (20). Stunned by his blasphemy, Henry's parents accuse him of backsliding, giving in to the devil, and committing a "sin in de sight ub God" (16). His beliefs fluctuate throughout the course of the text, and yet the moments of conflict in which characters attempt to think through the meaning of their faith and evaluate its practice *within* black communities clearly set Delany's novel apart.

In the post-Emancipation period, we find more and more black characters like Henry asking Dostoevsky's "eternal questions" and questioning the intergenerational consequences of a religion that is, for some, too closely associated with white, patriarchal oppression.[11] The prominent AME bishop Daniel Alexander Payne offers a valuable historical reference for this era, given the way his own efforts at social and political reform intersect with the problem of evil. "Sometimes it seemed as though some wild beast had plunged his fangs into my heart, and was squeezing out its life-blood," reflects Payne in 1888. "Then I began to question the existence of God and to say: 'If he does exist, is he just? If so, why does he suffer one race to oppress and enslave another, to rob them by unrighteous enactments of rights, which they hold most dear and sacred? . . . But then there came into my mind those solemn words: 'With God one day is as a thousand years and a thousand years as one day. Trust in him, and he will bring slavery and all its outrages to an end" (quoted in Mays, *Negro's God*, 49). These questions are debated with ever-increasing fervor—and inconclusiveness—in the secular literature being published into the twentieth century as black American writers find themselves struggling in an age of modernity that features not only systematic social inequality, but more pronounced reassessments of God in science, psychoanalysis, and political ideology.

As previously stated, Benjamin Mays foregrounds the post–World War I decade as a pivotal moment in which radical breaks with cultural tradition and nationalist rhetoric intrude upon black literary representations of God. And while I agree that an "awakening race consciousness and increased educational advantages" during this time played a significant role in generating more critical religious views (Mays, *Negro's God*, 3), the surge in publishing opportunities for African Americans during the 1920s, along with an expanding liberal reading audience, further influenced the availability of this writing. Such critiques are enabled, too, by the population shifts of the Great Migration, in which African Americans fled the intense racial violence, political inequality, and declining agricultural economy in the South to urban centers, predominantly in the North. Mays situates the hopefulness that fueled black migration alongside the "social gospel" inspired by the democratic promises of the Progressive Era and through black participation in World War I. In the aftermath, however, this optimism disintegrated when "institutions were not reconstructed and a new earth did not appear" and when as the egalitarian hope of the war gave way to race riots and Jim Crow, according to Mays, "the church of God took no courageous stand to right these wrongs" (6, 241).

This disillusionment can also be understood as a transitional moment in black literary production as well, particularly when we consider Mays's discussion of the postwar poetry of Theodore Henry Shackelford. Like Cullen's "The Black Christ," poems like Shackelford's "God Will Make It Right" (1919) effectively name contemporary racial issues but resist the kind of political and ideological engagement that was becoming more widespread in the 1920s. And so, where "men dictate/Where we must go to eat," and "in some states/Our vote we may not cast," Shackelford's speaker seeks relief in the assurance of God's heavenly reward, noting, "Prayer is the panacea which/Will comfort every soul" (28–29, lines 9–10, 15–16, 31–32). Certainly these verses underscore familiar spiritual and psychological strategies for survival in black communities, and yet Shackelford's appeal to prayer as a "panacea" constitutes an increasingly outmoded and critically inert perspective among black modernist writers. In addition, Christian pulpits after the First World War were increasingly denounced for refusing to address the psychological ramifications of antiblack religious rhetoric and social concerns such as segregation, disenfranchisement, racial violence, and union discrimination. Burgeoning classes of black professionals and activists openly usurped leadership roles traditionally ascribed to the clergy, as ministers were being maligned increasingly as "policemen" whose main goal was to maintain order among black masses (Fishel and Quarles, "Wake," 229). In Arthur Fauset's pioneering study of religion in the urban North, *Black Gods of the Metropolis* (1944), the anthropologist cites a pronounced disappointment with "more orthodox evangelical churches" as one of the motivating factors for the participation of African Americans, particularly among the working class, in the Pentecostal and Holiness churches of the 1930s and 1940s, including the United House of Prayer for All People and Father Divine's Peace Mission Movement (97). It is also important to note the social progressivism of mainline churches in cities like Chicago, where the influx of southern migrants underscored the need for black religious spokesmen and women to combat systemic inequalities in labor, housing, education, and legal justice.[12] These active upper- and middle-class congregations would have been similarly unenthusiastic about Shackelford's passive moralizing in "God Will Make It Right," preferring instead the formal sophistication and nostalgia of works like Johnson's *God's Trombones: Seven Negro Sermons in Verse*.

At the same time, even well-received literary treatments of African American religion such as Johnson's were overshadowed by pervasive black cultural stereotypes perpetuated by white writers. In his preface to *The Negro's God*, Mays comments specifically on *The Green Pastures*, a Pulitzer Prize–winning drama that, two years prior in 1936, had been made into a film starring Rex Ingram. Mays anticipates his audience's familiarity with the tale in his opening remarks: "It has been assumed by many people that the ideas of God expressed in *Green Pastures* are wholly representative of what the Negro thinks of God, but the data themselves show that the Negro's idea of God is not now and has never been what *Green Pastures* may lead some people to believe." Mays eagerly offers up the "data" of African American literary production to counteract the influence of *The Green Pastures*, which was based on a 1928 short-story collection by the white humorist Roark Bradford titled *Ol' Man Adam and His Chillun*.[13] After the playwright Marc Connelly adapted Bradford's stories to the stage, white and black audiences embraced *The Green Pastures* in 640 performances between 1929 and 1931 (Nolan, *Marc Connelly*, 15). The play promoted the simplicity of African American faith by framing its cultural exigencies around a series of Sunday school Bible lessons for children. May's concern was driven by the way in which *The Green Pastures* reinforced familiar generalizations about black southern spirituality under the guise of vaudeville humor, folk nostalgia, and a trailblazing all-black cast that served, ironically, to substantiate its "wholly representative" quality. From the wizardry of "De Lawd" and his mammy angels to the Negro lodge hall that doubled as the Pharaoh's throne room, Connelly's drama reimagined black religion in the modern national landscape. Nathan Huggins argues that, "the production made it the faith of those who had no pretense of sophistication and who, therefore, could believe in an uncluttered and simple way. Doubt seemed impossible in the black child's fantasy" (*Harlem Renaissance*, 300). Each cultural iteration of this fantasy—as folk tale, stage play, and film—further advocated the idea of unmerited suffering as a means of black salvation, even as it appears to transcend complex theological debates through the reverie of a heavenly fish fry.[14]

Mays's explicit reference to *The Green Pastures* affirms the influence of the creative arts in shaping national discourses surrounding religion, race, and regional identity, but it also exposes the uneasiness that attends the efforts of African American writers to offer more complex, heterogeneous perspectives. Richard Wright acknowledges these risks in his own work and admits, for instance, his reluctance to represent the unique worldview of his ardently religious grandmother. He states, "I was afraid that if I depicted that *something* in terms of the forms of religious life common among Negroes—forms well-known also to whites—that the attempt would defeat itself, that the reader would be carried away by the local color—a la GREEN PASTURES—and the peculiar mannerisms and would laugh instead of being enthralled" ("Memories," 2–3). This anxiety over racial representation, when contextualized alongside the modern break with tradition, meaningfully expands our understanding of what Mays refers to as the "social crisis" that shaped the black literary portrayal of religious belief and practice in the twentieth century.

Too OFTEN, however, contemporary African American literary scholarship overlooks the critical fluctuations of religious thought in black modernist and postmodernist enterprises, due in part to the "invisibility of religion in American literary studies" in general (see Lundin, *There Before Us*, xi).[15] And scholars who do engage the unwieldy representations of religious skepticism appear much too eager to resolve and justify these crises, often by aligning the authors and their characters with an idealized heritage of faith and sanctified endurance. To be sure, the organic evolution of Christian tradition is regarded appropriately as the "heart" and "womb" of African American culture by theologians and historians (Lincoln and Mamiya, *Black Church*, 7–8), but literary critics can no longer afford to sidestep the challenge to classic theism that emerges throughout black writing. For instance, in *Honoring the Ancestors: An African Cultural Interpretation of Black Religion and Literature* (1998), Donald H. Matthews points to several aspects of the spirituals—such as antiphonal patterns, polyrhythm, and improvisational style—that are useful in evaluating black cultural forms and meanings. Yet it is clear that the interpretive horizon of his "spiritual hermeneutic" is limited to those texts that explicitly avow the theistic reasoning of these venerable songs (*Ancestors*, 101).[16] More recently, James W. Coleman's *Faithful Vision: Treatments of the Sacred, Spiritual, and Supernatural in Twentieth-Century African American Fiction* (2006) treats the aggressive religious skepticism in black literary texts as a "failing" that inadequately represents religio-racial truths (19). Coleman is especially forthright in his condemnation of Richard Wright's stance toward the church in *Native Son;* he describes the novel's "dead-end faithlessness" (17) and "trivializing [of] black Christian belief" (20) as an atypical "distortion of black cultural tradition" (22), rather than as symptomatic of Wright's larger critique of spiritual and societal incongruities. Much of Coleman's evaluation of Wright, Baldwin, Walker, and others is based on the extent to which their works ultimately and inevitably reaffirm Christianity as a positive cultural influence, blended syncretically with African-based hoo-doo traditions.[17] Commenting on Bigger Thomas's rejection of the church, Coleman maintains:

> An individual such as Bigger might certainly feel this way under his personal circumstances, but the text misrepresents the black cultural tradition by deny-ing the effect of Christianity. If it were true that black people did not have a practical belief in the agency of the sacred, spiritual, and supernatural and rather believed in the ultimate power of men as Bigger does, then long cen-turies of oppression would have made African Americans collectively bestial, and the situation would be as bleak as the novel shows. (20)[18]

Approaches such as this tend to standardize cultural narratives of col-lective resilience and unfailing religious devotion in a way that neglects the constructive qualities of spiritual crisis. Again and again, African Ameri-can literature strikes a subversive stance, questioning God so as to dispute the reasoning behind redemptive suffering arguments; to affirm religious heterogeneity within black communities; to reject divinely sanctioned patriarchal domination; and to argue for a worldview that better conveys their existential realities. For many of these characters, the situation may, indeed, be "bleak," and some are prompted to angrily reject religion al-together, but surely such views are no less instructive than other, more "representative," ones. "When the choice is between Christian resigna-tion or faith and humanistic action or reason, literary characters, like their folk counterparts, often reject Christianity in favor of a more exacting and humanistic idealism," states Trudier Harris. "They reject the easy way out in favor of more challenging solutions" ("Humanism," 52). I hope to build on this idea by demonstrating that the thorny questions of seekers and skeptics are more than fleeting disruptions or trivial "distortions," margin-alized by a conventional wisdom that implicitly represents blacks as natural Christians and churchgoers.

My analysis also labors against the misconception that philosophizing about the nature of God and evil is an undertaking found exclusively among highly educated, upper-class black elites, or that women and southerners are less likely to apply these modes of inquiry to their faith. The evidence clearly indicates that critical religious reflection crosses gendered, socio-economic, and regional boundaries. Women are often portrayed as taking *more* risks in scrutinizing time-honored assumptions about classic theism, given their subordinate positions within ecclesiastical hierarchies of power. Indeed, church mothers and preacher's wives abound, but so do women like the irreverent Beneatha Younger (*A Raisin in the Sun*), the willful Shug Avery (*The Color Purple*), the discerning Baby Suggs (*Beloved*), and the new prophet Lauren Olamina (*Parable of the Sower*). And while that "old-time religion" is typically represented as the opiate of poor rural folk, some of Christianity's most strident critics emerge from this very community. For instance, Clarence Hardy's persuasive analysis *James Baldwin's God: Sex, Hope, and Crisis in Black Holiness Culture* (2003) maintains that Baldwin's vigorous rejection of Christianity is inseparable from the haunting influence of church traditions, Judeo-Christian language, and a profound fascination with matters of spiritual and material transcendence. Hardy's reluctance to privilege certain aspects of Baldwin's spiritual identity, such as his early years as a Pentecostal youth preacher, over his forthright denunciations of religion later in life generates a more comprehensive awareness of the cultural, social, and political dialectics that inform the writer's creative choices.

Likewise, Trudier Harris has, throughout her distinguished career as a literary critic, acknowledged the contentious nature of African American religious identity in ways that inform and complement this study. In 2007, her lecture "Failed, Forgotten, Forsaken: Christianity in Contemporary African American Literature" highlighted the rejection of Christian traditions in black writing after 1960. Marking the face-off between Mama Lena and Beneatha in *A Raisin in the Sun* (1959) as "Christianity's last stand in African American literature," Harris goes on to explicate how contemporary writers, and black womanist texts in particular, refuse the unwelcome intrusions of spiritual authority from dominant power structures ("Failed," 8). "When characters suffer, God is not the source of their comfort," Harris states. "When communities experience racial or gender violence, God is neither blamed nor called upon to resolve the issues" (23). Texts such as Ntozake Shange's *for colored girls who have considered suicide / when the rainbow is enuf* (1975), Gloria Naylor's *The Women of Brewster Place* (1982), and Toni Cade Bambara's *The Salt Eaters* (1980) assert the "divinity *within* African American women," through the "laying on of hands" (8–9). Just as important, for my purposes, is Harris's emphasis on the "individuality and fragmentation" that manifest in the challenge to traditional religious institutions (22). Yet where Harris evaluates the spiritual alternatives that emerge from this richly fragmented non-Christian discourse (Lauren

Olamina's "Earthseed" religion in Butler's novel, for example), my study is more interested in black characters who are less decisive about their move away from Christianity, and in narratives that convey this indecision structurally and symbolically. Employing critical methods that are framed around the problem of evil allows me to accentuate moments in which God is, in fact, "blamed" and "called upon to resolve the issues." Ultimately, I hope to make the case that twentieth-century literary representations are less concerned with declaring definitive answers than with illustrating an angst-ridden process that is both critical and creative.[19]

## Carolyn Rodgers and "JESUS WAS CRUCIFIED"

> "And what are you now?" Elijah asked.
> I was in something of a bind, for I really could not say—could not allow myself to be stampeded into saying—that I was a Christian. "I? Now? Nothing." This was not enough. "I'm a writer. I like doing things alone."
>
> —JAMES BALDWIN, "Down at the Cross"

Of James Baldwin's formative influence, the critic Sondra O'Neale comments: "Baldwin opened the floodgate for contemporary anti-Christian, non-biblically based black American literature. In most of his works, he only questions divine existence while still courting its allegiance, but his boldness invited younger writers to complete the schism between black art and black faith" ("Fathers," 140). We might interpret Carolyn Rodgers's poem "JESUS WAS CRUCIFIED, or It Must Be Deep (an epic pome)" as an example of one young writer's response to Baldwin's invitation. Published during the height of the Black Arts movement in her 1969 collection *Songs of a Black Bird*, Rodgers's poem combines familiar modern religious grievances with the Black Nationalist ideologies and aesthetic principles of the era. Rodgers's verses widen the schism to which O'Neale alludes through a lively debate between a mother and daughter over the troubling costs of black self-sacrifice grounded in Christian faith. For my purposes, her work also serves as a vivid and broad illustration of how questions about divine justice and the problem of evil are asked throughout twentieth-century African American writing.

From the start, Rodgers's poem exposes bitter intergenerational conflict; her speaker is a fledgling nonconformist who seeks to correct the religious inadequacies and oversights of her predecessors. One instructive verse from the quarrel in "JESUS WAS CRUCIFIED" proceeds as follows:

she sd du u pray? i sd sorta when i hear Coltrane and
she sd if yuh read yuh bible it'll show us read genesis
revelation and she couldn't remember the otha chapter
i should read but she sd what was in the Bible was
happnin now, fire & all and she sd just cause i didn't
    believe the bible don't make it not true
            (and i sd)
    just cause she believe the bible didn't make it true
and she sd it is it is and deep deep down
in yo heart u know it's true
            (and i sd)
   it must be d
       eeeep

                              (lines 59–71)

As is frequently the case in twentieth-century African American writing, these generational ruptures go beyond the customary breach between devoted churchgoers and backsliders. This conflict also situates intellectually curious, formally educated youth in opposition to the provincial and so-called anti-intellectual fears of their elders. Willful independence further collides with the communal traditions of mothers and grandmothers, who are often depicted as the forebearers of tradition and the (hidden) pillars of the church. And to the extent that the elders embody the hard-earned wisdom of a southern folk past, their offspring are portrayed as more worldly, urban, and spiritually adventurous.

In the aforementioned passage, Rodgers highlights such oppositional concepts through repetition and linguistic signifyin(g) that revise key phrases in the poem. While "she sd" and "i sd" volley back and forth in rhythm throughout the verses, the mother's warning, "just cause i didn't/ believe the bible don't make it not true" (lines 63–64) is rearticulated by the daughter as "just cause she believe the bible didn't make it true" (line 66). The daughter also puts forth the experimental and spiritually inflected jazz of John Coltrane as her form of prayer, with the capitalized "Coltrane" visually counterbalancing the only other capitalized word in the stanza—her mother's "Bible" (lines 61, 64). These revisions, when combined with the insistence of replicated words like "it is it is" and "deep deep down" (line 67), accentuate the polarized worldviews and theological perspectives of the two generations. As we shall see, debates over long-established religious beliefs and practices span the century as each generation rehearses the battle between old and new ways of understanding God.

Next, Rodgers's poem condemns the destructive racial and gendered assumptions embedded in long-established religious claims, language use, and institutional structures. It is in this context that African American Christians are accused over and over again of accepting their own suffering by blindly praising the "white man's God." Fueled by what Harris refers to as the "dominant script" of the religious indoctrination of African slaves in America ("Failed," 3), skeptics view Christianity, in particular, as an insidious form of mental enslavement and self-loathing. These texts scrutinize church rituals and attempt to expose the superficial theatrics and toxic commitments that supposedly keep black Christians in a perpetual state of spiritual infancy. Common scriptural metaphors for the divine—Father, Husband, and Master, for example—are denounced as enablers of racial oppression and sexism. Likewise, skeptics who aggressively pursue this line of reasoning in African American literature often insist that classic ideas about God's power and benevolence falter beneath overwhelming evidence of disproportionate ethnic suffering. "jesus need to be thrown down and whipped / till something better happen," says Amiri Baraka in a 1972 poem: "jesus aint did nothing for us / but kept us turned toward the / sky (him and his boy allah / too, need to be checkd / out!)" ("When We'll Worship Jesus," lines 46–50).

To illustrate how this conflict is expressed in "JESUS WAS CRUCIFIED," consider the heated accusations and insinuations exchanged between mother and daughter. The poem's title, when coupled with supporting verses, accuses the mother of trying to emulate Christ too closely (or, perhaps, too narrowly) by accepting a submissive and sacrificial posture within white power structures. When the older woman speaks of fighting the social security board for the right to her retirement funds, the daughter replies, "don't let em nail u wid no technicalities" (line 84). Rodgers's wordplay clearly functions as a vehicle for her sociopolitical critique of religion throughout the poem. The mocking rejoinders also convey the daughter's unwillingness, at this point at least, to empathize with her mother's position or acknowledge her difficult economic, political, and religious choices.

Interestingly enough, James Cone responds to the kind of sentiments expressed in Rodgers's poem through his 1976 essay "Black Theology and the Black College Student." In a view that is common among black liberation theologians, Cone argues that the reactionary skepticism of black students belies a superficial understanding of their ancestor's faith ("College," 124). While he does not advocate uncritical acceptance of the church, he rejects the idea that "all talk about Jesus and God, so dominant in black

churches, must cease if black people are going to liberate themselves from
the values that enslaved them" (121). Indeed, throughout Cone's work during this period, he asserts that God should be revered through his continued work on behalf of the oppressed, or through what Cone identifies as
God's "blackness." Cone maintains that true revolution, both sacred and
secular, depends on knowledge of self. Among "the people" and within
"the culture of our ancestors" is where lasting change must take root. And
as he concludes in the 1976 essay, "even if we cannot hold the faith they
affirm, are we not at least obliged to respect their faith if we expect to
understand why the people regard it as the only source of their survival?"
(124–25).

It is this unspoken obligation that the daughter rebuffs in "JESUS WAS
CRUCIFIED." Moreover, her rejection appears to be based, in part, on her
mother's own unwillingness to move beyond the false assumptions that
vilify her daughter's generation. The mother complains about how hard
she worked to send her child to college, and now her daughter is "actin not
like decent folks" (24) and associating with Communists. The daughter
attempts to respond to her mother's interrogation:

> (and i sd)
> i don't believe—(and she sd) U DON'T BELIEVE IN GOD
> NO MORE DO U?????
> u wudn't raised that way! U gon die and go tuh HELL
> and i sd i hoped it wudn't be NO HUNKIES there . . .

> (lines 30–34)

Here the poem's speaker responds to the accusations of Black Nationalism, communism, and atheism in a way that parodies her mother's otherworldly interests; she even risks damnation in the interest of revolution.
Yet, given how the two women are speaking at crosscurrents, it is clear
that neither view will be allowed to fully emerge and articulate itself in the
poem. Especially significant is the way the daughter's attempt to clarify
her stance in the verse is interrupted ("i don't believe—") in midsentence.
Such interruptions are common in twentieth-century black literature, and
instructive. Religious critiques can be so loud and forceful, the crisis of
faith so intense, and the arguments against theism so thoroughly reasoned
that it may puzzle readers to find ambiguous humanist affirmations and
undeveloped political ideologies proffered as the only alternatives.

Skeptics and seekers in African American literature are likewise unable to put forth an organized religious system to "replace" the Christian

traditions that trouble them so. As Harris explains, "Most of the other visions are only fragments in reaction to current circumstances, not sustainable systems under which characters may live long and healthy lives" ("Failed," 23). Some, such as Langston Hughes in his poem "Personal" or Baldwin in his famous essay "Down at the Cross," fumble with inexact labels before staking claim to their individuality and the right to personal discretion in spiritual matters: "I like doing things alone" (Baldwin, "Cross," 70). Acts of artistic creation are frequently acknowledged as serving a spiritually fulfilling purpose in black lives when no formal religion will do, whether it is through writing, as Baldwin states, or playing the piano, like the title character in his story "Sonny's Blues." However, simply expressing opposition and enduring charges of blasphemy to ask probing spiritual questions often remains the most powerful statement, particularly considering the explosive impact that religious dissent can have in black communities of faith. Certainly the screaming capitalization of the OUTRAGED mother in Rodgers's poem bears this out.

In other poems, Rodgers moves closer to Cone's theological prescriptions before ultimately adopting a more traditional evangelical faith. Texts such as "mama's God", "IT IS DEEP," and "how I got ovah II / It is Deep II," do not diminish the criticisms of the daughter in "JESUS WAS CRUCIFIED," but rather, these later poems underscore a deep ambivalence in African American literary texts that attempt to negotiate abstract religious grievances with the empowering dimensions of its practice in oppressed communities. After her own religious conversion and during the waning years of black cultural nationalism, Rodgers published the poem "and when the revolution came" in the 1975 collection *how i got ovah*. In this poem, she depicts an image of church folk who are ready to welcome back the prodigal militants:

> we been waiting fo you militants
> to realize that the church is an eternal rock
> now why don't you militants jest come on in
> we been waiting for you
> we can show you how to build
>     anything that needs building
> and while we're on our knees, at that.

(lines 55–61)

To enable the collective unity described here, this poem restates Rodgers's previous sociopolitical and theological concerns as rants about giving up "easter and christmas," combing your hair "the natural way," and eating "brown rice"—ideas that appear fleeting and foolish beside the strength of the "eternal rock." Furthermore, the elders in this poem do not interrupt the young in midsentence, but instead listen patiently and wait (presumably as they have always done) to be appreciated for their wisdom. The concluding verses suggest that the reconstituted community will be made of church folk and militants both humbling themselves before God as they "grow in black grace" (46) and build institutions together "on [their] knees" (61). Though it is not clear how the effectiveness of these new institutions will be measured, and whether or not Coltrane will now be played at Sunday service, Rodgers's approach foregrounds qualities such as the strength and the forgiveness of black Christians in order to enable reconciliation.

What is significant about Rodgers's work, when considered as a whole, is the way in which she invites the reader to scrutinize the ever-changing shape and tenor of her spiritual struggle. Other texts examined in this study respond differently to the crisis of faith, using different evaluative measures to probe life's mysteries and producing an even wider range of interpretive possibilities and conversion experiences. Still, regardless of the outcome, each text opens discursive avenues that affirm the value of existential interrogations of the problem of evil. Theoretical arguments and abstract riddles serve as an important point of departure for spiritual inquiry, to be sure. Yet the narratives under investigation—which include sentiments similar to the sly irreverence of "JESUS WAS CRUCIFIED" and the penitent confessions of "and when the revolution came"—ultimately demonstrate how the subjective experiencing of evil continually shapes and legitimizes individual and collective understandings of divine justice among black people. Again and again, twentieth-century African American writers locate Lucille Clifton's question—"why do you not protect us"—at the heart of their creative interpretations of religious belief and practice. Though answers remain elusive and unclear for some, their goal is, as Cornel West maintains, to learn how to linger and "to wrestle in a sustained way" with the tragedy and absurdity of human existence ("Black Strivings," 92).

ACCORDINGLY, EACH of the following chapters constitutes a different approach to the philosophical variances of the problem of evil. Guided by Benjamin Mays's example and Michael Peterson's more recent claim that "great literature not only makes the problem more concrete, but also exposes us to particular conceptions of its depth and many dimensions" (*Evil*, 19), this study probes the nuances of the fictional images, characters, and narrative structures of black religious crisis and critique in the twentieth century. While some writers tend to exert their imaginative energies formulating the dilemma in the context of black American experience, others suggest defenses or theodicies that attempt to resolve the question of God and the meaning of human suffering more comprehensively.

The first chapter, "'In My Flesh Shall I See God': Ritual Violence, Racial Redemption, and the Black Christ," uses Countée Cullen's 1929 poem "The Black Christ" to explore the controversial image of the lynched black sufferer as sacrificial martyr during the segregation era. While previous examinations have focused almost exclusively on the Christ imagery, I maintain that Cullen patterns his narrative after the Book of Job. He incorporates the Old Testament story's legal rhetoric, sensory imagery, and distinctive solution of redemptive suffering into the modern crucifixions of black men. As a result, the true beneficiary of the poem's miracle is not the "resurrected" lynched body, but the surviving family members who bear witness: the mother who never lost her faith in Jesus Christ, and the skeptical brother, whose trust in God's goodness is restored. I argue that such artistic engagements with the crucified black Christ attempt to "solve" the problem of evil by reinterpreting the idea of suffering as punitive in favor of a new understanding of suffering as pedagogical—an avenue for spiritual growth in black communities of faith. Cullen's poem ultimately provides this study's most thorough illustration of a traditional Christian theodicy and offers a useful transition to mid- and late twentieth-century texts.

Black literature features a vigorous engagement with conversion narratives of all sorts, with portals, thresholds, and the momentous act of spiritual turning as a manifestation of black subjectivity. In the second chapter, "'Wrastl' On Jacob': Richard Wright and the Trope of the Mourner's Bench," I examine the existential struggle encoded in rituals of black religious conversion through the work of Richard Wright in the 1930s and 1940s. My analysis examines how his characters' questions about God, suffering, and masculinity, initially forged during adolescence, are articulated through literal and figurative performances on the "mourner's bench"—a symbolic seat for unsaved and repentant sinners at the church altar. In my explications of *Native Son*, *Black Boy*, and Wright's unpublished novel *Tarbaby's Dawn*, I also discuss the way community pressures and the emotional exploitation of black mothers inevitably transforms this familiar liturgical ritual into a predatory act. Given that Wright is one of many writers who associate the call for divine justice with issues of abandonment and repudiation, the mourner's bench trope constitutes an influential intertextual signifier in African American writing.

Moving from the mourner's bench to the wedding altar, the third chapter, "'A Loveless, Barren, Hopeless Western Marriage': Spiritual Infidelity in the Fiction of Nella Larsen and Alice Walker," demonstrates how the discourse of marital strife functions as a means through which black writers recover the repressed spiritual identities of women who have been unjustly yoked to God and to man. The multifaceted depictions of "wedlock" in the work of Nella Larsen and Alice Walker are especially revealing for the ways the material manifestations of troubled marriages and unfulfilling sexual relations are represented *spiritually* through corrupted church covenants and the devastation of God's silence. I use the philosophical questions that Larsen raises in *Quicksand* (1928) as a catalyst for evaluating the intersections of religion, marriage, and sexuality in Walker's fiction from the 1970s and 1980s. Informed by recent studies in womanist theology, my analysis of "spiritual infidelity" demonstrates the real effects that oppressive theological language/vows can have on the bodies of black female brides. In the process, I argue that these texts force a jarring reconsideration of the Christian God's existence as an omnipotent and benevolent deity, while rejecting the church's valorization of black women's self-sacrifice, denial, and loss.

The fourth chapter, "'There is No Way Not to Suffer': Evil Ruptures and Improvisations of Joy in 'Sonny's Blues' and 'The Sky Is Gray,'" considers how two powerful short stories reconfigure the philosophical debate over both moral *and* natural evil through countertexts of lived experience. "Sonny's Blues" (1957) and "The Sky Is Gray" (1968) both raise critical questions about the inexplicable nature of human suffering, yet each story challenges the unspoken desire for order, stability, and absolute meaning that lies at the core of such intellectual endeavors. Baldwin's tale alludes to the improvisational repetitions and breaks of jazz and blues music, for example, as a way of invoking the humor and pathos of existence. This chapter places Baldwin's account of urban life in Harlem in dialogue with the southern perspective of Gaines's short story, which emphasizes the grueling realities of Jim Crow during the early 1960s. My analysis draws on a broader understanding of theodicy to explicate how the blues offers a critical paradigm for the development of black masculinity as well as a maturing religious consciousness.

Issues of suffering, survival, and spiritual health circulate throughout Toni Morrison's work, yet none of her novels confronts the problem of evil as innovatively as *Paradise* (1998)—the primary focus of the book's concluding chapter, "'But God Is Not a Mystery. We Are.': Toni Morrison and the Problem of Paradise." Where previously discussed texts focus al-most exclusively on evil's purpose, *Paradise* relocates the discursive hori-zon of black spiritual struggle to the amorphous existence and meaning of "good." Morrison portrays an experimental rendering of a black utopia in this novel that is couched in Judeo-Christian discourse and textured by African American experience. Yet even a community formed with "so clean and blessed a mission" (292) can collapse when the brittle comforts of rigidly prescribed social and spiritual identities are unable to withstand change, risk, or adventure. To interrogate the failures of Morrison's town, I analyze her efforts to deconstruct the way sacred stories and signs are read (and misread) to convey essential truths about humanity's purpose. I also single out three of the narrative's prophetic figures, whose pragmatic spiritual wisdom and worldly insight provide a compelling alternative to the constraints of the town's theodicy. Delving into the mythical claims of *Paradise* offers further evidence of how the American descendants of African slaves wrestle with the problem of evil and divine justice in the twentieth century.

In the study's concluding pages, I address creative engagements with race, religion, and evil in our own century through a brief consideration of Hurricane Katrina and the literary representations of loss and devas-tation that followed the 2005 Gulf Coast disaster. I highlight poems, in particular, from a special issue of the African Diaspora journal *Callaloo* as a way of illustrating how contemporary writers explore the nature of God through themes of helplessness and desertion incited by the flood. Water imagery evokes added associations for African Americans that recall the atrocities of the Middle Passage, even as the verses denounce the ways in which marginalized people of all races suffered. Implicit in many of these creative responses is the question of God's judgment, newly phrased for the twenty-first century: "Did God cause the wind to roar and the waters of New Orleans to rage?" (Dyson, *Come Hell*, 193), yet far greater scrutiny is applied to human agents of neglect and apathy in the poems. Significant at-tention is also placed on imagining the individual stories of Katrina survi-vors, buoyed by hope and a tested faith. As black literary representations of the hurricane and the other inevitable storms continue to grow, perhaps the texts in this study will have served as signposts of new territories ahead.

# 1

## "In My Flesh Shall I See God"

### Ritual Violence, Racial Redemption, and Countée Cullen's "The Black Christ"

> My mother, Job's dark sister, sits
> Now in a corner, prays, and knits.
> Often across her face there flits
> Remembered pain, to mar her joy,
> At Whose death gave her back her boy.
> —COUNTÉE CULLEN, "The Black Christ"

THE FRONTISPIECE of Countée Cullen's 1929 collection *The Black Christ and Other Poems*, confronts readers with a nude black male hanging by his neck from a long, jagged tree limb. In the black-and-white drawing by the art-deco illustrator Charles Cullen, the figure's hands are fastened behind his back, and his feet are tied at the ankles. Rising behind the lynched body are sunbursts and a white cloud that ascends into the torso, shoulders, and bowed head of a second man, this one adorned with a crown of thorns. The image alerts us to the central argument put forth by "The Black Christ," that the corporal text of terror against African Americans should be read alongside the crucifixion of a "white" Jesus of Nazareth. But the drawing also anticipates the vexing ambiguities that emerge in the verses to follow. Already we may be wondering *how* poetic invention will align these two sufferers, even as they are depicted as racialized opposites of spiritual and material reality. Do the figures in the illustration represent two different individuals with distinct cultural histories, or are they dual aspects of a single man? The frontispiece imagines a connection between racial transcendence and divine immanence that invites further questions about the redemptive qualities of the early twentieth-century "passion play"

31

that Countée Cullen sets in the Jim Crow South. Exactly what kind of redemption will be championed through the Christian martyrdom of a black lynched body and the unmerited suffering of those left behind?

Literary critics who have taken the time to explore "The Black Christ" remain generally dissatisfied with Cullen's engagement with these questions. Most concur with Darwin Turner's assessment of the thirty-three-page poem as an "impressive failure" (*Minor Chord*, 75). Preferring the thematic clarity of the New Negro poet's most famous works such as "Heritage" and "Ballad of the Brown Girl," many critics fault the poetic techniques in "The Black Christ," dismiss its foray into spiritual realism, and claim that Cullen "adds little to an overworked trope."[1] On the other hand, religious scholars consider Cullen's lyrical meditations in his poem to be an effective vehicle for discussing theological concepts. James H. Smylie uses it to examine the ethic of suffering love, while William R. Jones explores the issue of divine racism through the story's conflict.[2] Fascinated as I am by this interpretive elasticity, I agree that the piece is not without its stylistic imperfections. Yet my investigation is motivated by a reluctance to disregard it as being so thoroughly flawed, particularly when the clunky machinations of these "flaws" reveal critical insight into the poem's assertion that Calvary "was but the first leaf in a line/Of trees on which a Man should swing" (lines 17–18).

In "The Black Christ," when a young black man named Jim is hunted by a southern lynch mob for striking a white man in self-defense, Jesus suffers in the victim's stead, disguising himself in Jim's dark flesh moments before the rope is pulled taut. Cullen further modernizes Christ's resurrection in the poem as the tree that once sagged with Jim's body miraculously sways free in the climactic scene. Bearing witness to the miracle is Jim's brother, the nameless narrator, whose inability to reconcile God's apparent goodness with the agony of racial oppression frames the poem's most compelling moments of introspection. There is also Jim's mother, the black matriarch described in the poem as "Job's dark sister," whose unquestioned faith earns the most precious reward (line 934). Indeed, in his effort to construct a socially relevant work and to achieve a certain figurative, aesthetic, and theological coherence, Cullen does not confine the thematic breadth of his narrative to the New Testament. While previous scholarship has focused almost exclusively on the poet's handling of the Christ imagery in his verse, my reading suggests that the enigmatic questions of theodicy offer a more provocative point of entry into "The Black Christ." In this chapter, I argue that Cullen patterns his narrative, in particular, after the wisdom literature of Job and incorporates its legal rhetoric, sensory imagery, and distinctive solution of redemptive suffering into the modern crucifixions of black men.

Though the gruesome spectacle of lynching may command the attention of Cullen's readers and provoke the most visceral response, what will become clear during the course of my analysis is that the principal issues that circulate through "The Black Christ" have little to do with identifying the underlying causes of lynching, exonerating murdered black victims, or condemning white lynch mobs. Readers who have dissected this narrative for a cohesive social exposition against lynching have been frustrated by the meager political strata buried beneath the poetics of racial redemption. Of ultimate importance to Cullen, and arguably to the legions of African American writers and artists who take up the crucified black Christ metaphor, is the spiritual *affect* of terror and the way in which black communities of faith negotiate the questions of moral evil and divine justice that are central to the Book of Job. For the believer who struggles with human misery in a world created by a just, loving, and all-powerful God, this black Christ solves the philosophical puzzle by reinterpreting the idea of suffering as punitive in favor of a new understanding of suffering as pedagogical, an avenue for spiritual development or what John Hick refers to as "the soul-making process" ("Soul-Making," 225).

Literary biographers attribute much of Cullen's "ongoing quarrel with Christianity" to the conservative evangelical upbringing he received from his adopted parents, Carolyn Cullen and the Methodist pastor Frederick A. Cullen. According to Gerald Early, young Countée was especially devoted to his father, who led a socially and politically active ministry in Harlem during the 1920s, and was characterized as a "strict fundamentalist" with a "Puritan demeanor" (introduction, 17). Yet the deep religious awareness that Reverend Cullen nurtured in his son would often manifest in Countée's poetry through a racialized discourse that set his Christian identity in conflict with his "pagan" desires. Cullen's enduring fascination with the imaginative possibilities of religio-racial struggle leads Early to surmise that it was "the resulting fictive tension, the resulting dramatic functionalism, that enabled Cullen to write so well" (58). Still, Cullen's biographer also acknowledges the functional theodicy that emerges from the poet's creative engagement with black suffering:

> But Cullen, as an intellectual black, easily saw that black Christianity must ultimately accept that the Negro's humanity must forever be his tragic suffering: this is precisely what his greatest religious poems—"The Litany of the Dark People," "The Shroud of Color," "The Black Christ"—say. He is

constantly condemned to be entrapped by the myth of his victimization, and whether he rages against it or submits to it, he ultimately confesses that he is helpless before it. (58–59)

In keeping with Cullen's larger body of work, I argue that his approach to suffering in "The Black Christ" ultimately consecrates the agony of unmerited pain in a way that upholds classic conceptualizations of God's omnipotence and omni-benevolence. The poem's speaker advocates a theological justification for evil based on ideas of redemptive suffering that have long been considered to be "the most dominant theory concerning the suffering of African-Americans" (Pinn, *Moral Evil*, 8). It is this approach to human suffering that distinguishes Cullen's poem from the later works under investigation in this book. (Four decades after "The Black Christ" was published in 1929, the unrepentant Black Nationalist in Carolyn Rodgers's poem "JESUS WAS CRUCIFIED" will mock the same platitudes of endurance that bring Cullen's narrator to his knees in prayer.) Nevertheless, like the trope of the mourner's bench discussed in the next chapter, the cultural metaphor of the crucified black Christ interrogates the spiritual dimensions of black sociopolitical oppression in ways that distinguish modern black engagements with faith.

## Lynching, the Bible, and Black Literature

The pain and consequence of racial violence is a pervasive theme in African American literature. Twentieth-century representations of southern spectacle lynching induce a particularly brutal quality of horror and grief, with their macabre images of ropes, charred bones, and angry white mobs. In the eighteenth century, the term "lynching" typically applied to "nonlethal summary punishment such as flogging or tar-and-feathering," but later definitions of the extralegal procedure indicate that to be "lynched" was to be publicly executed by hanging, burning, and other forms of torture (Dray, *At the Hands*, iii). Suspects were denied due process of law, dragged from their homes and even from jail cells, only to be killed before criminal evidence could be collected and verified. Antilynching activists such as Ida B. Wells, along with the NAACP and other civic organizations, worked tirelessly to expose false and inflammatory accusations and to highlight how white vigilante justice was used in the South as a method of social control.

"There is much killing in American history, a great deal of it no doubt senseless and unnecessary," notes the historian Philip Dray, "but lynching celebrates killing and makes of it a ritual, turning grisly and inhumane acts of cruelty into theater with the explicit intent that they be viewed and remembered" (*At the Hands*, xii). In the wake of ritualized acts of violence, one of the ways in which black writers make what the theologian J. Deotis Roberts calls "creative use of suffering" is by imagining a faith-based response through the black Christ ("Individual," 310). Works from Langston Hughes's poem "Christ in Alabama" (1932) to Ernest Gaines's novel *The Autobiography of Miss Jane Pittman* (1971) take the historical reality of lynching into consideration with the ways in which black communities of faith have traditionally read their past, present, and future in scripture. These literary renderings acquire new dimension when assessed within the context of a black religious culture that is replete with its own exegetical activity.

In accounting for the syncretism of the crucified black Christ metaphor, the figurative language of the Bible is an obvious source. This sacred text portrays the act of being "hanged on a tree" as indicative of divine judgment and rejection in the ancient world. Hanging, in this context, applies primarily to the manner in which the sinner was publicly shamed and not necessarily to the torture-ridden execution that often followed (Hengel, *Crucifixion*, 24). While the New Testament Book of Acts in 5:30 and 10:39 links the instrument of public degradation—the tree—to the cross on which Jesus Christ was sacrificed, Paul's epistle to the Galatians reads the Crucifixion within the framework of Old Testament law. For example, Deuteronomy states: "When someone is convicted of a crime punishable by death and is executed, and you hang him on a tree, his corpse must not remain all night upon the tree; you shall bury him that same day, for anyone hung on a tree is under God's curse. You must not defile the land that the Lord your God is giving you for possession" (NRSV, Deut. 21:22–23). With this in mind, Paul remarks that it is Jesus who "redeemed us from the curse of the law by becoming a curse for us" (Gal. 3:13). The ancient Romans not only crucified criminals and political insurgents, but used such torture to punish and deter rebellious slaves—an association that intensified the perceived indignity suffered by a Messiah (Hengel, *Crucifixion*, 62). It should also be noted that the tree to which these Bible verses refer is actually a large wooden stake, often affixed with a cross beam; and yet there is an uncanny connection between the Deuteronomic tree and the southern poplar trees that were chosen, in the words of a song made famous by Billie Holiday, to bear "strange fruit."[3]

While the Bible offers one door through which scholars can enter the imagined kinship between ritual violence and racial redemption, black cultural memory offers another. The allusion circulates through the survivalist religion of late eighteenth- and nineteenth-century slave communities with its unique blend of evangelical Protestant beliefs and West African religious practices. The sociologist Orlando Patterson contends that "Jesus and his crucifixion dominate the theology of the slaves," and he argues that enslaved black Americans were particularly captivated by the dualistic nature of the crucifixion theme that places "the ethic of judgment" alongside "the ethic of the redeemed sinner" (*Slavery*, 75). Spirituals, sermons, slave narratives, and tracts such as David Walker's *Appeal* strike a balance between God as divine judge on the one hand, and as comforting savior on the other.

Although the specificity of the biblical allusion may vary, representations of the black Christ share a similar premise—that black people, who have been judged by white society as intellectually, culturally, and biologically inferior, share through their suffering a special kinship with Jesus Christ. Kelly Brown Douglas notes that "Jesus' bond with the outcast and down-trodden" was a critical element of the enslaved African's encounter with Christianity in America, despite the efforts of whites to use the Bible to justify oppression (*Black Christ*, 21). The metaphoric enterprise also con-demns white racist Christians by explicitly and implicitly labeling them as "crucifiers." With regard to the religious discourse of post-Emancipation southern lynching, literary representations of the black Christ swell in accor-dance with the historical occurrences of the practice in the late nineteenth and twentieth century. In 1920, W. E. B. Du Bois published a poem in *Dark-water: Voices within the Veil* that captures the horror of a white man who admits to lynching a black man "in Thy name." Tormented, the murderer cries:

> Awake me, God! I sleep!
> What was that awful word Thou saidst?
> That black and riven thing—was it Thee?
> That gasp—was it Thine?
> This pain—is it Thine?

> (251)

Other visual and literary arts of the Harlem Renaissance further indi-cate the pervasiveness of this theme. In Claude McKay's "The Lynching" (1920), the spirit of a burning victim "ascend[s] to high heaven," where "His father, by cruelest way of pain,/Had bidden him to his bosom once again" (lines 1–3). Two years later, Cullen would foreshadow the themes of "The Black Christ" in a sonnet entitled "Christ Recrucified" (1922). In it, the poet declares: "The South is crucifying Christ again/By all the laws of ancient rote and rule" (lines 1–2). Walter White's 1924 novel *The*

*Fire in the Flint* features a middle-class black surgeon who is lynched for attempting to heal the racial inequality of his south Georgia town with a ministry of "economic independence" (196). In his study of crucifixion in ancient societies, Martin Hengel maintains that, "by the public display of a naked victim at a prominent place—at a crossroads, in the theatre, on high ground, at the place of his crime—crucifixion also represented his uttermost humiliation, which had a numinous dimension to it" (*Crucifixion*, 87). Historical records demonstrate that the ritualized violence of modern lynching shares with the ancient practice of crucifixion this intense public humiliation. But what new meanings are generated when African American storytellers, singers, artists, preachers, historians, and activists seek out a "numinous dimension" in lynched black bodies?

## "Greet, Virgin Tree, Your Holy Mate!": Understanding Cullen's Crucifixion

Few literary texts explore the issue as explicitly as Cullen's "The Black Christ." In the poem, the character Jim is hanged on a tree, and the concluding line removes all doubt as to this tree's significance: "Its roots were fed with priceless blood./It is the Cross; it is the Rood" (lines 968–69). In keeping with the biblical account of Christ's experience, the young man foreshadows his own death during one of his nightly conversations with his brother. "I have a fear," Jim states:

> "This thing may come to me some day.
>   Some man contemptuous of my race
>   And its lost rights in this hard place,
>   Will strike me down for being black."
>
> (lines 219–23)

And yet the racial determinism that compels Jim's prophecy is complicated by his brother's depiction of him as prideful and headstrong. In one of the many instances in which the narrative insinuates that Jim and the New Testament Savior are *not* one and the same, Cullen notes the young man's embittered intention to aggressively defend himself and avenge a painful legacy of "many thousands gone" if attacked. Jim continues:

> "And I may swing, but not before
>   I send some pale ambassador
>   Hot footing it to hell to say
>   A proud black man is on his way."
>
> (lines 231–34)

Such sentiments may be heroic, but they are hardly "Christ-like." The last couplet even seems to suggest that Jim is willing to spend eternity in hell for the pleasure of a single "life-divesting blow." It is for this reason that Gerald Early maintains that Cullen's text "reinvent[s] the entire myth of disobedience to authority, which is the cornerstone of Christian theology, so that it is *that* disobedience which is understood as . . . the assertion of political and moral right" (introduction, 62). The poem's speaker further emphasizes Jim's heroism by frequently describing him as handsome, passionate, and of an "imperial breed"—a prince, perhaps, from an "Ethiopian Prophecy" (line 274).[4] Jim also exhibits a deep admiration for the beauty of creation. Christened by his brother as "Spring's gayest cavalier" (line 945), Jim describes nature's seasonal rebirth through lush images of music, animals at play, a lady draped in green and gold. His language is replete with classical imagery and is tellingly devoid of any Christian or biblical allusions (thus leading Houston Baker to characterize Jim as "pagan-spirited" [*Many-Colored Coat*, 49]). Significantly, it is this delight in spring as both an expression of innovation and as an agent of transition that contributes, in part, to his encounter with a lynch mob.

"The thing we feared has come," Jim states later in the narrative (line 463). He stumbles into his family's rural cabin, bleeding from the head, with a branch in his hand. As he waits for the "two-limbed dogs" (line 466) to arrive, he insists on explaining his actions—testifying, so to speak—to his brother and mother. He tells them that, during his revelry with spring, he met a white woman who shared his appreciation for nature's beauty. Sensual allusions of springtime fecundity notwithstanding, no explicit mention of a sexual relationship between the two is made until a white man disturbs the interracial couple. After striking Jim, he accuses the woman of being "a black man's mistress, bawdy whore" (552). Jim would later confess that it was not because of any personal affront that he hit (and most likely killed) the white man. "Spring's gayest cavalier" claims to have defended the honor of not one, but two ladies "rich and fair" against a villain who "had unlatched an icy door, / And let the winter in once more" (590–91).[5]

Jim's brother hides him in a closet once the story is told, and soon after, a mob of white men bursts into their home. It is in the ensuing scenes that the New Testament machinery, clanking louder now than ever, takes full control of the plot. When the white men shout, "Lynch him!" Cullen's narrator remarks: "O savage cry, / Why should you echo, 'Crucify!'" (lines 645–46). When a lone voice advises the men to wait "with slow talk of trial, law," before conceding to the mob, he is cast as Roman procurator Pontius

Pilate (line 648). And at last, when Jim reappears before his accusers strangely illuminated against the wall, "as if evolved from air; / As if always he had stood there," the changed expression in his face and the gentleness of his voice signals a startling Christophany (lines 678–79).

At least one critic has said that "The Black Christ" features "a Negro boy who is lynched and who lives again after death" (Ferguson, *Countee Cullen*, 113). But a closer investigation reveals that the man who was once Jim has been displaced by Jesus Christ of the New Testament. This "Son of God" gives his life *voluntarily:* "No one takes it from me, but I lay it down of my own accord. I have power to lay it down, and I have power to take it up again" (John 10:18). Rather than have his African American protagonist express a similar willingness to sacrifice his life and be lynched, Cullen allows a disguised black (or blackened) Christ to walk into white hands. Likewise, in his discussion of the poem, Smylie states that Cullen "does not interpret Christ's crucifixion in terms of a sacrifice to satisfy wounded honor or a debt for human sin, but rather in terms of *theo pathes*, the God who is with us and for us in our human agony" ("Countée Cullen's 'The Black Christ,'" 164).

Even the members of the lynch mob detect something strange about the black man with "a crown / Of light" above his head (lines 699–700). Considering the way in which historically such vigilante groups have been careless about identifying black suspects, it should come as no surprise that the mob ultimately disregards their moment of hesitation and drags the black man outside. What results is "a cry":

> So soft, and yet so brimming filled
> With agony, my heart strings thrilled
> An ineffectual reply,—
> Then gaunt against the southern sky
> The silent handiwork of hate.
> Greet, Virgin Tree, your holy mate!

(lines 774–80)

With this image, "The Black Christ" appears to blend the two figures from the Charles Cullen illustration into a single bodily text. Angry and grieving, the narrator—still an unbeliever—barrages his devout mother for her faith. But when, during the course of his rant, the closet door creaks open in their home and Jim emerges unharmed from his hiding place, the surprising twist is revealed. The single body is split in two again, and we are left to comprehend Jim and the fate of his divine double. The narrator states:

> Either I leaped or crawled to where
> I last had seen stiff on the air
> The form than life more dear to me;
> But where had swayed that misery
> Now only was a flowering tree
> That soon would travail into fruit.

(lines 897–902)

Exactly who, then, is the Black Christ meant to represent? As the Harlem Renaissance lyricist who was obliquely reprimanded by Langston Hughes for wanting to be "a poet—not a Negro poet,"[6] Cullen would certainly have been aware of the cultural currency of racial modifiers. By qualifying the noun "Christ" with the adjective "black," the title of Cullen's poem calls attention to the existence of a standardized version of the New Testament figure that is understood in Western Christian discourse as white. To be sure, the works of African American writers and artists frequently illustrate how the benevolent, life-affirming qualities that are associated with Christ can be undermined when Jesus is fixed in the image of an oppressor. At the height of his grief, the narrator of Cullen's poem invokes such an image during a debate with his mother. His challenge, "is the white Christ, too, distraught,/By these dark skins His Father wrought?" (lines 833–34) brings to mind the frontispiece of the collection and the white crucified figure who gazes down at the lynched black man below.

Yet Cullen's discursive portrait ultimately evokes an image of Jesus that lacks a fixed racial identity in order to foreground the material and spiritual depths of black subjugation. "The Black Christ" uses an unknown man's blackness to depict the workings of an immanent deity that has the power to reanimate himself in *every* "face" and take on the form of *any* human being, including, but not limited to, the "dark skins His Father wrought." The sentiment is in keeping with Paul's Epistle to the Philippians, in which Jesus "emptied himself, taking the form of a slave, being born in human likeness. And being found in human form, he humbled himself and became obedient to the point of death—even death on a cross" (Phil. 2:7–8). And so Cullen's poem employs blackness to signify the form and likeness of humanity in its fundamental, and most humble ("slave") state. This shape-shifting—or rather, this *race-shifting*—Christ could arguably transcend race, even as he embodies the pain and suffering that are associated with its cultural construction in the segregated South. As Katherine Clay Bassard reminds us, "the vanishing body of Jesus leaves an empty signifier whose reembodiment is both demanded and displaced by those from dispossessed communities" ("Race," 98). Such a reading is in keeping with the narrative's cautionary subtext that, with each lynching, Christ is (re)crucified by whites who claim to be his followers. It may also explain why Cullen's poem is "Hopefully dedicated to White America."

But puzzling issues still remain. If Cullen hoped that "White America" might learn from this miracle, then it is worth pointing out that no whites appear to be present to witness the modern Resurrection. We are given no indication in the poem that the mob lingered long after the execution. The only people who do bear witness to the "flowering tree" and benefit from God's saving grace are the members of Jim's family. To be more specific, it is Jim's *brother* who is saved, and it is the faith of Jim's *mother* that is affirmed through the ordeal. In the poem, the ministry of Jesus Christ is confined to his parting words to the narrator, a direct plea for "a greater faith, a clearer sight" (line 723). And turning to the only woman in the room, he states: "Mother, not poorer losing one, / Look now upon your dying son" (lines 727–28). Indeed, it seems that the narrative's climactic event is enacted for the benefit of these two souls. Jesus steps forward in Jim's body only moments before a white man raises a "heavy club to smite" (line 670) the narrator and his mother, leading one to conclude that it is these two "innocent" (line 709) ones that Jesus is most interested in rescuing.

Jim, on the other hand, abruptly disappears from the story—a fact that reinforces the idea that "The Black Christ" is more conversion narrative[7] than antilynching treatise. By removing the body in his poem, Cullen highlights the community's devastation and the "curse" that the narrator believes "lay on this land and clime" (line 299). Jim's vanished corpse draws our attention to the characters who are left behind to survive the "corruption, blight, and rust" of the South (305). So with the timely appearance of a black deus ex machina, the narrative shifts from the restoration of one man's body to the restoration of another man's soul.

## Encountering Job in "The Black Christ"

Cullen's poem abounds with biblical allusions, beginning with the echoes of Psalms 4:7 in the first line and continuing through the narrator's lament for an apathetic world in which "Jacobs" no longer dare to wrestle for God's grace as in Genesis 32. Particularly strong are the poem's Old Testament references to events and figures not only in Genesis, but in Exodus, Joshua, 2 Samuel, Ezekiel, and Job. It is this last Old Testament referent that opens up the richest and most critically rewarding interpretive possibilities for "The Black Christ." Numerous creative writers have used the archetypal sufferer of ancient wisdom literature as a springboard for exploring the complexities of human suffering, endurance, and faith.[8] A decade prior to the publication of Cullen's poem, the black poet Theodore Henry Shackelford traced a similar path to Christ's crucifixion through the trials of Job, remarking that "Those whom God blessed most largely/Did oft' most troubles know."[9] Richard Wright cites verses from the Old Testament book in at least three of his works: Job 23:2 in *Native Son* (1940); Job 18:12 in *Black Boy* (1945); and Job 21:5 in *The Outsider* (1953).

In addressing the issue of theodicy specifically, Cullen incorporates three critical elements of the Old Testament book in his work: the personification of Job's character through the narrator as "questioner" and the mother as "devout believer"; the adaptation of legal rhetoric that translate Job's desire for a hearing in the divine court into a black man's plea for racial justice; and finally, the manipulation of sensory images in Job to convey the substance of faith and to critique the hazards of the racialized gaze. Additionally, Job's pleas for vindication feature strong images of nature and God's creative power that are echoed in Jim's romantic meditations on spring. Even the shape of Cullen's poem shares basic similarities with Job's literary structure. (Layers of poetic discourse—laments, speeches, and dialogue—are situated between the narrative prose of a prologue and epilogue.) But more importantly, the narrative's engagement with the Book of Job allows us to approach Cullen's use of the Christ-figure from a different perspective. Ultimately, I will argue that the poem uses the summary execution of the black Christ as a divine test of faith for the narrator and his mother—a test that problematically employs "lynch law" as its *crux*.

Some background on Job may be instructive here. In the prologue of Job's spiritual drama, we are given unusual access to God's heavenly council. It is in this meeting place that God first brings Job to the attention of Satan ("the Adversary"), and the two deliberate over the exceptional quality of his faith. For Job is "blameless and upright," God insists, "a man who fears God and turns away from evil" (Job 1:8). Satan responds by raising the unsettling possibility that Job's righteousness is self-serving, a matter of convenience; he remains faithful because such godliness has been rewarded through personal wealth and abundance. The Adversary's challenge—"But stretch out your hand now, and touch all that he has, and he will curse you to your face" (Job 1:11)—sets the story's plot in motion. God authorizes Satan to destroy the esteemed man's livelihood and Job's children, animals, and servants are killed. In a second test, Satan is given God's consent to strike Job's bone and flesh. While his wife admonishes him to "curse God and die" (Job 2:9), his three friends—Eliphaz, Zophar, and Bildad—advise him to accept his ruination as chastisement from God.

The trio's counsel is expressed through platitudes of retribution theology that Job, himself, once subscribed to in the abstract. Now as he experiences the reality of pain and loss, Job struggles to reconcile the deterministic view of suffering as punitive with his sincere belief that he has committed no sin deserving of such punishment. In a series of speeches that are reminiscent of Psalms 42–44, Job argues his case to his friends and grieves his alienation from God with anguished pleas to heaven: "Why have you made me your target? Why have I become a burden to you?" (Job 7:20). He refuses, however, to accept the simple solutions of his friends, and never does he claim to have intimate knowledge of the ways of God. Just as the prologue maintains that "In all this Job did not sin with his lips" (Job 2:10), the appearance of God in the story's conclusion reconfirms Job's godliness. God acts as judge in the epilogue, and as the biblical scholar Robert Fyall states: "Yahweh does not charge Job with sins he has not committed, but he does charge him with ignorance. This leads to Job's repentance and a restored relationship with God" (*My Eyes*, 33). Having passed the divine test, Job is rewarded twofold. We are told that "the Lord blessed the latter days of Job more than his beginning" (Job 42:12). God's mysteries are never unraveled in the story's conclusion, and many of the believer's questions are left unanswered. Job learns that the righteous sufferer is valued by God and that suffering contains a redemptive power that can strengthen the faithful.

So it is with "The Black Christ." Cullen begins by conveying the differences in the worldviews of the narrator and his mother by taking advantage of the dual nature of Job's character. The narrator, Jim's brother, who once "cursed Christ's name," testifies to his own Jobian encounter for the benefit of "all men's healing" in the prologue (lines 2, 20).[10] The narrator pleas for a renewed faith in a world whose roots have sickened and become, like a tree, "diseased, trunk, branch, and shoot" (line 39). This framework, with its proselytizing tone and associative imagery between lynching and crucifixion, establishes a clear set of expectations for the reader. Such foreshadowing allows us to anticipate Jim's "resurrection" long before his doubting sibling. With this in mind, the opening verse of the prologue explicitly locates the backsliding narrator as the primary beneficiary of the story's miracle:

How God, who needs no man's applause,
For love of my stark soul, of flaws

> Composed, seeing it slip, did stoop
> Down to the mire and pick me up,
> And in the hollow of His hand
> Enact again at my command
> The world's supremest tragedy.

(lines 7–13)

In the Old Testament, Job's speeches in the poetic sections are insistent and swarming with angry questions, whereas the speaker in the prose sections depicts Job as patient and passive. In "The Black Christ," the narrator embodies the questioning Job, while his mother's reassuring voice represents the more patient qualities. Cullen links her unwavering faith with the rigid social structure of the agrarian South in order to construct a woman whose "kinship to the soil" is expressed as a spiritual imperative (line 152). Moreover, by christening the narrator's mother as "Job's dark sister" (line 934), Cullen not only racializes the biblical figure, but genders Job's more docile attributes as feminine traits. His depiction echoes common literary representations of the southern black "church mother" whose religious devotion operates in concert with superhuman moral strength, endurance, and intuition. Indeed, it is the church mother in "The Black Christ" who will be the first to intuit the presence of the divine in Jim's flesh. It is she who uses prayer to endure her son's persecution and bears witness to his return with the declaration: "Let your heart's conversion swell / The wonder of His miracle" (lines 883–84).

The narrator makes it clear that he and Jim were comforted by their mother's Bible stories of the oppressed Hebrews in Egypt when they were children, but as they grew older and became more aware of the "things she knew not of," their sense of God's power was diminished by life in the Jim Crow South:

> "Likely there ain't no God at all,"
> Jim was the first to clothe a doubt
> With words, that long had tried to sprout
> Against our wills and love of one
> Whose faith was like a blazing sun
> Set in a dark, rebellious sky.
> Now then the roots were fast, and I
> Must nurture them in her despite.
> God could not be, if He deemed right,
> The grief that ever met our sight.

(lines 201–10)

The narrator follows Jim's lead and continues to nurture his unbelief. He puts forth a view of the South that differs from his mother's pastoral vision. For him, the land is haunted by ghosts and lynched bodies, where the hope of harvest turns to rot. Hurt and angry, he grapples with poverty, discrimination, and the ever-constant threat of violence through intense debate with his mother, who continues to insist that trust in God "is our one magic wand" (line 430). But when the two suffer their own divine test—Jim's lynching—the narrator angrily erupts in his despair and demands, in Jobian fashion: "Why? Hear me ask it. He was young / And beautiful. Why was he flung / Like common dirt to death?" (lines 816–18).

Cullen makes the problem of evil explicit with his speaker's tortured refrain: "Why?" And in keeping with the Book of Job, the New Negro poet creatively employs legal rhetoric to work through the spiritual crisis when no material recourse is available. Job is a legal drama, to be sure, from the heavenly council in the prologue to the divine "verdict" of the last chapter. The title character is both a worshipper and a litigant whose most desperate plea is for a hearing before God. Indeed, this relationship is one of the five principal metaphors that, according to the biblical scholar Renita Weems, is employed most frequently by Old Testament prophets to characterize God and the people of Israel (*Battered Love*, 16).[11] Job insists upon his innocence throughout the book, but in chapters 9 and 10 especially, he reveals his frustration over his inability to participate in an open legal contest. Of God, Job states, "For he is not a mortal, as I am, that I might answer him, that we should come to trial together" (Job 9:32). Job asks in vain for an arbiter to petition his case, for witnesses to defend him. He even imagines how his own cross-examination might sound in court:

> I will say to God, Do not condemn me;
>     let me know why you contend against me.
> Does it seem good to you to oppress,
>     to despise the work of your hands
>     and favour the schemes of the wicked?
> Do you have eyes of flesh?
>     Do you see as humans see?
> Are your days like the days of mortals,
>     or your years like human years,
> that you seek out my iniquity
>     and search for my sin,
> although you know that I am not guilty,
>     and there is no one to deliver out of your hand?
>
> (Job 10:2–7)

Such judicial language takes on added significance when considered within the context of racial violence in America, especially as it is represented in literature. Consider, for instance, Georgia Douglas Johnson's 1925 drama *A Sunday Morning in the South*. In the opening scenes, two elderly women, Liza and Sue, discuss the police hunt for a black man who allegedly attacked a white woman the previous night. Liza remarks, "I says the law's the law and it ought er be er ark uv safty to pertect the weak and not some little old flimsy shack that a puff of wind can blow down" (214). While declaring that "the law's the law," the elderly woman uses biblical imagery to underscore her hope that it *ought* to be an ark of safety, despite the fact that for many black people, it is no protection at all. Ultimately Liza's grandson, a teenager who had previously expressed a desire to go to night school and "help changes the laws," is the one who ends up being accused of the crime (214). Even as a neighbor attempts to reach out to a sympathetic white judge, Liza and Sue sing, "Jesus will help me, Jesus alone" and pray, "That's all, that's all we kin do jes tell Jesus!" (216). The lynching of Liza's innocent grandson in the play's conclusion fails to shake the women's faith. Instead, the murder reveals the nature of justice for African Americans in a society in which man's law is as unstable as an "old flimsy shack."

Significantly, one of the defining characteristics of lynching is that it occurs outside the courts where ordinary citizens act as judge, jury, and executioner. Dray notes that lynching was frequently practiced by "vigilance committees" in the colonies during the Revolutionary era and later in isolated frontier territories during the nineteenth century (*At the Hands*, 20–22). And yet by 1905, "lynching had come almost exclusively to mean the summary execution of Southern black men" as an expedient form of communal justice and social control (18). Lynching records kept by Tuskegee Institute indicate that 3,447 black men and women were lynched between 1882 and 1962. Seven black people were lynched in 1929, the year Cullen's "The Black Christ" was published. The number of deaths increased to twenty the following year.[12] In his discussion of lynching's illegality, Dray singles out the denial of due process as one the practice's most atrocious attributes:

> Lynchings, even where they have been the accepted norm, have always disturbed many Americans. This is not simply because they are barbaric, inhumane acts, but because they inherently disavow a right Americans hold dear—the right to due process before the law. Since early in the eighteenth century, before the founding of the American republic, due process has been understood to include a clear accusation of charges stating what law the accused has violated, a court made up of competent authorities, the right to confront

one's accuser in a trial held under proper proceedings, and the right to be freed unless found guilty. (*At the Hands*, 18)

Despite the spontaneous nature of mob violence, lynchings required organized reinforcement from the entire white community in order to maintain an oppressive social structure that could consistently divest African Americans of their constitutional rights. Likewise, the collective anonymity of the executioners ensured that few lynchers were ever prosecuted. Federal antilynching legislation was also extremely difficult to pass, leading one scholar to comment that "lynching almost became a nationally sanctioned pastime" (Harris, "Lynching," 464).

In passages that parallel Job's petition for his day in court, the mother and the narrator in "The Black Christ" look to heaven for due process before the law. They know that neither Jim nor any other black man will be judged fairly in the South by white racist power structures. Of the white man who attacks him, for example, Jim states: "My right/I knew could not outweigh his might/Who had the law for satellite" (lines 559–61). In dialogue with his mother, the narrator laments over God's apparent distance and reasons that he and his family are too inconsequential to receive any special attention. He longs for a pantheon of warrior Gods, like the Greek and Roman deities, who protect the humans who praise them by providing happiness and wealth in *life*, not only in death. Later, the narrator mocks his mother's faith and angrily questions why her loving God would not protect his creation, why would she continue to praise a Christ who had done nothing "for [her] who spent/A bleeding life for His content?" (lines 831–32). His mother steadfastly insists on faith as the answer. When her son is dragged into the night and lynched, we are told that the black matriarch prays aloud, asserting God is "the judge of all that men might do" (line 801). The mother of "The Black Christ" appeals to a heavenly advocate in ways similar to Job in 16:19 when he states: "Even now, in fact, my witness is in heaven, and he that vouches for me is on high." Where Job appeals to the God of the Hebrew Bible, Cullen asserts that Jesus is the intercessor and "defense counsel" for his Christian characters.

God speaks through a storm in the concluding chapters of the Book of Job. The Lord "answers" Job through a series of rhetorical questions that call attention to his life-giving power and creative dominion. At last Job repents, understanding that God, who has "begotten the drops of dew" (Job 38:28) and can "draw out Leviathan with a fish-hook" (41:1), has a plan for his life that even includes suffering. As Fyall notes, "Job had wished to bring God to trial and Yahweh himself accepts the legal framework and refers to Job as one who has a case with the Almighty, and it is he who finally pronounces the verdict" (*My Eyes*, 34). Likewise, when Jim appears unharmed in Cullen's poem, the narrator is brought low by the miracle. He reflects back, amazed and ashamed, to the parting words of the black Christ, who called him "brother." His soul turns to God instantaneously, emboldened by a vision that resonates not only with Job's theophany, but with the vivid conversion narratives of former American slaves.[13] Jim's "resurrection" proves that God has not only heard the cries of the narrator and his mother, but has judged them both innocent. Furthermore, God has chosen to save Jim to allay all doubts about his saving grace. Just as Job humbled himself before God's mighty query—"Will you even put me in the wrong? Will you condemn me that you may be justified?" (Job 40:8)—so the narrator now claims to be "forever on [his] knees" by his mother's side: "Ever to praise her Christ with her,/Knowing He can at will confer/Magic on miracle to prove/And try me when I doubt his love" (lines 941–45).

As a result, "The Black Christ" shares with the Book of Job a theodicy of redemptive suffering, or the idea that the suffering of the righteous can have a beneficial effect. The narrative's antilynching sentiment is almost incidental to an agenda that valorizes sacrificial religious devotion in black communities and promotes unquestioned faith in the modern world. But when placed within the context of unmerited and disproportionate suffering in black America, Cullen's use of ritual violence as an "accessory device"[14] comes with consequences that deeply undermine the consolatory worth of his representation of lynching as a spiritual test. Readers of Job, for example, are privy to the rules and regulations of God's test ("he is in your power; only spare his life," God says to Satan in Job 2:6). Yet readers of "The Black Christ" are left to wonder whether or not the moral evils that afflict southern black folk are safeguarded by similar restrictions. Cullen's narrative certainly compels us to grapple with the inscrutable nature of life's greatest mysteries through religious faith. But if the poem also compels us to weigh the extraordinary rescue of a lynched body against the divine hands that tied the noose (or allowed the noose to be tied), then I would argue that such a rendering heightens, rather than alleviates, the wasteful suffering of countless black victims whose lives were not spared.

We are told that the narrator is comforted by his new, fraternal connection with Christ, one that may fortify him through challenging times. He realizes, in the words of the black theologian Howard Thurman, "that there is a fellowship of suffering as well as a community of suffers" ("Suffering," 237). Nevertheless, by attributing the horror of lynching to a greater design, by attempting to make "sense" out this senseless act, the spiritual realism of the poem averts our eyes from those human beings whose free will renders them responsible. The members of the awkwardly staged lynch mob appear and disappear like phantoms after their performance in the story, severely diminishing their culpability. In keeping with Anthony Pinn's critique of redemptive suffering, I would also argue that the use of this ethic in Cullen's poem "does not move toward the lessening of oppressive circumstances; rather, it lessens a sense of accountability and responsibility on the part of oppressors. The possibility of redemption through suffering, although not removing a sense of guilt, significantly reduces any urgent need to change behavior oppressors might feel" (*Why Lord?* 89).

Furthermore, with phrases such as "the days are mellow for us now," the poem concludes abruptly with a placating sense of closure (line 930). While the mother prays and knits "in a corner," the narrator gives the impression that his entire days are now spent in supplication (line 935). We are left with an image of order and contentment in the peaceful rural abode where, incidentally, lynching continues unabated. It is an ending that one of Cullen's contemporaries called "grotesquely unnatural" (Wood, "Black Pegasus," 93). Cullen's pastoral fantasy renders the rural poverty, the subjugation, the silence, and even the grisly murder of African Americans as potential pathways to racial redemption. Even Susan Neiman's broad characterization of theodicy as a way to "place evils within structures that allow us to go on in the world," when applied to Cullen's poem, unwittingly reveals the extent to which his characters have been compelled to physically and emotionally detach themselves from the world in order to "go on" in it (*Evil in Modern Thought,* 239). What began as a spiritual indictment of human suffering, then, becomes a southern parable of endurance that leaves worldly systems of oppression profoundly undisturbed.

## "I Saw; I Touched": A Struggle Rewarded

One final instructive comparison between "The Black Christ" and Old Testament wisdom literature can be found in Job 19. The righteous sufferer anticipates the day of his vindication in this oft-quoted passage:

> For I know that my redeemer liveth, and that he shall stand at the latter
> day upon the earth:

> And though after my skin worms destroy this body, *yet in my flesh shall*
> *I see God:*
> Whom I shall see for myself, and mine eyes shall behold and not
> another; though my reins be consumed within me.
>
> (KJV, Job 19:25–27)

Significantly, verse 26 of this chapter has been identified as one of the book's most difficult to translate, "almost unintelligible," according to one Bible commentary (Rodd, *The Book of Job*, 40). A slightly different meaning of the verse is suggested by the New International Version of Job 19:26: "And after my skin has been destroyed, yet in my flesh I will see God."[15] Religious scholars have debated over whether or not Job, whose body the Adversary has been given permission to torment, is claiming to behold God in life, as his skin has been scourged with disease, or after, once he has "wasted away in death" (Fyall, *My Eyes*, 51). Does he see God from within his flesh or from without? As Rodd states, "These translations accord with the view of a vindication either during or after Job's lifetime" (*The Book of Job*, 41).

I am intrigued by the indeterminacy of this verse, for it echoes the imaginative ambiguities of the twentieth-century crucified black Christ metaphor. Cullen's poem celebrates the enduring faith of one who believes that she will see her Savior in the afterlife, but it also rewards the irreverent call of another—a modern soul-searcher—who demands proof of God's existence and a demonstration of his righteousness in the *here and now*. Indeed, the black mother holds fast to the definition of faith as "the assurance of things hoped for, the conviction of things not seen" (Heb. 11:1). With this in mind, she states: "I had no need to view/His side, or pass my fingers through/Christ's wounds" (lines 399–401). But her son remains unmoved. As with the speaker in Cullen's poem "Heritage," the narrator of "The Black Christ" longs for stone and wooden idols "to feel and touch and stroke" (line 340). Cullen makes great use of sensory images to play upon not only the reliability of God, but the subjectivity of racial constructs. Race hatred and the pain caused by racial prejudice are often expressed in the poem through sight, through "corrupt unhealthy glances" (605) and "woe-ravaged eyes" (730), and through the ideas and deeds that are "streaked" (448), "mirrored" (456), and "filmed" (461) on the eyes. When the narrator judges the efficacy of faith in the same fashion, however, he finds a God who "in [his] sight has never done/One extraordinary thing" (lines 326–27). Ultimately, the poem's Doubting Thomas is swayed by the material substantiation of God's grace through Jim's rescue on earth.

> I saw; I touched; yet doubted him;
> My fingers faltered down his slim
> Sides, down his breathing length of limb.
> Incredulous of sight and touch,
> "No more," I cried, "this is too much
> For one mad brain to stagger through."
>
> (lines 885–90)

It is in his brother's dark flesh, then, that the narrator "sees God." But most importantly, the poem goes on to suggest that a divine presence can be found in every victimized body, and that this profound realization is at the core of the unbeliever's awakening. The religious conversion of Jim's brother comes to fruition through his acknowledgment that the tree on which the black Christ was crucified is only one of many unknown trees in the South "whereon as costly fruit has grown" (962).

While the black Christ can certainly encompass every facet of Jesus Christ's life, death, and resurrection, the cultural use of the metaphor represents an attempt to isolate those aspects that are associated with bodily persecution and martyrdom. Outraged by the Scottsboro case in 1931, Langston Hughes makes a similar connection between divine suffering and the scourged flesh of black people in the poem "Christ in Alabama": "Christ is a Nigger / Beaten and black / O, bare your back" (lines 1–3). More than three decades after Hughes wrote his poem, a similar image of the Crucifixion would be summoned forth in the *Wales Window for Alabama*. Designed by the stained-glass artist John Petts, the window was donated by the people of Cardiff, Wales, to the Sixteenth Street Baptist Church in Birmingham the year after a bomb killed four girls there in 1963. The window features an image of a crucified black Christ with his head bowed and arms outstretched, one hand held up in protest, the other extended in a sacrificial posture. There are several messages etched in the colored panes; none is more poignant than the suggestion that the blast that tragically ended the lives of the four innocent youths reverberates on a higher, spiritual plane. Etched around Christ's feet are the words, "You do it to me" in reference to Matthew 25:40.[16]

An older stained-glass window of Jesus also stands in the Birmingham sanctuary. The Christ in this image has a white face and blond hair and stands before a door with a staff in the image of the Good Shepherd (John 10:7). The window, which was damaged during the bombing, was repaired afterward and now stands on the wall adjoining its newer twin. While both windows in the Sixteenth Street Baptist Church are meant to represent

Jesus Christ, the brown-skinned image uses the biblical narrative to chronicle a precise historical moment in the lives of black southerners. It memorializes the pain and suffering of the bombing through the crucified black Christ's sacrifice, just as it honors the redeeming triumph of the civil rights movement through his resurrection.[17]

The same year of the Birmingham church bombing, Howard Thurman wrote that a man who suffers "has to handle his suffering or be handled by it" ("Suffering," 236). Thurman's eloquent meditations on suffering maintain that spiritual and physical anguish can function like the stained glass of the *Wales Window for Alabama,* as a lens through which new light can be seen. "Openings are made in a life by suffering that are not made in any other way," Thurman states. "Serious questions are raised and primary answers come forth. Insights are reached concerning aspects of life that were hidden and obscure before the assault" (238). The crucified black Christ metaphor is one way in which writers and artists have imagined the redemptive "openings" that are generated by the assault of ritualized violence against black Americans.

Countée Cullen couples his distinct rendering of the black Christ with a plea for spiritual revival, a call for seekers fearless enough to confront the inexplicable and reach out for what his poem refers to as the "Shining Thing" (line 46). He even reinforces the value of spiritual struggle in the prologue by alluding to Jacob, yet another Old Testament figure, and praising those like the narrator who "wrestle all night long, though pressed/be rib to rib and back to breast,/Till in the end the lofty guest/Pant, "Conquering human, be thou blest" (lines 51–54). Cullen's brief allusion to the themes of struggle and salvation in "Wrestling Jacob" offers a valuable intertextual connection to the writings of Richard Wright, Langston Hughes, James Baldwin, and Zora Neale Hurston. These black writers also use the experience of conversion to foreground the religious questioning that is associated with the problem of evil. Yet Wright's work, in particular, differs from "The Black Christ" in focusing more consistently on the gendered dynamics of *failed* conversions. And as the next chapter demonstrates, the spiritual frustration and hostility in Wright's fiction and autobiographical writings call attention to systemic sociopolitical malfunctions among black believers, while disputing classic understandings of divine justice.

# 2

## "Wrastl' On Jacob"

*Richard Wright and the Trope of the Mourner's Bench*

> I hold my brudder wid a tremblin' han',
> I would not let him go.
> Wrastl' on Jacob, Jacob, day is a-breaking,
> Wrastl' on Jacob, Oh Lord I would not let him go.
>
> —Slave spiritual

"Wrastl' on Jacob" translates the Old Testament struggle of the son of Isaac through the sorrow songs of African American slaves (quoted in Raboteau, *Slave Religion*, 255). The spiritual focuses in particular on the night Jacob wrestled with God in the form of an angel before reentering Canaan (Gen. 32:22–32). The biblical trickster willfully seeks God's blessing and refuses to yield even after the angel injures his hip. At dawn, Jacob's persistence is rewarded. Having previously fought with his twin brother, Esau, and now with the God of Abraham, Jacob is blessed and renamed Israel—which has been translated to mean: "you have striven with God and with humans and have prevailed" (Gen. 32:28). Judeo-Christian traditions believe that God demonstrates the magnitude and consequence of his power in the account while remaining true to his covenant. In the process, Jacob's prophetic encounter serves to guide a chosen people whose coming struggles will require the same unremitting determination, the same courage and faith.

Black antebellum slaves in America added their voices to the biblical story of Jacob during prayer meetings as a way of guiding penitent sinners and adolescents in need of salvation. Consider, for instance, how the aforementioned verse from "Wrastl' on Jacob" situates the deeply personal struggle that the Old Testament figure represents in concert with the supportive presence of a "tremblin' han'." Jacob's experience, like those of the

53

Israelites in Egypt, spoke to the black slaves' individual spiritual strivings while resonating with the collective "wrestling" of an oppressed race in bondage (see Raboteau, *Slave Religion*, 251–56). During revivals that could last until daybreak, troubled seekers were called to a bench reserved near the altar—the "mourner's bench"—where the preacher's exhortations and the prayers of kneeling worshippers urged the unconverted to bury their sin and live anew in Christ. Autobiographies and interviews bear witness to countless spiritual journeys that were initiated on the mourner's bench, and it is in this sacred space that many blacks first embraced a freedom that they would never experience on earth. In keeping with Jacob's regenerative experience in Genesis, enslaved mourners made public their yearning to be *seen* by God and acknowledged, renamed, and blessed through struggle. As another version of "Wrastl' on Jacob" states: "Gonna rassal all night till broad day light/ and ask God to bless my soul" (Fisk, *Unwritten History*, 49).

By the time young Richard Wright hears a church elder describe Jacob's vision in the early 1920s, the small black religious community in Jackson, Mississippi, had already branded him as a sinner and a lost soul. In his 1945 autobiography, *Black Boy*, Wright describes himself at the age of twelve as a skeptical youth, unconvinced by the church's vision of life and undecided on the question of God's existence. When pressured by his family and classmates to believe, he attributes his doubt to hopelessly uncooperative senses. He could not "feel any religion"—he needed to "see something" before he would join the church.[1] His longing resonates with that of the speaker in Countée Cullen's 1929 poem "The Black Christ," who also yearns for a God that he can "feel and touch and stroke" (line 340). But the miraculous regeneration of body and soul that Cullen imagines in his narrative poem is for Wright an elaborate sleight of hand designed to deceive and manipulate the weak-minded. He becomes so frustrated with his grandmother's moralizing that he whispers to her during service: "You see, granny, if I ever saw an angel like Jacob did, then I'd believe" (*Black Boy*, 117). His grandmother misinterprets this furtive desire and quickly boasts to the church elder about Wright's vision. Embarrassed by Granny's own blindness, young Wright corrects the error by explaining to the preacher: "I told her that if I ever saw an angel, then I would believe. . . . But I didn't see *anything*" (118).

Whether absent or unseen, Jacob's combative angel is invoked in *Black Boy* as the harbinger of Wright's lifelong struggle with God and black Christian faith. Here, too, is the mourner's bench, surfacing in the narrative just as his spiritual wrestling reaches a critical peak. His vivid description of the revival at his mother's Methodist church in 1922 is reminiscent of age-old black religious traditions that reveal the influence of both white Christian beliefs and West African patterns of worship and adult initiation. Like his black forebearers, Wright is summoned to a seat near the altar where hymns of support and sanctification await him. But instead of being saved, Wright feels angry, exploited, and "trapped by the community" (*Black Boy,* 153). His account condemns the southern black church's most powerful rite of passage as a morally bankrupt drama that leaves young men feeling blinded, doped, and tricked for the sake of religio-racial belonging: "It was no longer a question of my believing in God. . . . It was a simple, urgent matter of public pride" (154). Communal pressure combined with the emasculating emotional appeal of his crippled mother prompt him to conclude that "the business of saving souls had no ethics" (154).

Interrogating the black Christian "business of saving souls" and its "ethical" alternatives is crucial to understanding how the spiritual challenges raised by the problem of evil are explored in the work of Richard Wright. My discussion in this chapter will examine how his characters' questions about God, religion, and human existence, initially forged during adolescence, are articulated through literal and figurative performances on the mourner's bench. The ritualistic seat appears repeatedly in Wright's fiction and autobiographical writings, functioning not only as a *site* of spiritual travail, but as a *state*—a condition of struggle for his young male characters, whether they labor behind a plow in a Mississippi field or behind bars in a Chicago prison. I argue that the Afro-Christian mourner's bench operates as one of the fundamental structures of feeling in texts such as *Tarbaby's Dawn, Native Son, Black Boy,* and *The Outsider;* it is the trope that gives form and meaning to his intense scrutiny of black survivalist faith and deterministic doctrine.[2] Furthermore, the self-deception and mistranslation that Wright chronicles in his conversion narratives underscore the existential relevance of individual freedom, responsibility, and choice in the lives of African Americans during the segregation era.

Scholars who are interested in exploring Wright's engagement with the philosophy of existence frequently note his interest in Søren Kierkegaard, Albert Camus, Jean-Paul Sartre, and others in relation to *The Outsider,* the novel that Wright published in 1953.[3] But my analysis of works such as *Black Boy* maintains that Wright's deep fascination with the spiritual consequences of individual subjectivity and freedom—which would later be formalized through Sartrean ideas of anguish, abandonment, and despair—prefigure his meeting with the French philosopher in 1946 (Fabre, *Unfinished Quest,*

299). In challenging the self-determining voluntarism of evangelical conversion rituals, Wright exposes what are, for him, troubling inconsistencies
in the black church's claim that salvation is a matter of choice. He further
posits as an impossibility the notion that a young seeker's religious, racial,
and gender identity can be freely chosen in a community marginalized by
racism and poverty. As he says of his own experience in *Black Boy:* "If I
refused, it meant that I did not love my mother, and no man in that tight
little black community has ever been crazy enough to let himself be placed
in such a position" (155).

Thus it should come as no surprise that as existentialism was becoming
of particular interest in America during the 1940s, according to Wright's
biographer Michel Fabre, "Wright found that it fit in with his intimate
vision of the world" (*Unfinished Quest,* 299). Again and again, Wright
imagines the male protagonists of his stories in the horrifying moments
in which they confront an absurd and irrational universe and discover that
they are "condemned to be free" (Sartre, "Existentialism," 295). I should
note, however, that panning through Wright's work for flashes of Sartre
suggests the kind of authenticating strategy that runs counter to my inves-
tigative agenda. It is my hope that in examining how the mourner's bench
acts as a structural metaphor for Wright's own philosophic scrutiny, the
versatile sensibilities of existential philosophy might provide an additional
intellectual perspective and not a framework for glib Western validation.[4]

African American literary traditions ultimately provide the most significant intertextual corroboration of the mourner's bench trope, for Wright
is not the only writer to use this specific image to frame the public and private turmoil that frequently accompanies profound spiritual questioning.
Other black writers such as Langston Hughes, Zora Neale Hurston, and
James Baldwin also express their own painful experience with conversion
rituals. Each calls into question the integrity of the ecclesiastical communities that necessitate the kind of religious performance that represses doubt,
disregards dissent, and rejects reason. Nevertheless, Richard Wright awakens the philosophical tensions of the conversion experience with such fre-
quency and subversive complexity that it is his sustained rendering of the
trope that offers the richest point of departure for this study.

## "To Choose God over Self": The Mourner's Bench

It was during the Second Great Awakening in the late eighteenth and early
nineteenth century that the mourner's bench became particularly widespread

in the South. This evangelical movement made Christianity "more accessible to illiterate slaves and slaveholders alike" by shifting the emphasis away from the rigid liturgical training and biblical instruction of the Anglican Church to the experiential aspects of conversion (Raboteau, *Slave Religion*, 132). Massive numbers of African Americans became Christians during the Second Great Awakening, especially in Baptist and Methodist denominations. Sinners and seekers of all ages were summoned to the mourner's bench, also referred to as the "anxious bench," where those who were "anxious" for their soul could set the redemptive process in motion. In fact, the guiding principle behind the anxious bench, most commonly associated with the New England evangelist and theologian Charles Finney, is the responsibility of the individual "to choose God over self" and strive for moral perfection through *voluntary* submission (Hewitt, *Regeneration*, 28).

In the religious experiences of enslaved blacks, the concept of regeneration on the mourner's bench also incorporated characteristics of a West African Sacred Cosmos. African elements such as antiphonal singing, spirit possession, and the ring shout were given new life, often unknowingly, in antebellum Protestant revivals. But it was the "communal celebrations of initiation and death" among the Yoruba, Igbo, and other native peoples that resonated most profoundly with the language and worship practices of early black Christians, two and three generations removed from their African homeland (Sobel, *Trabelin' On*, 74). Mechal Sobel notes strong parallels between African American Baptist conversion rituals (in which seekers claim to be "struck dead") and the "second birth" practices of West African ethnic groups. Death imagery is invoked by the Ga in Ghana as young boys are "beaten and treated as corpses" before joining the community as adults, while the new lives of the Nigerian Igbo initiates are recognized after the public simulation of their deaths through circumcision (*Trabelin' On*, 15).[5]

Christian baptism, with its emphasis on total immersion as "a symbolic death, with the subsequent laying on of hands symbolizing the entrance of the new spirit into the soul," shares much in common with African initiations into adulthood and communal responsibility (Sobel, *Trabelin' On*, 90). In slave communities, the conversion experience was considered a special rite of passage and "a major social method for initiating adolescents into the community" (Raboteau, *Fire*, 156). Indeed, interviews with former slaves by the Works Progress Administration place the typical age for conversion between nine and twelve years. Guided by a spiritual mother or spiritual father, adolescents were expected to undergo a process of "seeking," which was often accompanied by the dreams and visions of near-instantaneous conversion. Albert Raboteau states, "black children endured the pressure of adult expectation, but they also enjoyed the encouragement, guidance, and affirmation of their elders" (*Fire*, 156).

Nevertheless, black and white Christians occasionally criticized such pressures, even when accompanied by adult guidance or the intense fervor of religious worship. In opposition to Charles Finney, religious leaders such as John Nevin argued that the revivalism of the anxious bench promoted a "false religious excitement" that led to quick and insincere conversions (Hewitt, *Regeneration*, 93). By the 1830s, a growing number of white evangelists were convinced that "the process of walking forward to sit in the anxious seat, instead of being an act of profound spiritual travail, became a stereotyped and forced ritual" (McLoughlin, *Modern Revivalism*, 148). Black conversion narratives reveal similar concerns about Afro-Christian rebirth celebrations. Consider the following description of the "moaner's bench"[6] by a former slave:

> Preachers used to get up and preach and call moaners up to the moaner's bench. They would all kneel down and sometimes they would lay down on the floor, and the Christians would sing. . . . They would call for moaners first night, and moaners would come up for two and three nights waiting to feel something, or to hear something. Sometimes they would walk way out in the woods after getting religion. They would get to rolling and shouting and tell everybody that they had found Jesus and they would shout and shout, and sometimes they would knock the preacher and deacon down shouting. But about a week after that they would go to a dance, and when the music would start they would get out there and dance and forget all about the religion. (Fisk, *Unwritten History*, 48–49)

The anonymous speaker reminds us that sustained commitment to God's word demanded that religious conversion be attended by deep internal transformation, or "metanoia."[7] While the preacher's call often accelerated this process, the opportunity for religious posturing remained a constant concern. In some instances, "the inward should be the bearer of the outward, but the anxious bench had reversed this order" (Hewitt, *Regeneration*, 94).

Conversion narratives hold in tension the outer and inner manifestations of metanoia in a way that serves as a useful example for the mourners in black literary interpretations. Behind the church revivals, family prayers, and baptisms in Richard Wright's work are empty, forced rituals that bind religious belief with racial authenticity, manhood, and the survival of the race. A similar argument is made by the religious scholar Sylvester Johnson, who points to Wright's use of the concept of "tribalism" in evaluating the coercive power that believers exert through ritual: "The community of legitimate persons—the tribe, as Wright describes it—is the agent who reveals or constructs the extreme guilt and vileness of the potential convert. The believers are tribal because they encode outsiders as a threat *ipso facto*. One must pledge allegiance to this tribe through the conversion ritual in order to be transformed from an evil threat to a legitimate member" ("Tribalism," 184–85).[8] More than simply revealing the "false religious excitement" of the mourner's bench, then, Wright's critical stance seeks to expose the faulty, virulent logic that equates religious questioning with a kind of existential illegitimacy.

Wright's novel *Tarbaby's Dawn* offers an excellent example of this process at work. When the title character of this unfinished work arrives at the riverbank in his baptismal robes, he is similarly poised on the brink of adulthood. We are told that, "[Tarbaby] knew for a fact that he was going into that water with no religion in his heart," and yet he feigns conversion and woefully submits, terrified that his true self—the self that longs to flee the South and his parents, to resist Jim Crow, to abandon his pregnant girlfriend—will be revealed in a Sunday morning lie (249).

Wright began writing *Tarbaby's Dawn* in the mid-1930s at least two years before *Uncle Tom's Children* was published, stopping after 285 pages.[9] The first half of the story takes place in 1925 outside Jackson, Mississippi, and follows fifteen-year-old Daniel Morrison—nicknamed "Tarbaby"—through adolescence. The tale captures Tarbaby in crucial moments of self-discovery as he explores his sexuality, yearns to earn his own money, and dreams of one day becoming a black prizefighter like Jack Johnson. Although Tarbaby is a teenager, he has not progressed beyond the fourth grade and continues to engage in childhood pranks, much to the dismay of his strict and ardently religious parents.

Of particular interest is the scene in which Tarbaby attends a revival at his mother's church. During the service, the preacher Elder Hargrove initially uses the biblical story of the prophet Daniel in the Babylonian den of lions as a call for racial pride and activism. "Love your black race so much you will want to face guns, lions, and death rather than see them suffer!" shouts the elder (59–60). But when he concludes his sermon by requesting that all the young men rise before the congregation, the mood of the narrative shifts. Elder Hargrove no longer shouts to allay racial suffering; he "begs"—"Come to the mourners' bench and let us pray for you!" (61). And as Tarbaby and his friend Jim become the center of attention, his mother enters the text, "watching him" and silently coming closer while

Elder Hargrove intensifies his appeal: "I want all of you boys to be brave tonight! I want youall to be soldiers for King Jesus! Join God's army! I want youall to join church tonight! *All* of you!" (62). In response, Tarbaby's public articulation of faith in God and community is dependent upon a desire not to be set apart from those around him. Though the invitation to be brave like Daniel calls for individual sureness, the elder's call ("You two young men in the back, there!") and perhaps even Wright's phonetic rendering of the vernacular phrase *youall* demonstrate the difficulty that Tarbaby has detaching his "you" from the collective "all." It is only after the others rise that he follows, thinking, "*I can't be kneeling here by myself*" (62; emphasis in original).

Amidst the trinitarian structure of the mother, the preacher, and the congregation, this mourner's decision is a crucial step toward more than baptism. The response that his performance engenders in his family, friends, and even the older men conversing at the local barbershop makes clear that his decision must meet the community's approval. It indicates his efforts to become a man like his biblical namesake, and a brave, responsible member of society.[10] What, then, are we to make of the idea that Tarbaby only feigns religious feeling in these scenes, believing that the choice to come to God is not truly his to make? His mother is the first to apply the term "lying" to Tarbaby's conciliatory gestures, saying: "If you get baptised and your soul ain't right you telling God a lie, you hear? And He ain't agoing to forgive you for nothing like that!" (183). Anticipating one of the major concerns of *Black Boy*, the theme of lying as "a constant requirement for survival, and a nearly impossible performance" (Adams, "I Do Believe," 308) shadows the second part of *Tarbaby's Dawn* as Wright continues to render the title character's individual and communal identities as irreconcilable. In the second part of the novel, Wright reinforces the cost of Tarbaby's self-deception and signifies upon the structure and sentiment of the mourner's bench by reconfiguring the seat at the supper table in the Morrison home. Surrounded by his parents, his brother, Si, and his sister, Nellie, Tarbaby is pressed once more for a public confession of faith and racial solidarity. Again Wright translates the conversion ritual into a predatory act with the black mother making the strongest appeal, sinking to her knees at the boy's side. Mrs. Morrison's theodicy in this scene can be compared to that of the self-sacrificing mother in Cullen's "The Black Christ" in that it advocates faith through a fellowship of suffering and a racial kinship with a crucified Messiah:

"Honey, they treated Jesus just like the white folks treat us. They beat 'Im. They spit in His face. They put a crown of thorns on His brow. Then they nailed 'Im to the cross. And He hung there, honey, and died so's me and you might live. He lifted us all above this world, son. Don't you see, honey?"

"Yessum."

"Now, don't you believe?"

"I believe, Ma."

"Then take Jesus to your heart! Your poor old ma's abegging you on her knees, honey child!"

"All right, Ma. I'll be baptised Sunday. Sure enough I will."

"Glory to God!" shouted his mother.

"Ahmen!" said the old man.

Si and Nellie smiled at him sweetly.

"My son's done come to Jesus!" said his mother, sobbing into her hands.

"Ahmen!" said the old man again, nodding his head slowly back and forth.

Tarbaby walked to his room full of a sense of dread and shame. (237–38)

Arguably, Tarbaby's dread, and the alienating power it represents, anticipates book 1 of Wright's novel *The Outsider*, and its heightened engagement with Kierkegaardian philosophy.[11] The adolescent protagonist of *Tarbaby's Dawn* lacks the intellectual sophistication of *The Outsider*'s Cross Damon, whose complex search for identity conveys the existential struggle of modern man. And yet Tarbaby's crisis of faith offers a provocative representation of black subjectivity similarly "riddled with disappointment, frustration, and pain" (Hayes, "Double Vision," 175).

Tarbaby's emotional cacophony of fear and desire crescendos as he takes his place among a hundred men and women at the bank of the river: "Soon it grew so loud that Tarbaby could not take it in; it became just noise. It seemed that he was outside of it all. And could they not tell it by looking at his face? Surely, it was written there!" (254). He is terrified that his face, unmasked before God, will communicate indecision like a brand or a curse to be "read" by the community. No one steps forward, however, to yank Tarbaby from the river. And despite a friend's earlier warning, the water does not turn "black" when he is dipped into its chilled depths (186). Neither does lightning strike him for "lying to God" as he once believed it would (222). If Wright's protagonist experiences a second birth in this pivotal moment of immersion, it is a rebirth into the startling realization that although he has "escap[ed] the wrath of God," he will not be rescued from the terrifying sea of humanity. Not sin, but self-deception is washed away in the river as Tarbaby comes to a new awareness of his own place in the world and realizes, in the words of James Baldwin, that, God "failed His bargain" ("Cross," 33). Encoded within the breakdown of Tarbaby's religious conversion is the failure of the southern black youth to become a black Daniel—or for that matter, a black Jacob—who can choose his own redemptive path, acquire a strong racial and gendered identity, and be renamed through struggle. Instead, baptism awakens Tarbaby to an unfettered sense of being that exists in much the same way that he would emerge from the river, "quite helpless, letting people pull him this way and that" (258).[12]

## *Black Boy* and Mistranslations on the Mourner's Bench

Elder Hargrove's call to the mourner's bench in *Tarbaby's Dawn* echoes throughout Wright's work, but this critical approach to black religion reverberates most clearly in his autobiographical writings. The anguish that Tarbaby suffers through his "lie to God" intensifies in Wright's account of his own unfulfilling relationships with southern black Methodist and Seventh-Day Adventist churches, resulting in a narrative that is "filled with episodes in which its hero is unable to lie, forced to lie, caught between conflicting lies, not believed unless he lies" (Adams, "I Do Believe," 308).[13] Wright's participant-observer stance in *Black Boy* and the lesser-known essay "Memories of my Grandmother" suggests a more nuanced strategy for exposing the inner workings of his struggle with the spiritual and psychosocial ramifications of unbelief. In turning to Wright's autobiographical works, my analysis demonstrates how he further develops the salient concepts of the mourner's bench trope through the aforementioned angel (mis)sighting and through other optical illusions, moments of selective hearing, and sensory malfunctions between the saved and the sin-sick mourner. Wright ultimately condemns those who willingly embrace what he believes are deeper lies—that a good, just God exists, and that the unmerited suffering of humanity serves a holy purpose.

These "mistranslations," as I refer to them, occur at crucial moments in *Black Boy*. Consider, for example, the opening scene, in which Wright and his brother find a stray kitten. The purring creature had been irritating his father, who eventually shouted, "Kill that damn thing!" Wright responds: "I knew that he had not really meant for me to kill the kitten, but my deep hate of him urged me toward a literal acceptance of his word" (11). After he destroys the kitten, his mother, Ella Wright, demands that the animal be given a proper burial, and during the course of the ceremony, she shrewdly takes advantage of her son's "literal acceptance" of the "Word":

> I closed my eyes tightly, my hand clinging to hers.
> "Dear God, our Father, forgive me, for I knew not what I was doing . . ."
> "Dear God, our Father, forgive me, for I knew not what I was doing," I repeated.
> "And spare my poor life, even though I did not spare the life of the kitten . . ."
> "And spare my poor life, even though I did not spare the life of the kitten," I repeated.
> "And while I sleep tonight, do not snatch the breath of life from me. . . ."
> I opened my mouth but no words came. My mind was frozen with horror. I pictured myself gasping for breath and dying in my sleep. I broke away from my mother and ran into the night, crying, shaking with dread.
> "No," I sobbed.
> My mother called to me many times, but I would not go to her.
> "Well, I supposed you've learned your lesson," she said at last. (14)

What is significant about this scene is not only the familiar sense of "dread" that overcomes young Richard, but the degree to which his mother is held responsible for introducing him to the vengeance and sovereignty of God's power. Just as a child learns to recite the letters of the alphabet through imitation, so Wright learns of human frailty and powerlessness by mimicking his mother's understanding of divine justice. He managed to avoid his father's wrath, but the faith his mother confers upon him swiftly replaces this weak father with a stronger one. The God that Ella Wright turns to in moments of trouble is the God of Wright's spiritual infancy.

As a child, Wright dutifully attends Protestant services with his mother, granting "God's existence a sort of tacit assent" as he, like his character Tarbaby, begins to grapple with superstitions and mysteries of the unknown (115). Yet, as Wright's persona matures in *Black Boy*, he understands the goals of the church differently than his mother. Sunday morning is an opportunity to socialize with his peers: "Some of the Bible stories were interesting in themselves, but we always twisted them, secularized them to the level of our street life, rejected all meanings that did not fit into our environment" (82). In these early stages of self-definition, Wright distinguishes the church from his volatile "street life" through the gauge of experience and the corroboration of sight, hearing, and touch. He can feel the broken bottle glass cut into his skin during a neighborhood fight with a group of white boys, but God's grace eludes his senses. Unlike his mother, he cannot resign his fate to invisible forces.

Ella Wright's piety is eclipsed, however, by the devotion of her own mother, Margaret Bolton Wilson. In the early 1920s, Wright is forced to move into Granny's strict household after his mother's second stroke rendered her temporarily paralyzed and unable to work. He is persuaded by his grandmother to attend a religious school where his aunt, Addie Wilson, a recent Seventh-Day Adventist school graduate, works as the sole instructor. That the threat of being labeled a "horrible infidel" and a "hardhearted ingrate" convinces him to attend the school is significant, for so many of the choices that Wright makes in the matriarchal Wilson household carry the weight of this serious accusation (104).

Indeed, Wright's mother and grandmother are depicted as the personification of otherworldly dependence. Religion as Wright understands it—with his frequent references to its warmth, softness, and analgesic qualities—constitutes their entire response to the world around them. Abandoned or widowed and forced to become the primary caregivers in their families, they inevitably surrender themselves to religion as a way of coping with loneliness, oppression, and poverty. Like Helga Crane in *Quicksand*, who is drawn to the black southern church because of its anesthetizing power, the women in Wright's fiction and autobiographical writings turn to religion for its sense of dependency (on God, on the male preacher) that allows them to "deliberately stop thinking" (Larsen, *Quicksand*, 116). Such is the case not only for Ella Wright and Margaret Bolton Wilson, but also for the characters Mrs. Morrison from *Tarbaby's Dawn* and Bigger's mother, Mrs. Thomas, in *Native Son*.

These women find their only respite in what Mircea Eliade calls "sacred time," a break in the historical present in which human existence is dominated by a desire to return to a paradisiacal state. Such religious nostalgia often leads to ceaseless repetition of beliefs, customs, and patterns of behavior, resulting in an *unmoving* temporal condition that "may appear to be a refusal of history" (*The Sacred*, 68). Eliade's theory resonates with Wright's perception of the black church as a space where congregants blindly struggle to apply an outmoded belief system to an ever-changing landscape. Even the women who renounce Christianity—as Sue does in "Bright and Morning Star" and as Sarah Hunter does in *The Outsider*—are unable to resist the "faith of their childhood" in times of crisis.[14] Significant problems arise when mothers who are themselves suspended in an infantile state teach this way of being to their adolescent sons. The resulting discomfort and anger of these young men can often be attributed to what Claudia Tate shrewdly identifies in *Native Son* as Wright's "urtext of matricidal impulse" that stresses "the son's perception of maternal betrayal and his reactions of initial ambivalence and subsequent hostility" (*Psychoanalysis*, 96). Indeed, when Wright discusses the profound, and often unsettling, impact that religion had on his life and work in "Memories of My Grandmother," he speculates:

> It may be that those events that create fear or enchantment in a young mind are the ones whose impressions last longest. It may be that the neural paths of response made in the young form the streets, tracks, and roadways over which the vehicles of later experiences run. . . . It may be that a man goes through life seeking, blindly and unconsciously, for the repetition of those dim webs of conditioning which he learned at an age when he could make no choice. (17)

Wright typically juxtaposes his grandmother's spiritual conditioning with the "throbbing life of the people in the streets," noting the unusual manner in which ecclesiastical space and time seem to exist as a separate planar entity (*Black Boy*, 102). He even likens his family's proselytizing to an act of near strangulation in which "they were determined to take me by the throat and lift me to a higher plane of living" (7). Yet by making such clear visual distinctions between the South's social realities and the liturgical landscape of the black church, Wright unwittingly calls attention to the more beneficial aspects of sacred space. His language highlights how this need is articulated by black people during an era in which *public* space was defined racially and every seat and sidewalk was marked by the profanity of segregation. From this perspective, religion can be viewed as a politically empowering mode of systemizing time and space within the black collective. Religious practices create a sense of control that transcends the rules of Jim Crow. This is where the "transhuman quality" of sacred time becomes especially important, for the belief systems that shape Granny's faith are impervious to the prejudices of men (Eliade, *The Sacred*, 71).

As I have noted elsewhere, however, Wright does not expend a substantial amount of critical energy trying to understand the historical processes that shaped his grandmother's patterns of behavior (Whitted, "Using," 27). Focusing instead on the view from the mourner's bench, he attributes many of his difficulties during adolescence not simply to white racism, but to his grandmother's rigid adherence to daily Bible study, prayer, and the behavioral and dietary restrictions of her Seventh-Day Adventist faith.

Particularly problematic for Wright is Granny's attitude toward group sanctification that effectively negates the individual decision-making element of the conversion experience: "Granny intimated boldly, basing her logic on God's justice, that one sinful person in a household could bring down the wrath of God upon the entire establishment, damning both the innocent and the guilty" (*Black Boy*, 103). Wright notes that his questions about religious issues—far from being regarded as an opportunity for spiritual maturation and growth—were seen as a threat to Granny's own redemption upon Christ's imminent return. Granny places the responsibility for her and her family's salvation onto Wright and even attributes his mother's failing health to his unbelief.

So it is with the intention of restoring balance to this communal structure, rather than to establish a personal relationship with Christ, that Wright utters the words: "You see granny, if I ever saw an angel like Jacob did, then I'd believe" (*Black Boy*, 117). Because he tells the reader at the outset that he never truly expected to see an angel, the embarrassment of the situation is intensified when Granny encourages him to describe an image that does not exist:

> Granny rushed to me and hugged me violently, weeping tears of joy. Then I babbled, speaking with emotional reproof, censuring her for having misunderstood me; I must have spoken more loudly and harshly than was called for—the others had now gathered about me and Granny—for Granny drew away from me abruptly and went to a far corner of the church and stared at me with a cold set face. I was crushed. I went to her and tried to tell her how it had happened.
>
> "You should't've spoken to me," she said in a breaking voice that revealed the depths of her disillusionment. (119)

More than a simple misunderstanding, the incident with the angel uses a mistranslation between two planes of living to reveal what Wright believes is the ideological limitation of Granny's belief system. Granny is physically incapable of *hearing* Wright's doubts within the confines of a life that extends no further than domestic and religious spheres of influence. In keeping with the religious allusion to the moment when God "confused the language of the whole world," Wright tells us that he "babbled" in his attempt to explain the mistake to his grandmother (Gen. 11:9). But the correction comes too late. Soon after, Granny and Aunt Addie would declare Wright dead because he refused to "die" as they did and live again through Christ: "[T]hey told me that they were dead to the world, and those of their blood who lived in that world were therefore dead to them" (122).

The angel (mis)sighting marks Wright's departure from his grand-mother's Seventh-Day Adventist church. With his entrance to the seventh grade, the narrative focuses increasing attention on his reemergence in the profane spaces of street life. He becomes an avid reader, writing his own short stories in his free time. He achieves personal satisfaction and a small measure of independence through his first job doing chores for white fami-lies. Ella Wright, no longer bedridden, is also featured more prominently in the text. In fact, Wright's eventual return to the church is partially at-tributed to his mother's improving health. She leaves Granny's church to join a Methodist one that is populated by many of his public school class-mates and friends. More than the Seventh-Day Adventists, this less restric-tive Methodist church is a rich microcosm of Jackson's black community. Black men and women of different ages, classes, degrees of education, and shades of color coalesce in Wright's rendering of this "responsible com-munity church" (151). And it is not simply his mother who encourages his participation on Sunday mornings. The boys from his own "gang" are particularly influential in convincing Wright that salvation is the only path to communal and racial belonging. Though saddened by their logic, young Richard sits side by side with his new friends on the Methodist church pews and, at his mother's request, attends a special revival. He takes com-fort not only in their acceptance of him, but in his anonymity among the homogeneous throng of believers.

The pretense of Wright's participation begin to unravel when the preacher closes the revival with a familiar call: "Now, I'm going to ask all of you to rise and go into the church and take a seat on the front bench" (152). Indeed, by the time Wright is literally called to the mourner's bench in *Black Boy*, we know that he has been here many times before. Seething behind a book at his desk in Aunt Addie's church school; spurning the prayers and perilous warnings of a religious friend; nodding drowsily at Granny's side during a nightlong prayer service—all are preludes to the moment when Wright is beckoned to the mourner's bench with the prom-ise of his own rebirth and being made new. Within Wright's own account is the helplessness and apprehension of his young male characters. Like the protagonist of *Tarbaby's Dawn*, Wright's concern for his soul is similarly eclipsed by moral pressure to obligate himself before the congregation and his crippled mother. Afraid of being labeled a "moral monster," Wright allows himself to be led to the preacher's outstretched hand. "It was no longer a question of my believing in God," Wright states. "It was no longer a matter of whether I would steal or lie or murder; it was a simple, urgent matter of public pride, a matter of how much I had in common with other people" (154).

Here it is worth noting the association Wright makes in *Black Boy* between the church and his sexuality, for it is during Sunday service that his "first lust for the flesh" came into being as well (112). In the Seventh-Day Adventist Church, Wright uses the demoniac image of a "black imp with two horns" to signify his pubescent desire for the elder's wife. He claims that his depraved eroticism was intensified by "masochistic prayers" and hymns—the same hymns so often sung and hummed by his mother (and nearly every black maternal figure in his fiction). Initially he suggests that the relationship between the "sweetly sonorous hymns" and his "fleshy fantasies" were reciprocal, but the power dynamic shifts once Wright is subjected to the intense spiritual handling of the mourner's bench. Consider the way in which he describes himself after the revival as emotionally flaccid, numb: "I walked home limp as a rag; I had not felt anything except sullen anger and a crushing sense of shame" (155). Not only Wright's mother, but his aunts, uncles, classmates, neighbors—all are implicated in this spiritual molestation.[15]

The encounter brings to mind the tormented outbursts of another one of Wright's fictional skeptics, Cross Damon from *The Outsider:*

> I'm not even an atheist. To me it's just too bad that some people must lean on imagined gods, that's all. Yet I'd not have it otherwise. They need religion. All right; let them have it. What harm does it do? And it does make for a greater measure of social stability. But I object if somebody grabs me when I'm a defenseless child and injects into me a sedative—the power of which lasts for a lifetime!—which no one would ever be able to tell if I'll ever need or not! (483)

Damon's indignation is clearly foreshadowed in *Black Boy.* After being preyed upon and emotionally abused in what was supposed to be a safe and sacred space, Wright makes the decision to play hooky from church with his friends. His irreverence attempts to revive the sense of dignity and manhood that was debilitated by the same phallocentric "injection" of religion that Damon Cross describes. Strengthened by his peer group, Wright concedes that the church and the conversion that he experienced on the mourner's bench is a "fraud" (155). His friends remind him that "the main thing is to be a member of the church," while Ella Wright reassures her son that he will "grow into feeling it" (155). Such empathetic counsel, coming *after* Wright's humiliation on the mourner's bench, amplifies the degree to which his "salvation" has done little to inspire a belief system that will engage the deepest and most elusive mysteries of life.

For a glimpse into Wright's own existential struggle, we must look beyond his fraudulent conversion to the stroke that his mother suffered shortly after the revival. The two incidents, narrated side by side, are quite instructive. As Wright questions the reasons for his mother's suffering, he does not reflect upon the wrathful God to which she prayed at the kitten's funeral. Even his grandmother's retribution theology cannot explain Ella Wright's groans of unmerited pain and paralysis. In an especially poignant passage, we are told that Wright "used to lie awake nights . . . wondering why she had apparently been singled out for so much suffering, meaningless suffering, and I would *feel* more awe than I had ever *felt* in church. My mind could find no answer and I would *feel* rebellious against all life. But I never *felt* humble" (156; my emphasis). The core of Wright's belief system can be found in this willingness to linger with the inexplicable and to recognize the spiritual dimensions of "awe" and "rebellion" without settling for his family's theodicy of redemptive suffering. Given Wright's emphasis on sensation and sensory perception in the earlier account of his conversion experience ("Mama, I don't feel a thing" [155]), it is especially significant that he offers, in his reflections on his mother's suffering, a philosophy of existence that is rich with the kind of feeling that he could never manage to "grow into" through his church community.

## Bigger's "First Murder"

The mourner's bench functions as discursive scaffolding from which to consider the issues that circulate through Wright's approach to God, religion, and the reality of moral evil and human suffering. Its ritualistic aspects call our attention to the collective ethos of black religious tradition while emphasizing the organic functionality of the church in maintaining rites of passage that are social as well as spiritual. The overly assertive role of women in the conversion ritual leads not to spiritual maturity in Wright's view, but to an emasculation that borders on sexual abuse. Physically separated from the rest of the congregation, the mourner's bench also reinforces an implied moral hierarchy between the sinner and the saved, between youth and experience, between the nostalgic pabulum of sacred time and the "life of the people in the streets." Its orchestrated appearance during revivals, accompanied by hymns, prayers, and the insistent call of the preacher, effectively transforms the church's altar into a stage on which race, religion, and gender are performed. And finally, the solitary image of the mourner underscores the way in which he struggles unceasingly with fundamental philosophies of existence as represented through the idea of "lying to God" and through "mistranslations" of sight and language. While one could arguably read the mourner's bench even further into Wright's renderings of racial prejudice and his voracious critiques of white supremacy, it is important to note the efficacy of this discursive structure in underscoring social relationships and cultural systems *within* black communities.

Such an approach encourages us to take a closer look at the subtle ways in which Wright replicates the mourner's bench outside the church. Already discussed, for instance, is Tarbaby's interrogation behind closed doors with his family at the dinner table. But another example can be found in Wright's disgruntled exchange with the elders gathered on his uncle's front porch—a communal space not unlike the black church in its folk wisdom and wordplay. In this scene from "Memories of My Grandmother," Wright recalls a summer afternoon in which he listens quietly, captivated, as his uncle reads aloud a newspaper account of the criminal trial of Richard Loeb and Nathan Leopold Jr., two young white men who had murdered a fourteen-year-old boy in 1924. The old folks congregate on the front porch while a teenage Wright sits among the children gathered at their feet. As his uncle reads about the astonishing intelligence of Loeb and Leopold—each supposedly spoke German, French, and Spanish—young Richard longs to hear words spoken in these strange tongues. He wonders: How might his own sentences sound from the perspective of someone who has never heard the English language? Naively he voices a desire to "forget English for a few minutes" and looks up from the porch steps to the people above:

> The array of elderly Negroes—my blood relatives on the porch there—were struck dumb that summer afternoon. They stared at me. Then my uncle leaned forward.
>
> "That boy is coming to no good end," he said, shaking his head. "Imagine someone saying that he wants to forget *his* language so he can hear how it sounds!"
>
> Yet it seemed that they could not realize that it was their teaching me their religion, their encouraging me to live beyond the world, to be *in* the world but not *of* the world, that had implanted the germ of such ideas in me. (16)

What begins as adolescent curiosity exposes an impenetrable breach between Wright and his uncle as each seems to speak a different "language" and cannot successfully communicate. Wright strikes a familiar participant-observer stance in this scene that shifts from the silenced, angry youth to the detached, articulate adult who brings religious discourse to bear on the deeper irony of his uncle's prophecy.

An apt visual metaphor for this ideological divide, "to be *in* the world but not *of* the world," can be found in their position on the front porch, where the initiated porch talkers sit above the platform and the uninitiated seeker sits below—a bifurcation that Wright develops through the mourner's bench, but that ultimately defines alternative ways of experience reality beyond the pews of the church. Similar to Wright's encounter with the kitten in *Black Boy*, his telling of this incident uses "a literal acceptance" of the elder's word as a rhetorical strategy for unmasking religious flaws; in denouncing Wright's inquisitiveness, his uncle ends up denouncing the belief system of the "array of elderly Negroes" who were "struck dumb" that memorable afternoon.

The uncle who first read about Loeb and Leopold on his front porch in Mississippi probably never imagined that his nephew would one day become a "porch talker" in his own right, incorporating the newspaper account of the crime into his 1940 novel *Native Son*.[16] Unlike *Tarbaby's Dawn* and *Black Boy*, Wright does not physically place Bigger Thomas on a mourner's bench in the church. Bigger does not kneel and weep before the altar, but it would be a mistake to assume that Wright does not reconstruct the liturgical structure of the mourner's bench in his characterization of Bigger as a young man with "no spiritual sustenance" (Wright, "Bigger," 445). It is important to remember that Bigger's "first" murder was "the preacher's haunting picture of life," not Mary Dalton (*Native Son*, 284). Of particular interest to my discussion are the novel's frequent references to spirituals, prayers, and Wright's portrayal of Bigger's mother, Mrs. Thomas—all familiar elements that come together in Bigger's jail cell, where his cot is transformed into another metaphorical "anxious bench."

The spirituals provide a compelling subtext to several scenes in *Native Son*: Mrs. Thomas sings over breakfast (10), Mary Dalton makes an attempt to communicate with Bigger through song (77), and when Bigger attempts to elude capture for Mary's murder, he wakes up to the sound of singing at a black church. Like a tranquilizer, the music from the church "seeped into his feelings," coaxing and tempting him with surrender through the verses: *"Steal away, Steal away home, I ain't got long to stay here"* (253). Bigger contemplates his unbelief and wonders, "Would it not have been better for him had he lived in that world the music sang of? It would have been easy to have lived in it, for it was his mother's world, humble, contrite, believing" (254).[17] Later, in jail, Bigger demonstrates just how much Mrs. Thomas's songs failed to prepare him for the social realities of Chicago. It is through Reverend Hammond that the connection is made, for the black preacher's speech and strong dialect associate his profession with the Thomas family and their southern past. The fatalistic tone of Reverend Hammond's message, which is intended to prepare the youth for death, differs drastically from Elder Hargrove's counsel in *Tarbaby's Dawn*. Instead of being told to "be brave like Daniel" and fight for the pride and dignity of the race, Bigger is advised to "Be like Jesus. Don't resist" (285).

In this instance, the imperative to fight comes outside the black community from the Labor Defenders, Jan Erlone, and the "Godless Communist" lawyer Boris A. Max (414). Both make their appearance in Bigger's cell shortly after Reverend Hammond. In this scene, the state attorney follows next, frightening Bigger with his self-righteousness and condescension. When Mr. and Mrs. Dalton are escorted into the jail, the crowd presses Bigger for a confession of guilt. The scene itself is, as one critic suggests, "highly contrived," but Wright's intention, to "elicit a certain important emotional response from Bigger," succeeds.[18] As Bigger sits behind bars and silently stares from one face to the next, Wright plunges him into a lonesome valley of internal struggle and reconfigures the young man's cot into his mourner's bench.

The revivalist elements of the scene in Bigger's jail cell spring to life when Mrs. Thomas joins the gathering. She sobs and wails in a fit of uncontrollable emotion, reenacting the familiar tears and prayers of Mrs. Morrison in *Tarbaby's Dawn* and Ella Wright in *Black Boy*. Compare also Tarbaby's "sense of dread and shame" at the dinner table and Wright's description of Bigger's feelings as Mrs. Thomas tries to convince her son to pray:

> "Don't you want to see your old ma again, son?"
> Slowly, he stood up and lifted his hands and tried to touch his mother's face and tell her yes; and as he did so something screamed deep down in him that it was a lie, that seeing her after they killed him would never be. But his mother believed; it was her last hope; it was what kept her going through the long years. And she was now believing it all the harder because of the trouble he had brought upon her. His hands finally touched her face and he said with a sigh (knowing that it would never be, knowing that his heart did not believe, knowing that when he died, it would be over, forever):
> "I'll pray, Ma." (300)

Bigger promises to pray as a way of atoning for the social and economic hardship that his imprisonment has inflicted upon his family. With the covenant, "I'll pray, Ma," he moves from "passive to active membership in the community" within a religious framework that echoes initiation rites in African societies (Mbiti, *African Religions*, 118). Significantly, his mother, brother, and sister surround him afterward with a hug, and Reverend Hammond begins to pray. But Wright's image of the Thomas family "locking" their arms in a circle around Bigger's body spurns the affirmative communal strength of the believers' embrace. Instead, the hug suggests that the "lies" that appease frenzied black mothers suffocate misunderstood black males.[19]

Wright further complicates the traditional structure of the mourner's bench with the presence of the "white mountain" (*Native Son*, 298). The closed circle of black arms, rimmed by an even wider border of white faces, gesture toward the inner and outer tensions of Bigger's irresolute conversion experience. It is worth mentioning here that Wright even places white observers in the baptism scene of *Tarbaby's Dawn;* they stand on the top of a nearby levee and look down on the black participants in the river (256). In *Native Son*, the white people stand against the wall of the jail cell while Bigger's family and friends enfold him. They scrutinize the exchange silently, sometimes smiling or gasping, but always staring. When Mrs. Thomas falls to her knees, the text suggests that it is her apparent weakness "under the eyes of white folks" that makes Bigger feel so deeply ashamed.[20] Later he states, "The white folks like for us to be religious, then they can do what they want to with us" (356). Enclosed within the jail cell, then, are many different appeals for faith, commitment, and creativity. The figurative conversion experience in *Native Son* echoes Bigger's deeper anxieties of a world tainted not only by racism, but by maternal deception and metaphysical trickery.

## The Mourner's Bench in African American Literary Autobiography

African American literature features a vigorous engagement with "second birth" ceremonies of all sorts, with portals, thresholds, and the momentous act of turning as a manifestation of black subjectivity. The mourner's bench has useful metaphorical applications in several of Wright's works, but his critical approach to black conversion experiences opens up connections with other writers as well. Similar representations of the conversion experience appear in Sarah Wright's novel *This Child's Gonna Live* (1969), as well as Alice Walker's novels *The Third Life of Grange Copeland* (1970) and *Meridian* (1977). And no matter how long the elders pray over Jimmy Aaron in Ernest Gaines's *The Autobiography of Miss Jane Pittman*, the obedient young boy continues to struggle with his understanding of God and never fully becomes a part of the rural church.[21] Returning again and again to the ritualistic symbol of mourner's bench, black writers bear witness to a destabilizing cosmos in which seekers tumble awkwardly between wholeness and fragmentation, righteousness and corruption, agency and victimization, faith and doubt.

Langston Hughes, at the age of twelve, desperately wanted to be saved and to participate in church activities, but also failed to experience a spiritual awakening. The chapter "Salvation" from *The Big Sea* (1940) details the painful struggle on the mourner's bench as young Langston "waited" to see Jesus while his aunt sobs at his side. As is the case with Wright, Hughes decides to lie in order to "to save further trouble" and rises from the bench to take the minister's hand. Particularly fascinating in Hughes's account is the way in which his "decision" to be saved transforms the congregation into a "sea of shouting" with waves and crescendos of praise virtually baptizing him with communal acceptance. Reflecting on his tears later that night in bed, Hughes is distraught by his lie, but even more devastating is the utter failure of his sensory perception to "see" what everyone else in the church had apparently seen: "I couldn't bear to tell [Auntie Reed] that I had lied, that I had deceived everybody in the church, that I hadn't seen Jesus, and that now I didn't believe there was a Jesus any more, since he didn't come to help me" (21).

Likewise, Zora Neale Hurston's reflections on her religious identity in her autobiography are complicated by notions of self-deception and fragmentation. Hurston strikes a similar participant-observer stance in the chapter "Religion" from *Dust Tracks on a Road* (1942). Her narrative puts forth a bifocal perspective of the triumphant revival services in her father's church, while describing her own difficulties with understanding and believing the message he preached. Indeed, the man who could "'bring through' as many as seventy-five in one two-week period of revival" on the mourner's bench apparently could not do the same for his own daughter. What she does tell us, however, offers an instructive analog to Wright's work:

It seemed to me that somebody had been fooled and I so stated to my father and two of his colleagues. When they got through with me, I knew better than to say that out loud again, but their shocked and angry tirades did nothing for my bewilderment. My head was full of misty fumes of doubt. (217)

Although Hurston is silenced by the three wise clergymen, she makes clear that her questions about God remained even when the moral pressure is compounded by her peers:

> When asked if I loved God, I always said yes because I knew that that was the thing I was supposed to say. It was a guilty secret with me for a long time. I did not dare ask even my chums if they meant it when they said they loved God with all their souls and minds and hearts, and would be glad to die if He wanted them to. Maybe they had found out how to do it, and I was afraid of what they might say if they found out I hadn't. Maybe they wouldn't even play with me anymore. (217)

In contrast, James Baldwin's extensive engagements with religion feature a notably different representation of the conversion experience that nevertheless complements the earlier work of Wright, Hughes, and Hurston. Elements of the mourner's bench trope appear in Baldwin's 1963 account of his spiritual crisis in "Down at the Cross: Letter from a Region in my Mind" in *The Fire Next Time*, beginning with his lucid articulation of the fear that led him to be spiritually "seduced" into "the church racket" at the age of fourteen in Harlem (28). He is compelled to join a church by his God-fearing parents and friends, and yet the most insistent pressure comes from the menacing depravity of crime, poverty, racism on "the Avenue" and by Baldwin's own adolescent anxiety. Together these dangers convey the moral impoverishment that he interprets as a chronic fear of "the evil within" and "the evil without" (15). Baldwin, like Wright and Hurston, criticizes the theatrical hypocrisy of black and white churches whose claims of Christian love, truth, and virtue were seldom practiced. He further demonstrates how such inconsistencies generated his own "guilty secret" as he attempted to hide his skepticism and his desire from God—themes that Baldwin first developed a decade earlier in the semi-autobiographical novel *Go Tell It on the Mountain* (1953).

Gunnar Myrdal stated in 1944 that, "the Negro church is such a good community center that it might almost be said that anyone who does not belong to a church in the rural South does not belong to the community" (*American Dilemma*, 939). In keeping with Myrdal's equation, writers such as Hughes, Hurston, and Baldwin join Richard Wright in their representations of black conversion experiences, often agreeing to pray, to be baptized, and to believe with great reluctance in order to belong.

The troubling disparities between public and private—between the outward act of rising and walking to the altar and an inner "transformation in consciousness"—become symbols of a deeper social rift and a divided self. On the rare occasions when Wright does acknowledge the value of the black church, the institution is portrayed as a "door" or a "portal."[22] Even in its role as a door, however, he understands Christianity as an incomplete conveyance; it may be the point of departure for black folk, but it cannot sustain a fully developed human and racial consciousness. His work offers, instead, an alternative view of African Americans who mark spiritual growth through the questioning of God, of evil, and of the decisive role that religious belief can play in racial and gender formation. With the mourner's bench trope, Wright conceptualizes the rebellion of his protagonists and the resignation of their elders as an uneasy kinship of spirits, wrestling on opposite sides of the altar.

# 3

## "A Loveless, Barren, Hopeless Western Marriage"

*Spiritual Infidelity in the Fiction of Nella Larsen and Alice Walker*

It is fatal to love a God who does not love you.
—ALICE WALKER

IN ALICE WALKER's short story "The Diary of an African Nun," a Ugandan woman gazes at the mist-covered Ruwenzori Mountains from the window of her Catholic mission. Beyond the mission, where a fire illuminates her African brothers and sisters in dance, the nun reconsiders her chaste vows against the calls of drums and ancient chants. She measures the cost of her religious commitment in a journal, divulging the temptations of idolatry as a challenge to Christ, the "pale lover" and husband of whom she writes in a restless query: "Must I still long to be within the black circle around the red, glowing fire, to feel the breath of love hot against my cheeks, the smell of love strong about my waiting thighs! . . . *I bear your colors, I am in your livery, I belong to you. Will you not come down and take me!*" (115; emphasis in original). Walker uses the black nun's struggle against unfaithfulness to emphasize the patriarchal constraints of religious service. But the story also raises concerns about the extent to which *all* Christians of African descent are bound in a manner similar to Walker's nun, symbolically yoked to God in a "loveless, barren, hopeless Western marriage" ("Nun," 118). Exploring how questions of divine justice and the problem of evil are expressed through these figurative intersections of marriage, sexuality, and religion is the primary goal of this chapter.

Significantly, the prophets of the Old Testament, including Jeremiah, Ezekiel, and Hosea, often convey unbelief as an adulterous act. Where the bond between God and the Israelites is allegorized through the rhetoric of nuptial bliss, apostasy is represented as a deep betrayal of the marriage covenant. The self-willed act of turning away from God is further underscored by disparaging female sexuality, for the offending spouse, like the offending nation, is imagined as a woman. The backslider is an irreverent wife who wanders "outside the home" and eschews holy sacraments for false gods and unspeakable desires. Rebels are condemned in feminine pronouns as defiled brides, whores clad in scarlet, wild vines, and donkeys in heat. "Like a woman unfaithful to her husband," declares the Lord, "so you have been unfaithful to me" (Jer. 3:20). Vivid biblical imagery of prostitutes who "lay under every spreading tree" (Jer. 2:20) augments the seriousness of the prophets' warnings and the consequences that go beyond shame and humiliation to eternal damnation.

Given the image's elasticity and far-reaching implications, the marriage metaphor offers one of the most provocative representations of God's relationship with humanity. The biblical scholar Renita Weems explains:

> Of the five metaphors that reappear in the prophets, only the marriage metaphor was capable of signifying failure to obey and conform to the prevailing norms as a moral and social disgrace. . . . Marriage forced audiences to confront their attitudes and assumptions about human sexuality in general, and women's sexuality in particular, in ways that none of the other biblical metaphors was capable of doing. It also called upon audiences to reaffirm their belief in a male honor system where a man's prestige rested in great part on his ability to control the behavior of the subordinates in his household (e.g. wives, slaves, children). (*Battered Lives*, 29)

Also key to the figurative language of marriage and infidelity in the Bible is the lure of "pagan religions" that incite God's jealousy through idolatrous worship. After being brought out of Egypt, for example, the Hebrew people were strongly forewarned against Canaanite religious practices with their sacrifices and fertility rites that emphasized the sexual nature of their gods and goddesses (Exod. 34:10–16). Later, in the Book of Hosea, the betrayal of Israel is reenacted through the troubled marriage of the prophet and his adulterous wife, Gomer. Images of mountaintop sacrifices, moon festivals, and lush, shady trees are employed to symbolize the heathen corruption that drives God's brides to commit adultery and his daughters to "play the harlot" (Hos. 4:12–14). As the biblical scholar Raymond C. Ortlund Jr. notes, the theme "lifts up before Israel a vision of Yahweh as one intensely jealous for the love of his people, with the corollary that their participation in foreign worship constitutes so repulsive a violation of the covenant that they reduce themselves thereby to the *moral status of whores* responding to the overtures of strangers" (*Unfaithful Wife*, 33; my emphasis).

Despite such threats, Walker's protagonist in "The Diary of an African Nun" dares to dispute, albeit privately, a religious covenant that requires her to give body and soul to a "bodiless" bridegroom for the sake of "civilization, anti-heathenism" (113, 115). She further contests the quality of a "marriage" that necessitates her pain and suffering. Her frustrations ultimately speak more to issues of power than religious faith and virtue; at stake in the question of God is the authority to define the Ugandan people's hope, to name appropriate behaviors and modes of feeling, and to govern their way of life. The silences imposed on the nun—and the divine silence that mocks her in turn—indicate how black motherhood, sexuality, and desire are affected by colonial aggression. For the sake of her "pagan" country's survival, the nun resigns herself to cultural barrenness and insists, "My mouth must be silent, then, though my heart jumps to the booming of the drums, as to the last strong pulse of life in a dying world" (118). Clearly stories like "The Diary of an African Nun" evidence Walker's global concern with what she has referred to as "our fearful-of-Nature, spiritually colonized age" ("Only Reason," 290).

My investigation in this chapter argues that the discourse of marital strife functions as one of the prime means through which Walker shapes the task of spiritual decolonization into a cultural imperative. Walker's multifaceted depictions of "wedlock" are especially revealing for the way in which the material manifestations of troubled marriages and unfulfilling sexual relations are represented spiritually through corrupted church covenants and the harrowing devastation of God's silence. To demonstrate this connection, my analysis will draw from the "The Diary of an African Nun" and the short story "Roselily," both from the collection *In Love & Trouble* (1973), and the novel *The Color Purple* (1982). Literary scholars such as Ann duCille have guided my understanding of how marital relationships are employed as metaphors of societal conflict in modern black women's writing, while the theological framework of my discussion is largely influenced by Weems's important study *Battered Love: Marriage, Sex, and Violence in the Hebrew Prophets*, and the womanist scholarship of Patricia Hunter, Frances Wood, Jacquelyn Grant, Delores Williams, and others featured in Emilie M. Townes's essay collection *A Troubling in My Soul: Womanist Perspectives on Evil & Suffering*.[1] Informed by their evaluative theology, I read Alice Walker's subversive rendering of marriage as a challenge to the theistic moral standards that normalize racial subjugation and misogyny. So-called acts of sacrilege are thereby transformed into gendered vehicles of socio-political liberation.

THE TERM "infidelity" is generally used to refer to any gesture of unfaith-fulness or disloyalty as defined by a dominant power structure. However, my analysis employs the phrase "spiritual infidelity" in order to take ad-vantage of the transgression's dual meaning as a betrayal of religious devo-tion and as a violation of the marriage covenant through adultery. Such a reading is bolstered by the theme's biblical usage, in which fornication "is used literally of such unlawful sexual activity, e.g. Tamar's apparent pros-titution in Genesis 38:24, as well as figuratively for betrayal of one's union with God" (Ortlund, *Unfaithful Wife*, 26).[2] Even so, in Walker's 1979 poem "Janie Crawford," Walker offers another glimpse into this kind of moral equation by declaring: "I love the way Janie Crawford/left her husbands the one who wanted/to change her into a mule/and the other who tried to interest her/in being a queen" (lines 1–5). Considering her admiration for the protagonist of Hurston's *Their Eyes Were Watching God* in this verse, it should come as no surprise that Walker's own fiction features a host of female characters who follow Janie's lead to free themselves from the men, the mothers, and the missionaries who seek to turn them into mules and queens. Walker further upsets toxic relationships between parents and chil-dren by advocating unconventional family ties that support self-discovery and nature-affirming spirituality.

Walker presents herself as an artist who is deeply concerned with quests and questions of the spirit in her autobiographical writing as well. Her humanist beliefs have been influenced by African and Native American re-ligious orientations, though she concedes that her early years in her family's church continue to have a lasting impact on her understanding of African American culture. Born in Eatonton, Georgia, Walker was raised among men and women who often internalized a sense of unworthiness through a religion that, she claims, stifled their voices and their creativity: "I think now, and it hurts me to think of it, how tormented the true believers in our church must have been, wondering if, in heaven, Jesus Christ, a white man, the only good one besides Santa Claus and Abraham Lincoln they'd ever heard of, would deign to sit near them" ("Only Reason," 296). Walker became more explicit about her religious doubts and questions during her college years. Later she developed a mode of black feminist or "womanist" in-quiry to chronicle black women's struggle for identity, agency, and spiritual wholeness. Included among her kaleidoscopic definitions of "womanist" in the essay collection *In Search of Our Mother's Gardens: Womanist Prose* is a reference to "outrageous, audacious, courageous or *willful* behavior. Wanting to know more and in greater depth than is considered 'good' for one" (xi). For Walker, the consequences of her own willful behavior remain both personal and political.

In one essay from *In Search of Our Mother's Gardens*, Walker alludes to the intermittent battles waged against her mother, whom she admires and strongly respects, over Christianity and the limitations of "religious fences."[3] The same dialectical tensions can be found in Walker's writing, where critical reasoning and humanist ethics take root alongside the folk wisdom of her spiritual heritage. Consider, for example, her clarification of the term "pagan" to positively denote "'of the land, country dweller, peasant,' all of which my family was." Walker goes on to state: "It also means a person whose primary spiritual relationship is with Nature and the Earth" ("Only Reason," 295). Although Willie Lee and Minnie Walker may have balked at being called "pagan," their daughter's desire to recover such terms from religious depravity and apply them to the lived experience of her people is maintained consistently throughout her writing.

An attentiveness to language as a system of knowledge and power is also vital to the prescriptions of womanist theology. Christian womanist ethics often insist on a fundamental reconsideration of sin, pointedly naming the subjugation of women as a moral evil analogous to racism and other forms of suffering perpetuated by human beings. Womanist scholars also reject the valorization of black women's self-sacrifice—a notion propagated within communities of faith and stereotyped in popular culture—through linguistic signs of matriarchal virtue and "natural" martyrdom. Jacquelyn Grant argues that such a restrictive notion of servanthood should be regarded as an offense "that results from the sociopolitical interests of proponents of the status quo and their attempts to undergird their intended goal through psychological conditioning that comes partially with the *institutionalization of oppressive language, even theological language*" ("The Sin of Servanthood," 210; my emphasis).[4] Acutely aware of the power that language has to shape reality, womanist reflection emphasizes self-willed articulations of identity and in doing so repudiates the very terms of an unjust system.

To be sure, Christ is at the center of Grant's valuable theological critique. She and other womanist religious scholars view the Christian church as a site for lasting, powerful transformation. My literary investigation remains mindful, however, of the non-Christian "pagan" beliefs and practices that incite charges of wickedness against Walker's female characters. Because stories such as "The Diary of an African Nun" advocate spiritual kinships with nature that are not bound by monotheistic religious traditions, my reading diverges at times from the recuperative claims of womanist theologians whose agenda lies in building a deeper relationship with Jesus Christ. I maintain that spiritual infidelity as a metaphorical concept does more than challenge the reader to confront oppressive gender relations and racial inequality within the church; it also forces a jarring reconsideration of the Christian God's omnipotence, benevolence, and existence. In this way, Walker's fiction has much in common with Richard Wright's midcentury religious critiques, even as her texts draw our attention away from the mourner's bench to the unseen spiritual struggles that begin at the wedding altar.

Of course, this kind of "sacrilege" extends beyond Walker's work. Her fiction shares strong ties with Nella Larsen, Zora Neale Hurston, Dorothy West, and other African American writers who frequently portray marriage, according to Ann duCille, as "a seat of emotional confinement, sexual commodification, and male domination, as well as infidelity, brutality, and betrayal" (*Coupling Convention*, 112). The same characteristics that duCille ascribes to the marriage plot are further sublimated within women's relationships with God and church traditions in these stories. Indeed, Larsen's 1928 novel *Quicksand* foregrounds the spiritual wounds of oppressive social conventions particularly well. Nearly seventy years before Alice Walker stated, "It is fatal to love a God who does not love you,"[5] Nella Larsen's protagonist, Helga Crane, was drowning in a domestic quagmire, convinced that her foolish dependence on a loveless God had exacerbated her misery. As my initial discussion of *Quicksand* will demonstrate, the philosophical questions that Larsen's novel raises about the meaning of human suffering provide a constructive point of departure from which to evaluate other literary representations of black women's spiritual infidelity.

## The Search for a "Church" Home: *Quicksand*

Perhaps it is only coincidence that the main character of Alice Walker's short story "Roselily" finds herself standing uneasily beside her husband-to-be with her "knee raised waist high through a bowl of *quicksand* soup" (3; my emphasis). In alluding to the title of Nella Larsen's late 1920s novel, Walker acknowledges her debt to this Harlem Renaissance writer who deftly captured the realities of marriage as a "stranglehold" for black women in modern society (duCille, *Coupling Convention*, 144). In the concluding pages of

*Quicksand,* Helga Crane's harrowing physical deterioration is marked by a psychological collapse that deepens as she struggles against the asphyxiating pulls of domesticity and religious tradition. Larsen's novel follows her black female protagonist as she travels from the South to Chicago, New York, and even to Copenhagen, naively convinced that with each new journey her desire for social status, sexual freedom, and racial belonging will be fulfilled. Aimless and weary, Helga's hasty nuptials to an Alabama preacher and the birth of four—soon to be five—children signify her final descent. We are told: "The cruel, unrelieved suffering had beaten down her protective wall of artificial faith in the infinite wisdom, in the mercy, of God. For had she not called in her agony on Him? And He had not heard. Why? Because, she knew now, He wasn't there. Didn't exist" (130).

Literary critics such as Hazel Carby have effectively highlighted how sexual and economic relations of power are mapped onto Helga's transatlantic search for identity as the prototypical New Negro woman. Others have addressed the racial negotiations of Helga's quest in light of her biracial parentage so as to expand critical understandings of the "tragic mulatto" motif in American literature.[6] More remains to be said, however, about the intersection of marriage and religion in Larsen's narrative and, specifically, the means through which the protagonist's unwillingness to abide by the conventions of the former (marital institutions) signal an aversion to the customs of the latter (religious institutions). Even the religious scholar Benjamin E. Mays, who notes the racial motives behind Helga's spiritual crisis, fails to fully consider how her denial of God relates to her conflicted views of marriage (*Negro's God,* 223).

Nevertheless, the black woman's tortured capitulation to Christian moral standards in *Quicksand* is irrevocably tied to her vows of marital and maternal responsibility. While such a relationship is a common feature of late nineteenth- and early twentieth-century black women's writing, Larsen's challenge to Victorian ideals of womanhood stands apart in boldly asserting an irreconcilable, unredeemed breach between traditional black Christian belief and black cultural health. The implications of this failure come as a shock to Larsen's heroine, who fumes about "Marriage. This sacred thing of which parsons and other Christian folk ranted so sanctimoniously, how immoral—according to their own standards—it could be!" (134). At stake for black women in works such as *Quicksand* are issues of personal and collective justice, empowerment, and self-definition that, as Helga's experience makes clear, are also matters of life and death. Although she interacts with a diverse range of religious expression in her travels,

Helga frequently voices her contempt for the black Christian church as an institution that is distinctly southern, patriarchal, and ideologically mis-guided—whether modernized in the college chapel, sanitized in northern cathedrals, or ritualized in the primitive sanctification of the storefront revival. *Quicksand* invests in religious signifiers such as these as a way of marking the most crucial stages of Helga's growth and development. An investigation of Larsen's narrative will facilitate a better understanding of similar issues that circulate through Walker's fiction.

In *Quicksand*, Helga's troubles begin at Naxos College. Her early experi-ences as an instructor at this southern black college are framed within the institutionalized conformity and the religious conservatism of racial uplift ideology.[7] In fact, the irritation that she expresses in the novel's opening pages is attributed to an afternoon visit by a well-known white southern preacher who applauds the college's philosophy of accommodation and restraint:

> And he said that if all Negroes would only take a leaf out of the book of Naxos and conduct themselves in the manner of the Naxos products, there would be no race problem, because Naxos Negroes knew what was expected of them. . . . And then he had spoken of contentment, embellishing his words with scriptural quotations and pointing out to them that it was their duty to be satisfied in the estate to which they had been called, hewers of wood and drawers of water. And then he had prayed. (3)

In the tradition of the nineteenth-century black feminist abolitionist Maria Stewart, who also refused to accept that her race would forever be "hewers of wood and drawers of water" ("Lecture," 252), Helga is enraged by the preacher's "banal" and "insulting" sociopolitical agenda and the conde-scending blessings of "his God" (2). She sees the preacher not as a spiritual medium, but as a representative of the hegemonic force behind the school's uplift machinery.[8]

The narrative also differentiates Helga's disgust in this scene from the response of the black people seated around her—respectful students and faculty who endorse the clergyman's message with "considerable applause" (2–3). Her perspective here as an outsider is essential to understanding the profound sense of dissatisfaction she exhibits not only at Naxos, but throughout the text. Indeed, the young black men and women in the school chapel are united by their ability to conform, without question, to the institution's codes of conduct. While Helga is disturbed by their com-plicity, she is also envious of the kinship they have forged through their unwavering commitment to the Naxos mission.

Helga's biracial parentage reinforces her estrangement even further. Among her white mother's family, she was made to feel ashamed of her black American heritage, while her unnamed black father deserted her as a child. She is portrayed as a mixed-race intellectual who, emotionally and physically, "had no home," having been abandoned by her family and alienated from her colleagues (30). Without these connections, Helga becomes a dangerously volatile and mobile character. But the same fluidity that facilitates her freedom of movement as an educated woman also lends itself to a sense of incompleteness—or homelessness—that follows her as she journeys around the world. Even after making the decision to leave Naxos and her fiancé for Chicago, Helga continues to search in vain not only for a physical home, but also for a *church home* and a religio-racial identity that will resonate with her own values.

In Chicago, Michigan Avenue's Episcopal church opens up discursive space for Larsen to explore her protagonist's beliefs in relation to an upper-class stratum of the black church "family." Helga rediscovers her Bible after being rejected by her biological kin—during a brief visit, her white uncle's new wife refuses to acknowledge her as family. She is denied access to employment and economic security because of her failure to produce a letter or a name to vouch for her suitability. This "lack of references" is cited as one of the main reasons she is rebuffed by potential employers, regardless of her education and teaching experience (33). Without a written endorsement of her qualifications or verification of the strong communal ties of a "usable past," one of the only jobs available to Helga is prostitution.[9] She rejects this option because "the price of the money was too dear" (34), and yet the prospect calls attention to the way economic power has severely limited her well-being, her mobility, and therefore, her freedom.[10] In addition, Helga also lacks spiritual "references." She does not have a liturgical history that can vouch for her moral upbringing and her religious experience. In the "very fashionable, very high services" on Michigan Avenue, Helga feels the chill of the urban church's elitism: "She hoped that some good Christian would speak to her, invite her to return, or inquire kindly if she was a stranger in the city. None did, and she became bitter, distrusting religion more than ever. . . . They noticed her, admired her clothes, but that was all, for the self-sufficient uninterested manner adopted instinctively as a protective measure for her acute sensitiveness, in her child days, still clung to her" (34).

The bitter distrust that Helga suffers in Chicago extends to another awkward visit to a church in Harlem once she has secured employment as a traveling secretary later in the novel. We are told that "most of Harlem's uplift activities" were held in churches and so she "unwillingly" ventures into the sacred space to attend a health lecture (49). The promise of social reform in New York offers a potential corrective to the placating moral imperatives of Naxos College. But Helga arrives to the church late and after disturbing a sleeping usher, forces the lecturing physician to pause uncomfortably as she is led to a seat in the front of the room: "The offended doctor looked at the ceiling, at the floor, and accusingly at Helga, and finally continued his lengthy discourse" (49). His humiliating gestures make it clear that her presence among the congregation of progressive race men and women is an unwelcome disruption. It is also in this church that Helga is reacquainted with the former principal of Naxos, Dr. Robert Anderson, who has relocated to New York. His return forces Helga to confront not only her own racial allegiances, but a "vague feeling of yearning" for Anderson that both thrills and frightens her. At the conclusion of their evening together, he remarks: "You haven't changed. You're still seeking for something, I think" (50).

Despite Anderson's prophetic words, it would be a misrepresentation at this point to characterize Helga Crane as a *religious* seeker in the tradition of nineteenth-century black spiritual conversion narratives or secular fiction such as Countée Cullen's "The Black Christ." Her anxieties about protecting her social identity seem to eclipse any interest she may have in truly developing a relationship with God or understanding a particular religious tradition. Throughout the novel, we are reminded that "Helga Crane was not religious. She took nothing on trust" (34). And yet Larsen repeatedly positions her heroine within the sanctuary of a church as a way of accessing relative signifiers of difference. Racial representation is of primary concern as she listens to the white preacher in the Naxos chapel, while the issues that frustrate her in the upscale northern churches center on the congregation's perception of her background and status. *Quicksand* undoubtedly takes advantage of the black church's long-standing multifunctional role as place for community gatherings, town hall meetings, schools and other educational training, and recreational centers. Lest we dismiss Larsen's settings as mere convenience, however, it is also clear that the disapproval Helga expresses from the church pews is pointedly grounded in moral terms. As a result, the rejection by her peers intensifies the hypocrisy and exclusivity of black communities of faith.

Soon after Helga's experience in the Harlem church, she becomes disgusted with the "race problem" and escapes to her mother's family in Den-

mark. Her reflections during her visit compartmentalize her biracial ances-
try into gendered categories of the material (white mother) and the spiritual
(black father). Overseas, Helga is surrounded by "the things which money
could give, leisure, attention, beautiful surroundings. Things. Things"
(67). Her Copenhagen family is intrigued by her race and embraces her
love of color, adorning Helga in glittering jewels and brightly colored fab-
rics as a way of accentuating her foreignness. Soon it becomes clear that
"Little Helga" has become the center of attention in a strange and disturbing way. A young and handsome artist, Axel Olsen, wants to paint her
portrait, but can only seem to capture her with sensual, grotesquely exotic
features. After spending a year in Denmark, Helga acknowledges "a feeling
of discouragement and hopelessness. Why couldn't she be happy, content,
somewhere?" (81). With her refusal to become Axel's wife and submit to
the continued objectification of her dark skin, Helga articulates an overwhelming longing to embrace the heritage of her father's "family" without shame. In Copenhagen, glutted by all that money can afford, Helga
develops a new respect for her black parent and his ties to his race—"ties
that were of the spirit" (95). Europe signifies physical freedom for Larsen's
protagonist, but spiritual freedom awaits her among blacks in America.

Upon her return to Harlem, Helga acknowledges both her desire to have
a future with Robert Anderson and a yearning to be a part of Negro society, because "it did mean something to her. She had no wish to stand alone"
(107). She shares a kiss with the former Naxos administrator and privately
entertains the possibility of a romantic relationship with him, despite the
fact that he is now betrothed to her friend Anne Grey. When he refuses her
advances, Helga's hope collapses under the humiliation of the experience.
At the height of her desperation, feeling foolish and full of self-loathing,
Helga rushes out into a storm and falls, literally, into a gutter. She stumbles
in her red dress toward a "blurred light" and the all-too-familiar refuge of
a storefront church. Having endured the loneliness and uncertainty of the
storms beyond, Helga succumbs to the "showers of blessings" within (111).

Helga experiences an inexplicable sense of nostalgia within the black
church that originates in the cultural memory of what is, presumably, a
shared racial past. She hears a hymn of repentance, "a song which she was
conscious of having heard years ago—hundreds of years it seemed" (110).
In keeping with this temporal dislocation—a representation that has much
in common with Wright's depictions of the church—Helga remarks that
"time seemed to sink back into the mysterious grandeur and holiness of far-
off simpler centuries" (114). The church's wailing multitude, undisturbed

by time and civilization, views her with "a hundred pairs of eyes" and "mixture of breaths" (111, 113). In a subtle reversal of the middle-class tendency to associate the working-class with unrestrained sexuality, Helga immediately becomes the center of attention because of her disheveled appearance and her colorful red dress, which labels her as "a scarlet 'oman," "pore los Jezebel," and an "errin' sistah" (112). Her own reaction oscillates between relief, amusement, and repulsion. One moment, she gives "herself freely to soothing tears," and the next, she recoils, "frightened at the strength of the obsession" (112,113).[11]

Charles Larson maintains that "the cathartic moment unites her with the folk, with the blackness she had scorned all her life," but what *Quicksand* promotes as "blackness" in the storefront church draws on a troubling assemblage of stereotypes (*Invisible Darkness*, 72). In these final chapters, the narrative's rendering of the church lapses into the pseudo-anthropological rhetoric of plantation travelogues, sentimental novels, and burlesque minstrelsy. Larsen relies on the economy of images such as the religious "orgy" to accentuate Helga's physical and sexual surrender. Black Christian worship is further objectified as the bizarre recompense of "nameless people, observing rites of a remote obscure origin." The folk are described as primal, reptilian creatures as they crawl on the floor in prayer. They shout and groan savagely, particularly the women who "gesticulated, screamed, wept, and tottered" beneath the preacher's powerful voice (113). Though Larsen may have wanted to immerse Helga in black culture, this agenda is repeatedly jeopardized, as Cheryl Walls notes, "by her stereotyped view of what 'true' black culture is" (*Women*, 113).[12]

Tormented by the cacophonies of racial prejudice and economic insecurity in Naxos, Chicago, New York, and Denmark, Helga embraces the religion espoused in the storefront church as a means of freeing herself through mental quiet. Her sexuality also facilitates this escape and allows her, initially, to regain a measure of control. DuCille points out that Larsen's satirical play on the word "conversion" in these scenes is used as a way "to refer to and to link Helga's religious and sexual initiations" (*Coupling Convention*, 111). In Chicago, she refused the money of men who solicited her for sexual favors, but after her failed tryst with Robert Anderson, Helga capitalizes on her own body's "exchange value" by enticing the storefront preacher (Carby, *Reconstructing*, 173). She notes how easily Reverend Mr. Pleasant Green yields to her suggestive touch and smile. Endowed with sexual currency, Helga believes that she will profit happiness through marriage, financial security, and a faith in God that allows her to "deliberately stop thinking" (116). Yet in the "confusion of seductive repentance," the narrative implies that Helga has exchanged one false perception for another when she returns to Alabama as the preacher's wife (118).

Now in place of the independent, but unanchored Helga Crane from the novel's opening is a woman named Mrs. Pleasant Green who acquiesces to the restrictive hierarchy of the southern town. Her new husband is the leader of a rural community with a rigid patriarchal structure; Reverend Green seems to be the only man in what appears to be a town comprised completely of women and their children. For these "dark undecorated women," God and the male preacher converge at the center of existence (121). Every morning in Larsen's small Alabama town is a Sunday morning, since the church and the community are virtually interchangeable there. Even Helga's new house, with its stark walls, plain furniture, and religious pictures, manifests the attributes of a church sanctuary. Ironically, the town's black religious services are held in the old stable of a wealthy white man, described as a "dreary structure . . . about which the odor of manure still clung" (121). As Helga struggles to embrace an identity through God, she pinches her nose and forces herself to "be unaware" of the odors—the nagging questions and doubts. Nevertheless, she cannot thrive in such a desolate locale, where stock figures speak with an almost indecipherable southern dialect and offer little more than biblical platitudes by way of conversation. In this environment, the quest for knowledge and artistic achievement—cherished by black elites as signs of progress and reason—is a pursuit that is viewed as beyond necessity. The rigors of domestic responsibility invalidate the need for books, much less the leisure to study them.

Soon after her "conversion," Helga privately doubts both the verity of her salvation and the sanctity of her marriage with its expectation of childbearing: "She saw suddenly the giving birth to little, helpless, unprotesting Negro children as a sin, an unforgivable outrage. More black folk to suffer indignities. More dark bodies for mobs to lynch" (75). Within twenty months of her marriage, however, Helga gives birth to a girl and twin boys. She becomes too ill to cook or clean as a result of her pregnancies and must depend on the female parishioners to provide for her family's basic needs. The links that Helga makes between sin, motherhood, and race are intensified by her role as a preacher's wife, where religion and domesticity are two sides of the same coin. Though her perspective is dramatically more complex than that of the humble, Job-like mother in Cullen's "The Black Christ" or the self-righteous maternal figures in Wright's work, it is worth noting how *Quicksand* manages to raise, in a similar fashion, the issue of maternal culpability in perpetuating black suffering. The self-blame that Helga internalizes is frequently recognized by contemporary womanist theologians as one of the more toxic effects of male dominance. Such guilt foregrounds her victimization by an oppressive social system, one that includes not only white power structures and lynch mobs, but also "primitive" black religious folk whose only concern is to be "right with God" (120).

So when Helga dares to voice her fears about her declining health, Reverend Green and his flock interpret her discontent as *blasphemy*, not a cry for help. Her husband reminds her that his mother "had nine children and was thankful for every one," not to mention the fact that Helga's "doubt and uncertainty were a stupendous ingratitude. Had not the good God saved her soul from hell-fire and eternal damnation?" (124). In her weakness, she drifts in and out of consciousness, untouched by the fervent prayers of the congregation. Withdrawing completely, she denounces Christianity as her race's greatest and most dangerous illusion:

> With the obscuring curtain of religion rent, she was able to look about her and see with shocked eyes this thing that she had done to herself. She couldn't, she thought ironically, even blame God for it, now that she knew that He didn't exist. No. No more than she could pray to Him for the death of her husband, the Reverend Mr. Pleasant Green. The white man's God. And His great love for all people regardless of race! What idiotic nonsense she had allowed herself to believe. How could she, how could anyone, have been so deluded? How could ten million black folk credit it when daily before their eyes was enacted its contradiction? (130)

Larsen explores a double-edged religious symbolism by demonstrating how images of the church as a refuge can easily translate into fear and ideological stagnation, political resignation, and unquestioned acceptance of the status quo. Furthermore, Helga's lament that the "white man's God" condemned blacks "to slavery, then to poverty and insult, and made them bear it unresistingly, uncomplainingly almost, by sweet promises of mansions in the sky by and by" is profoundly self-incriminating in light of her own demise (134). The "sweet promises" of her husband and his belief system have had a crippling effect, inevitably forcing her to look for relief in the otherworldly view of postponed liberation that she despises.

## From *Quicksand* to *In Love & Trouble:* The "Deadly Yoke of Oppression"

How, then, can the concept of "spiritual infidelity" deepen our understanding of Larsen's novel? Through Helga Crane Green we are witness to the "deadly yoke of oppression" that Frances Wood characterizes as the "silencing, ignoring, degrading, and dismissing [of] women's experience, especially those experiences that reveal the nature and extent of oppression perpetrated against them within the community" ("Take My Yoke," 39). Larsen's questing heroine crosses the thresholds of no fewer than five church communities in *Quicksand;* in each instance, her presence challenges deeply held assumptions about what constitutes appropriate forms of behavior for black Christian women. To be sure, works such as Wright's *Black Boy* (1945), James Baldwin's *Go Tell It on the Mountain* (1952), and Ernest Gaines's *A Lesson Before Dying* (1993) also demonstrate how the practice of compassion, kindness, and love can be obscured by ritualized acts of racial and religious performance. Yet where their narratives focus the theme around the question of "being a man," Larsen's novel disputes the idea that female individuality, mobility, intellectual inquisitiveness, and sexual independence are transgressive behaviors—sins that can be obliterated only through marriage and motherhood. This harmful rhetoric leads Helga to doubt her own strength and capacity for moral integrity when she is unable to successfully manage her new role: "How, she wondered, did other women, other mothers, manage? Could it be possible that, while presenting such smiling and contented faces, they were all always on the edge of health? All always worn out and apprehensive? Or was it only she, a poor weak city-bred thing, who felt that the strain of what the Reverend Mr. Pleasant Green had so often gently and patiently reminded her was a natural thing, an act of God, was almost unendurable?" (125).

*Quicksand* further satirizes the "natural" suffering and redemptive sacrifice of the Christian mother through southern female characters like Sary Jones. In another context, Sary might have been Helga's "spiritual mother"—the foundation of a supportive female network for the young bride in her time of crisis. Instead, Sary is one of several women who react to Helga's fears with "eyeball-rolling" resignation and amusement: "Yuh all takes it too ha'd. Jes remembah et's natu'al fo' a 'oman to hab chilluns an' don' fret so." When Helga points out that her exhaustion and ill-health "can't be natural," Sary counsels: "Laws child, we's all ti'ed. An Ah reckons we's all gwine a be ti'ed till kingdom come" (125). While Sary's survival strategies are surely shaped by her own tribulations (and her six children), her guidance captures the community's complicity in the dismissive silencing of Helga's experience. Helga attempts to follow the advice of her husband's congregation by submitting to God and enduring the pain without complaint because she is ashamed of her "lack of sufficient faith" (126). But as Anthony Pinn observes in his reading of the novel, "the prayers she prays to God and her continued suffering present a contradiction she cannot ignore and that is unresolvable through redemptive suffering arguments" (*Why Lord?* 152).

With respect to Helga's "infidelity," it is clear that she does not find comfort in another lover's bed, nor does she physically abandon her husband and children. But her disgust for Reverend Mr. Pleasant Green and her life in Alabama is clearly expressed through the way she forsakes the Christian God. Larsen places Helga's bitter loss of faith alongside her feelings of sexual revulsion and maternal loathing, to the point where the idea of marriage becomes "immoral" (134). Helga's own commitment to Christianity is arguably superficial and bewilderingly disinterested from the start. The theme is intensified by the way Larsen hastily surrounds her protagonist with black religious caricatures like Sary Jones and Reverend Green. Yet these narrative choices serve Larsen's larger agenda in demonstrating the real effects that oppressive theological language can have on black female bodies. Spiritual infidelity as a conceptual framework takes seriously the potentially devastating implications of phrases such as "'till death do us part" and the glib advice that, in the face of pain and suffering: "We must accept what God sends" (124). Helga, having internalized the "quasi-familial" rhetoric of God as husband and parent, unwittingly rehearses the hierarchical dependence of these metaphors, in which "the burden of the relationship rested firmly on the shoulders of the subordinate partner" (Weems, *Battered Love,* 17). In "racking pain and calamitous fright," Helga turns, as her last refuge, to the heavenly Father that she discovered in the storefront church and finds his justice and protection to be as misleading as her husband's love.

The novel's unflinching perspective returns us to the "bowl of quicksand soup" that threatens to consume a Mississippi bride in a short story by Alice Walker. Published as part of the collection *In Love & Trouble: Stories of Black Women* in 1973, "Roselily" revisits the theodical questions of *Quicksand* and continues Larsen's bold exploration of black women's spiritual crisis through the concept of infidelity. The story details the thought processes of the title character, a bride whose apprehension and uncertainty mocks the definitive language of her wedding vows. We are told that, "she does not even know if she loves him" (7). Yet Roselily has the future of her children in mind, and she hopes that her marriage will bring new comfort, social and economic security, and a measure of freedom that has been unattainable for her in the South. Her betrothed, who is from the North, is also a black Muslim. Roselily's country wedding, then, commemorates both her marriage and her movement away from Christianity. In Chicago, where her new husband lives, a new faith awaits as well.

"Roselily" allows us to read between the lines of the bride's story by alternating traditional Christian wedding vows with frank narrative prose. With *Quicksand* as a frame of reference, my discussion of this story, along with "The Diary of an African Nun," will examine how the female protagonists assess the significance of their choices—wrought with communal expectation and the threat of nonexistence—within the context of religious servanthood. Walker also reinterprets Helga Crane's experience by manipulating the idea of fertility in the stories from *In Love & Trouble*, employing images of coldness and sterility to demonstrate how marital covenants render these women spiritually unfulfilled, psychologically desolate. Roselily arguably takes the most progressive step in migrating north with her husband. But Walker troubles the young woman's journey of ascent by asking: What is the meaning of freedom in "robe and veil"?

As a daughter of rural folk, a mother of four, and a Christian woman, Roselily self-consciously contemplates her new roles as wife, northerner, and Muslim. She briefly reflects on pastoral images of her old life and romanticizes "memories of being bare to the sun" (6). Cautiously she envisions her future, with all of its hopeful promises, as a "stalk that has no roots. She wonders how to make new roots. It is beyond her" (6–7). Her only previous experience with the North has been through her fourth child's father, a married man characterized as a weak and melancholy intellectual reminiscent of Jean Toomer's male wayfarers in *Cane*. To Roselily, the North is a strange and mysterious place that changes the way people see the world. This much, however, is clear—she will not miss the preacher, whom she describes as "odious," and she will not mourn the passing of his church from her life (8). Although she was raised as a Christian, her predominant attitude toward religion is one of suspicion and sardonic exasperation. As the preacher officiates her wedding and speaks of God, Roselily is shaken by the urge to "strike him out of the way, out of her light, with the back of her hand. It seems to her he has always been standing in front of her, barring her way" (8). Her new husband appears to share her contempt, for a feigned smile hides his repugnance for the country folk who worship, in his mind, "the wrong God" (3).

Against this unbelief, Walker uses Christian wedding rites to further stress the ambivalence that Roselily feels toward marriage and the institution's latent potential to stand in the way "of her light." Indeed, the blues energy of her thoughts decenters the authoritative voice of the preacher. When he states, *"we are gathered here,"* the narrative wryly interjects, "Like cotton to be weighed. Her fingers at the last minute busily removing dry leaves and twigs. Aware it is a superficial sweep" (3). Roselily's uneasiness becomes apparent when she reflects not only on Christianity, but also on her husband's religion. Her brief allusions to Islam are limited to the most orthodox customs, particularly with respect to her appearance, that she will be expected to follow as a woman. When the preacher states, *"to join this man and this woman,"* Roselily imagines "ropes, chains, handcuffs, his religion. His place of worship. Where she will be required to sit apart with covered head" (4). The thought of negotiating a new set of rules and restrictions troubles Roselily, and she tries, rather unsuccessfully, to counterbalance this fear with the promise of freedom in Chicago. There she will be "respectable, reclaimed, renewed. Free! In robe and veil" (7). It soon becomes clear that as Roselily rids herself of an unfulfilling existence in the South, she is yielding to her husband a measure of control that amounts to a near-deification of his promises in a domestic afterlife: "Her place will be in the home, he has said, repeatedly, promising her rest she had prayed for" (7). Further narrative references to being "up high" add religious significance in relation to her migration to the North—a region already mythologized in black cultural history as a heavenlike paradise. Turning her attention to her husband, the one who will "free" and "uplift" her, Roselily questions the meaning of liberation on a pedestal of motherhood, domesticity, and piety: "She feels old. Yoked. An arm seems to reach out behind her and snatch her backward" (6).

So when the preacher at last, says, "or forever hold . . . his peace," we cannot overlook the serious consequences of this pledge and the post-mortem future that it anticipates for the bride. Foreboding allusions to *Quicksand* are particularly strong throughout the tale, from the images of spiritual suffocation to the debilitating constrictions of motherhood. In accordance, Roselily wonders: "When she is rested, what will she do? . . . Her hands will be full. Full of what? Babies. She is not comforted" (7). Her experience inverts Helga Crane's journey, for it is not a bucolic landscape, but a concrete urban fantasy that will eventually bury alive the wife and mother in "Roselily."[13] And if her attitude toward Christianity is any indication, Roselily will inevitably chafe against her husband's attempt to "redo her" under the veil of religious devotion: "He sees her in a new way. This she knows and is grateful. But is it new enough? She cannot always be a bride and virgin, wearing robes and veil. Even now her body itches to be free of satin and voile, organdy and lily of the valley. Memories crash against her. Memories of being bare to the sun" (6).

Walker's erotic language in the story underscores the adulterous long-ings of a restless spirit through a body that is shrouded like a bride, bound like a corpse. Such marital anxieties, expressed through Roselily's fear that "she cannot always be a bride and virgin," place her in direct conversation with "The Diary of an African Nun." In this story, Walker continues to wed spirituality with sexual discourse in the six brief journal entries that comprise the narrative. As I have previously stated, Walker destabilizes the favorable connotations associated with the nun's vows by questioning the righteousness of a holy sacrament forged in concert with colonizing aggression. The relationship between these two stories offers deep insight into Walker's womanist critique of God as a white male and her human-ist appraisal of black Christian worship as a form of self-preservation in times of trouble. In discussing the Ugandan tale, Walker further states her concern with the indoctrination of Christianity "as an imperialist tool used against Africa" (*Gardens*, 266).

Sequestered in an East Central African mission school and hotel founded by Americans, the unnamed nun is acutely aware of how the international community of visitors exoticize her as "a work of primitive art" ("Nun," 113). Her devotion is a comforting reassurance to those who equate Christian piety with human refinement. The narrative indicates that ever since she earned the privilege of wearing her uniform, she has honored her commitment with dutiful praise and obedience. It is no coincidence that the Holy Trinity she worships bears such a strong resemblance to the afflu-ent European travelers who visit her country. For Walker's nun, God is like a tourist for whom she must provide clean sheets and towels. The narrative also employs the image of the nearby Ruwenzori Mountains, with their rich soil encased in snow, to symbolize the protagonist's condition. The nun is "shrouded in whiteness like the mountains" (114). She bathes in cold water while the black people outside dance around a roaring "fire of creation" (116). But just as the "blazing heat of spring" melts the snow off the moun-tains once a year, so the protagonist longs to shed her white gown and all the lifeless trappings of Christian civilization: "Must I still tremble at the thought of the passions stifled beneath this voluminous rustling snow?" (115). This yearning for creation, for life and fecundity, is at the heart of a spiritual dilemma that is gendered through the Ugandan nun.

Certainly, the nun's position in the mission as "wife" fixes the identity of the divine as male. She writes: "I am a wife of Christ, a wife of the Catholic church. The wife of a celibate martyr and saint" (114). Her character makes repeated references to God as her father and master, and to Christ as her husband and lover. Such titles call special attention to the androcentric rule entrenched within her belief system. In keeping with this concept, the womanist religious scholar Patricia Hunter asserts that "to speak of God as father is intentional use of the masculine. Presenting God as male has legitimized male domination and power over women, children, and other living things. . . . Having a male God has led many to believe that women are something other than made in the image of God. If women are something other, then women are less than men who are truly made in God's image" ("Women's Power," 190–91). Accordingly, the woman's image of herself in "The Diary of an African Nun" fails to mirror the God she has been called to worship. She understands her existence, her status, and her power as "something other," in the sense that her gender as well as her race are incompatible with the standards of salvation established at the Western mission school.

Furthermore, when she speaks of Christ, her devotion is upset by images of failed sexual encounters. Calling out to her "Dearly Beloved," she writes of a yearning for spiritual companionship that is figured through frustrated desire, impotence, and the sterile passion of a faltering marriage (117). Like "Roselily," the story of the Ugandan woman uses sacred verses to juxtapose dogma with subjective desire. The nun writes: "'Our father, which art in heaven, hallowed be thy name, thy kingdom come, thy will be done on earth—' And in heaven, would the ecstasy be quite as fierce and sweet?" (117). In contrast are the Ugandan people who do not share the nun's religious beliefs. The collective voice of the African men and women glorify nature and commune with the spirits of their ancestors. She is tempted by their sensual pleasures—the sound of chanting, the beating of drums, the smell of roasting goat meat. Feeling abandoned by her own partner, she longs to join the sacred dance of life with a new mate.

While Walker's representation of the Ugandan spiritual and cultural belief system as an alternative to Christianity is engaging, it is also problematically ambiguous. There is little textual evidence, for instance, that connects the nameless Africans and their midnight fertility dance to any particular ethnic group or religion.[14] Such inscrutability reinforces the degree to which these non-Christian black bodies function as a romanticized abstraction of the metaphysical void in the nun's life—an ache that is conveyed by drumbeats and the images of lips, teeth, rolling limbs, and the "clacks of . . . dusty feet." The nun struggles with words to explain her desire for the exuberant life of the African people and the passion that she likens to the "hot black soil" hidden within the snow-covered mountains (117). In this longing for escape, contextual specificity gives way to a hazy vision of shared cultural memory not unlike Helga Crane's revelations in the storefront church in Harlem.

Nevertheless, the material effects of remaining in the Catholic mission are clear. The nun will never bear a child if she is to remain faithful to her vows. Regeneration and growth are particularly strong motifs in "The Diary of an African Nun," and Walker articulates these themes through the images of children and seasonal allusions to spring. A pagan dance sequence concludes symbolically at daybreak with the "acclaiming cries of babies," for instance (116). In contrast, the nun interprets her childlessness as an aberration and, perhaps, a liturgical misinterpretation of divine will, asking: "[D]id he not say, 'Suffer little children to come unto me'?" Fooled by the other nuns and priests, who had once appeared "so productive and full of intense, regal life," the African woman now realizes that she has relinquished her life-giving abilities to their God and his debilitating power (114). When the nun questions the value of maintaining this illusion, her thoughts turn from the reproductive capabilities of herself as a woman to that of her country. "Barrenness is death," she writes in her diary, and yet she believes that her people's best chance for survival is through a barren alliance with a white God: "For the drums will soon, one day, be silent. I will help muffle them forever. To assure life for my people in this world I must be among the lying ones and teach them how to die" (118).

This wife of Christ tragically reaffirms the sacred vows that demand her self-sacrifice in much the same manner as Roselily. Even as her heart aches with doubt, each of these two brides says *yes* to the men and the missionaries who conquer, silence, and destroy in the name of God. The Mississippi mother says, "I do," and thinks of her children, of resting in peace, while the Ugandan nun ponders the future of her country when she declares, "I will." Approaching such "conflicted inner visions" from a womanist perspective, the theologian Cheryl Townsend Gilkes points to the characters from *In Love & Trouble* to illustrate how black women "exhibit self-destructive stumbling blocks right alongside self-constructed inner resources as they seek to live an ethic of love and resistance and to sustain life and hope" ("Womanist Challenge," 234). In highlighting the decisive exchange of vows, Walker's stories emphasize the often-overlooked interior struggle of black women whose voices are as paralyzed as Helga Crane's physical body. But this kind of narrative strategy also risks depicting the heroine's fear as little more than naïveté and anxiety that fades with time. What, in other words, prevents us from reading the doubts of Roselily and the African nun as little more than "prenuptial jitters"?

I would argue that their flickers of doubt and desire do retain a subversive quality that profoundly compromises the institutions that bind them. Their objections linger even though neither one of Walker's protagonists explicitly breaks free from her marriage. Rather than openly dismantling the oppressive bonds of Christianity, their adulterous longings are ultimately incorporated into its structure, so that the assumed stability of these sacred institutions and the scriptures that support them must be reconsidered entirely. In other words, by not openly forsaking their individual nuptials, these women's actions cast doubt on the "faithfulness" of all marital and spiritual covenants that legitimize patriarchal domination and racial subjugation. The quicksand metaphor remains especially apt, as both Roselily and the African nun, fearful of being reduced to the "moral status of whores," replicate Helga Crane's fatalistic withdrawal from society.[15] After the ceremonies have ended, we remain haunted by the chilling insight of Larsen's unfulfilled bride: "Could it be possible that, while presenting such smiling and contented faces, they were all always on the edge of health? All always worn out and apprehensive?" (*Quicksand*, 125).

## "Or Forever Hold His Peace": Divine Silence and *The Color Purple*

Walker integrates the naïveté of the young bride in "Roselily" and the erotic, soul-searching monologue of "The Diary of an African Nun" into a thoroughly transcendent narrative of spiritual infidelity in *The Color Purple*. Where the two short stories from *In Love & Trouble* demystify the means through which institutionalized theological language victimizes black women, Walker's 1982 novel neutralizes that language; its heroine stridently refuses to worship a God "glorying in being deef [deaf]" (*Purple*, 176). Even the structure of Celie's written "prayers" highlights critical communicative functions—issues of voice, of punitive silence and liberating speech—that have been instrumental in each text previously discussed in this chapter. We may recall, for instance, Helga Crane's debilitating realization: "For had she not called in her agony on Him? And He had not heard" (Larsen, *Quicksand*, 130). Or the African nun's cry: "How long must I sit by my window before I lure you down from the sky?" (Walker, "Nun," 115). Conversely, Celie's more successful negotiations of silence and speech are crucial to evaluating black female responses to moral evil and human suffering. With this in mind, my concluding analysis of *The Color Purple* will scrutinize how the rhetoric of divine silence affects the voice of a black woman who has been told to "forever hold *her* peace."

The letters that Celie writes to God and her sister, and to nature, are integral to her rejection of a social order that relies on her battered body, poor self-image, and sense of shame to maintain its stability. Critics have commented extensively on Walker's remarkable manipulation of the epistolary form as a storytelling device and a "vehicle for self-expression and self-revelation" (Gates, *Signifying Monkey*, 245). Deborah E. McDowell refers to the entries as "letters of self-exploration" whose writing "liberates her from a belief in a God outside herself . . . and acquaints her with the God inside herself" ("Changing Same," 101).[16] My analysis builds upon previous readings by demonstrating how changes in the letters' form, style, and degree of contemplation also allow us to measure Celie's spiritual infidelity, or "turning away" from her father, her husband, and her God—the divine surrogate for both male figures. Walker foregrounds accusations of indecency in *The Color Purple* by merging the volatile language of female desire and sensuality with a willingness to openly critique a "loveless, barren, hopeless" Western religion. Ironically, the kinship that Celie forges with another woman, Shug Avery, features both spiritual and sexual "adulterous" dimensions that not only defy social conventions, but culminate in a self-affirming humanist vision of Creation.

Walker crafts Celie's unsigned and undelivered letters like a diary that begins in the young woman's fourteenth year. The confessional tone invites the reader to identify with Celie as she narrates a sorrowful coming-of-age in a rural southern town much like Walker's own home in North Georgia. But the opening of each entry ("Dear God") indicates a *correspondence*, an exchange between a sender and a receiver that cleaves Celie's experiences into distinct, compartmentalized fragments. Wendy Wall refers to these entries as "lettered bodies," or "anti-selves that Celie creates to mediate between herself and her oppressive environment" ("Lettered," 262). Here again, writing is commended as Celie's chosen mode of emotional release, a rewriting of the self. Yet her motives for filling these pages should also give us pause. In order to fully evaluate what Celie discloses or conceals and how, we must also explore the identity of her addressee. To whom is Celie writing?

A bearded white man with white eyelashes and white robes is the reader Celie imagines. He is Celie's image of God—a view not uncommon in black spiritual narratives—and it is his omnipotent "bluish-gray" gaze that looks down upon her from Heaven (*Purple*, 176). This is the portrait she paints for Shug later in the novel after being asked to describe what her God looks like. In another instance, Celie envisions him as a "stout white man work at the bank," surrounded by albino angels (91). Her wording indicates not only God's race and gender, but also his authoritative status and economic power. These characteristics further underscore the black woman's status in this hierarchical relationship as inferior or, recalling Patricia Hunter, "something other." In fact, their relationship echoes Walker's reflections about her own parents' vision of a segregated heaven—"But perhaps Jesus Christ himself would be present, and would speak up on their behalf. After all, these were black people who were raised never to look a white person directly in the face" ("Only Reason," 295). The same perspective can be attributed to Celie. Her subordination as a black woman is integral to her service to the church and her unquestioned faithfulness. She finds reassurance in the belief that, "this life soon be over. . . . Heaven last all ways," when confronted with inexplicable suffering (*Purple*, 47). From a literary perspective, it would appear that Walker's protagonist has less in common with *Quicksand*'s Helga Crane than with Sary Jones, the southern black matriarch who counsels Helga to deny herself and put her trust in the Savior.

In her first letter, Celie obediently confesses her failure to be a "good girl."[17] The label suggests sexual containment and moral purity (good) as well as dutiful submission in family and domestic matters (girl). Celie is convinced that she has violated these standards on all fronts. We soon learn that she has been repeatedly raped by the man she believes is her father (but who, she later discovers, is her stepfather). After giving birth to his second child, the infant boy is taken from her and presumably sold. It is her stepfather's threat, *"You better not never tell nobody but God. It'd kill your mammy,"* that initiates Celie's clandestine letter writing. The initial lines, "~~I am~~ I have always been a good girl," anticipate condemnation that is powerful enough to kill, while invoking a sense of guilt that leads to Celie's self-erasure (11). Nevertheless, though her letters convey a sense of innocence, I would argue that their simplicity and forthrightness also camouflage the carefully crafted narration of a young woman who has been compelled to account for her actions before the "Old Maker." This is the speech that the cultural critic bell hooks recognizes as a kind of silence—selective, guarded, and careful (*Talking Back*, 7).

To demonstrate, it is important to note that God also serves as a surrogate father and husband for Celie when she is too afraid to acknowledge her own. When her mother inquires about the father of her child, she writes: "I say God's. I don't know no other man or what else to say" (12).

Celie's diction in this scene invites closer scrutiny. While it is clear that she is rarely allowed to leave her home, she does have limited contact with a larger black community that includes males—at the very least, on Sunday mornings in church. One could argue that her claim not to "know" any other men connotes an intimate familiarity that is typically associated with sexual experience. Here, this kind of familiarity is used to characterize her relationship with God. After Celie gives birth, the exchange between mother and daughter continues:

> Finally she ast Where it is?
> I say God took it.
> He took it. He took it while I was sleeping. Kilt it out there in the woods.
> Kill this one too, if he can. (12)

Does Walker arrange these indeterminate pronouns to offer a glimpse into Celie's subconscious and project the actions of her stepfather onto a heavenly Father? In Celie's telling, it becomes just as likely that God "took" her baby and "kilt it" in the woods as her stepfather.[18] This perception of God appears to be complicit in Celie's abuse, similarly disapproving of her attempts to assert herself in any form. "Not only are many words for God masculine, the words we most often use are words that connote power over another and fear of authority," observes Hunter. "To only know or speak of God as father is limiting to those whose understanding of father is not positive" ("Women's Power," 190).

On the other hand, when Celie is forced to marry an older man with three children of his own, her sister, Nettie, laments about leaving Celie alone with this new family. Celie responds: "Never mine, never mine, long as I can spell G-o-d I got somebody along" (26). The two promise to write, but when Nettie's letters never reach her, Celie's next entry begins phonetically with "G-o-d"—signaling her deep loneliness in a world that was never hers ("never mine") to begin with (27). Her emphasis on spelling rather than speaking is crucial here, for as Nettie later remarks, Celie is often too ashamed to use her voice to pray or "talk about it to God" (122). As Maria Lauret points out, "Celie writes, in other words, when telling is impossible" (*Alice Walker*, 102). The letters serve, therefore, as a linguistic veil that allows Celie to mediate her shame in a manner that elicits sympathy from God, the only other man she "knows."

But does Celie feel inclined to write about some experiences and not others? Is she even *permitted* to speak freely on these pages? Being able to identify *who* is listening is fundamental to Celie's quest for a liberated voice.

I would not go so far as to suggest that Celie is being less than honest in her letters, but I believe that her selectivity should be remarked upon in these early painful scenes, particularly considering her references to God as her sole means of survival. Although we are given little insight into the decision making that attends her writing process, we must still reckon with the contradicting identities of her heavenly "reader." It is unclear whether or not the God who appears in her mind as the bearded white man is privy to the same level of self-disclosure as the God whose name she spells in desperate times of need. Similar incongruities can be found in her relationship with the church community and her husband, Albert (called "Mr. _____" in Celie's letters). These contradictions underscore the extent to which she is besieged by religious rhetoric that, like her wedding vows, proves to be utterly disconnected from her lived experience.

Once Celie takes steps to name her audience, however, her own voice becomes clearer. With the unexpected friendship of blues singer and Mr. _____'s former lover, Shug Avery, Celie's letters become longer, more complex and elaborate, and reflect a less inhibited sensibility. She writes of her admiration for Shug's bold, self-assertive manner, particularly when she is performing at the "jukejoint" and commanding an attentive audience of menfolk. With Shug, Celie violates her stepfather's command and speaks aloud of the horror of being raped. Celie also divulges, in these later letters to God, her erotic desire for the blues woman as well as their subsequent sexual experimentation. As one of the most significant steps in Celie's journey of self-exploration, her "adulterous" relationship with Shug also signals her discomfort with her abusive marriage and her insolent stepchildren. When, in the past, her obligations as a daughter, mother, and wife became too difficult to bear, she relished her role as "Sister Celie" and relied on the promised ease of heaven as a guide. But Celie visualizes heaven differently through her relationship with Shug. Celie remarks, as she sleeps with her arms around Shug's waist, "It feel like heaven is what it feel like, not like sleeping with Mr. _____ at all" (110).

Walker places Celie's affair with Shug in concert with her discovery of Nettie's undelivered letters. Together these incidents generate her strongest disavowal of her husband *and* the God to whom she has corresponded as the "Old Maker." Indeed, for years after her departure, Nettie wrote to her sister, but Mr. _____ hid the letters in his locked trunk. As Celie reads, we learn of Nettie's experiences living with a preacher and his wife—two missionaries who have unknowingly adopted Celie's son and daughter. Nettie travels with the missionaries to Africa, where they live, educate, and proselytize among the Olinka tribe in Liberia. Nettie remarks on her commitment to continue writing and sending letters, despite the fact that she knows Mr. \_\_\_\_\_ will never allow Celie to read them: "But always, no matter what I'm doing, I am writing to you. Dear Celie, I say in my head in the middle of Vespers, the middle of the night, while cooking, Dear, dear Celie. And I imagine that you really do get my letters and that you are writing me back: Dear Nettie, this is what life is like for me" (144). With her unexpected discovery, Celie not only learns of her sister's experiences in Africa, but of the existence of her two children and the shocking news that the man who she once believed was her father is, in actuality, her stepfather. Mr. \_\_\_\_\_'s actions in hiding Nettie's letters demonstrate another way in which silence can be used as a means of controlling access to information and power. As Tamar Katz observes, "Walker has given us a series of letters that almost never reach their addresses, a series of letter writers with absent, unhearing, or impotent readers" ("Didacticism," 189). Indeed, what is particularly significant about Nettie's attempt to envision her sister in the aforementioned passage is the way it parallels Celie's own struggle to imagine God as her reader.

As a result, Walker uses the communicative malfunction between Nettie and Celie to highlight the degree to which Celie's early letters to God were not only undelivered, but *undeliverable*. An embittered Celie insinuates that the Christian God, in his capacity as Father, is also "not our Pa!" and she divulges her unbelief directly to the source, saying: "You must be sleep" (162–63).[19] From a philosophical view, Celie questions traditional notions of God's benevolence by suggesting that he is not listening to her and refusing to hear (or read) her prayers. Or perhaps the fault lay with some intermediary—an intervening religious tradition not unlike her husband—that has broken the lines of communication and undercut God's omnipotence by consigning her hopes and desires to a hidden trunk. Celie tells Shug that God "act just like all the other mens I know. Trifling, forgitful and lowdown" (175). No longer can she situate herself within a biblical message that asks her to deny her own needs and "inhabit a world where women's rape and violation are theological justifiable" (Weems, *Battered Love*, 116). With the foundation of her faith profoundly shaken, Celie's next letter is addressed not to this man, but to Nettie. Walker utilizes these "changes of address" to signal deep transformation in her protagonist from a black church mother and wife to a woman actively freeing herself from the bonds of divine racism, sexual abuse, and domestic imprisonment. "Dear Nettie," we are told, "I don't write to God no more, I write to you" (175).

Undoubtedly, Nettie's transmittals carry with them the power of a spiritual awakening as the outpouring of information leaves the main character of *The Color Purple* feeling renewed and liberated. Where Celie's previous communications with God were unsigned, McDowell maintains that the appearance of Celie's signature at the end of her letters to Nettie signifies "expressions of ratification, of approval, of assertion, of validation" ("Changing Same," 103). Celie also begins critically reflecting upon how her interpretation of God has shaped the belief system that governs her everyday life. She writes: "All my life I never care what people thought bout nothing I did, I say. But deep in my heart I care about God. What he going to think. And come to find out, he don't think" (176). Celie struggles with the realization that her service to the church—washing the linen, singing in the choir, feeding the preacher—failed to attract God's attention. More importantly, the "servanthood" that caused her to sacrifice her health and emotional well-being to honor her parents and remain faithful to her husband also went unnoticed. In exploring the meaning of her suffering, Celie accuses God of willful neglect and abuse of power. Hers is a common sentiment in modern black literary engagements with religion, yet the circumstances of Celie's charge that God is "sleep" and "deaf" and "don't think" add a gendered dimension to already politicized notions of divine silence.

In the study *Unspoken: A Rhetoric of Silence*, Cheryl Glenn cautions against hasty generalizations of silence and speech, noting that "verbal and silent interactions are exercises and negotiations in power" (30). Among the distinctions Glenn makes in the strategic uses of silence is the claim that the absence of words can convey multiple meanings unmatched by speech, from respect, fear, and awe to indecision, disapproval, and abandonment. And just as "expected" silences are integral to the processes of communication, unexpected silences—"silences delivered instead of language"—necessitate interpretive skill and responsiveness from the listener (11). Of course, these expectations shift and change in relation to marginalized or "muted" groups. Glenn notes that those in positions of power often employ authoritative silences to impose silent acquiescence and inarticulate speech, thereby inducing subordinate groups to accept the control of dominant social structures (32). She also draws on bell hooks's observations about linguistic resistance in southern black communities to highlight how different forms of speech are accorded different values. Where the male preacher's voice was meant to be heard and remembered in hooks's experience, black women's voices "could be tuned out . . . not acknowledged as significant speech."[20] Particularly relevant to my analysis is hooks's assertion that the kind of speech she was taught as a young girl, "was often the soliloquy, the talking into thin air, the talking to ears that do not hear you—the talk that is simply not listened to" (*Talking Back*, 6). This notion of speech as "soliloquy" also brings to mind the Ugandan woman's written pleas to her "Dearly Beloved" in "The Diary of an African Nun." The claims of hooks, as well as Glenn, provide a useful perspective for evaluating Celie's desire to enter into meaningful dialogue with the sacred and express herself through "significant speech."

One could argue that theistic religious traditions place interactions with God outside material understandings of speech and silence. Black spiritual autobiographies and Christian conversion narratives reveal a God who speaks not as human beings do, but through visions, prayers, and the unspoken blessings of faith. Considering the way in which Celie has patiently suffered cruelty and injustice in the past, it is also clear that Walker's protagonist is hardly inclined to "accept good from God and not trouble" (Job 2:10). Indeed, the fear of being associated with Job's ungrateful wife—not to mention being accused of speaking "like a foolish woman"—is what has compelled Celie to silently endure her suffering in the past as an act of divine will. Yet Christian traditions also advocate a belief in a personal God; influenced by biblical language and the customs of her church, Celie's actions are shaped by the understanding that such a God is intimately involved in her daily life. So believing herself to be abandoned, Celie initially disavows God and rejects the variant images of a "lowdown" man as her Creator. In a manner similar to Helga Crane and the African nun, she interprets God's unexpected silences as indifference and utter disregard. She can no longer see or feel the redemptive value of such overwhelming, disproportionate moral evils in a world governed by an unsympathetic deity.

Shug Avery is the one who encourages Celie to reframe her vision of God and seek out a more attentive audience. The blues woman also makes the connection between the apparent deafness of her white, male God and the indoctrination of the Christian church:

> You mad cause he don't seem to listen to your prayers. Humph! Do the mayor listen to anything colored say? Ask Sofia, she say.
>
> But I don't have to ast Sofia. I know white people never listen to colored, period. If they do, they only listen long enough to be able to tell you what to do.
>
> Here's the thing, say Shug. The thing I believe. God is inside you and inside everybody else. You come into the world with God. But only them that search for it inside find it. (177)

Shug encourages Celie to embrace a spiritual energy that is neither white nor male, and honors self-discovery, human passion, and a loving kinship with the earth. She offers a belief system that celebrates the divinity of all creatures and acknowledges beauty as God's way of "trying to please us back" (178). Here is a God that does not demand shame and suffering for the sake of salvation. Like her relationship with Shug, Celie's new vision of God is an unorthodox and potentially destabilizing force that has the power to subvert both the rigid moral standards of her church community and the oppressive bonds of her marriage. Certainly there is a substantial network of women in the novel who, up until this point, have continually advised Celie to assert herself and "fight." Consider Nettie: "You got to fight. You got to fight" (26), and "You've got to fight and get away from Albert" (119); Mr. _____'s sister: "You got to fight them for yourself" (29); Sofia: "You ought to bash Mr. _____ head open. . . . Think bout heaven later" (47). But it is not until her redemptive conversation/conversion with Shug that Celie understands the value of the women's advice. This, along with the knowledge of Nettie's letters and the success of her children, compels Celie to fight not only "that old white man," but her husband by leaving Georgia and returning to Memphis with Shug.

Celie's transformed religious discourse has strong ties with the beliefs and practices advocated by womanist theology and black religious humanism. Both perspectives claim to regard suffering, for instance, as an "outrage" that is devoid of pedagogical qualities, thereby making humans accountable for annihilating evil.[21] At one point in *The Color Purple*, Shug attributes pain and suffering to the actions of humanity: "Man corrupt everything. . . . He try to make you think he everywhere. Soon as you think he everywhere, you think he God. But he ain't" (179). By naming man's "corrupting" power in this way, Shug empowers Celie with the voice and moral strength to resist. She advises: "Whenever you trying to pray, and man plop himself on the other end of it, tell him to git lost. . . . Conjure up flowers, wind, water, a big rock" (179). In this regard, Walker's narrative advocates a philosophy of existence in which humanity works together with God through a partnership of mutual admiration. This loving bond also implies a joint effort in combating suffering.

Another concept that is useful in evaluating the religious discourse of *The Color Purple* is expressed through aspects of Jacquelyn Grant's use of the term "discipleship." An inclusive discipleship can only be achieved, according to Grant, by rejecting oppressive theological language, patriarchal domination, and dehumanization within the church as well as the larger society. This relationship with God also recognizes women as full and active participants in religious institutions and empowers them to work for liberation. She states that, "The kind of wholism sought in womanist theology requires that justice be an integral part of our quest for unity and community" ("The Sin of Servanthood," 214). Grant's approach is certainly in accord with the womanist discourse of *The Color Purple*. But while Celie's new understanding of God does not completely reject theism, it is not based in a Christian belief system. In fact, she and Shug celebrate the divinity of nature in ways that the Bible negatively labels as acts of moral harlotry. Walker depicts female characters who "break off their yoke and tear off their bonds" (Jer. 2:20) by refusing to submit to a jealous God that has been used by the Christian church to dismiss black women's experience. Celie gains new wisdom from the trees, while the earth fuels her voice (187). And where "classical Yahwistic theology nowhere presents him as a sexual being calling for sexual participation in worship" (Ortlund, *Unfaithful Wife*, 32), Celie speaks openly about her intimate relationship with the sacred and how she "makes love" to God (197). She prays to this pagan divinity through the stars, trees, sky, and all the people of the earth. The risks that "Sister Celie" takes in learning to "speak to [God] in different way" prove to be as monumental as the day she breaks away from Mr. _____ with the declaration, "I'm pore, I'm black, I may be ugly and can't cook. . . . But I'm here" (229, 187).[22]

Critics have questioned whether or not Celie's awakening brings about collective transformation in *The Color Purple*,[23] but the tragic examples of Helga Crane, Roselily, and the African nun illustrate both the personal *and* corporate costs of the black woman's sustained silence and the risks she takes in speaking out. Further evidence of what is at stake in the individual wrestling of the spirit can be found in the startling philosophical exchange between Celie and her reformed ex-husband (now called by his first name, Albert) in the novel's concluding pages:

> Anyhow, [Albert] say, you know how it is. You ast yourself one question, it lead to fifteen. I start to wonder why us need love. Why us suffer. Why us black. Why us men and women. Where do children really come from. It didn't take long to realize I didn't hardly know nothing. And that if you ast yourself why you black or a man or a woman or a bush it don't mean nothing if you don't ast why you here, period.
>
> So what you think? I ast.
>
> I think us here to wonder, myself. To wonder. To ast. And that in wondering bout the big things and asting bout the big things, you learn about the

little ones, almost by accident. But you never know nothing more about the big things than you start out with. The more I wonder, he say, the more I love.

And people start to love you back, I bet, I say.

They do, he say, surprise. (247)

Characters like Celie embody the kind of existential wakefulness that Albert eloquently interprets here as "wonder" and "asking." Their life-affirming discoveries are evidence that the struggle to comprehend suffering is incomplete without a deeper concern for the larger meaning and purpose of human existence—or, "why you here, period." It is a theme that echoes profoundly in African American literary engagements with the problem of evil, rewarding the beleaguered seeker with rare glimpses of hope, possibility, and more love. And as we shall see, Baldwin's "Sonny's Blues" and Morrison's *Paradise* further intensify this idea of a love born from the impulse to wonder, to ask about the "big things."

Jacquelyn Grant states that "the language that we use to talk about God more often than not says more about the speaker than about God" ("The Sin of Servanthood," 210). Both Nella Larsen and Alice Walker manipulate the language of marital strife to expose how specious charges of faithlessness, moral deficiency, and conceit are used to contain the assertive speech and willful behavior of women in their stories. Ironically, the ones who ultimately suffer the most egregious betrayal in these stories are those who are branded so carelessly by their families and communities as "adulterers" to their faith. The works of these two African American writers respond by proposing forthright reconsiderations of God's character that diverge from traditional black Christian perspectives in an effort to recover the repressed vows of women who desire strong, meaningful spiritual partnerships.[24] So while spiritual infidelity provides a discursive context for interpreting black struggles against racism, misogyny, religious subjugation, and self-annihilation, it is clear that characters like Celie are hardly "unfaithful" to higher ideals of compassion, equality, and respect. As a result, the tormented struggle of the "pore los Jezebel" in *Quicksand* is transformed in narratives like *The Color Purple* into a womanist conversion narrative with its own unique vocabulary of praise and salvation.

# 4

## "There Is No Way Not to Suffer"

*Evil Ruptures and Improvisations of Joy in "Sonny's Blues"*
*and "The Sky Is Gray"*

> You can't stay there, you can't drop dead, you can't give up, but all right,
> OK, as Bessie said, "Picked up my bag, baby, and I tried it again." This
> made life, however horrible that life was, bearable for her. It's what makes
> life bearable for any person, because every person, everybody born, from
> the time he's found out about people until the whole thing is over is
> certain of one thing: He is going to suffer. There is no way not to suffer.
>
> —JAMES BALDWIN, "The Uses of the Blues"

THE UNNAMED black characters in the cramped waiting room of the
dentist's office are known only as the *lady*, the *preacher*, and the *boy*. In Ernest
Gaines's short story "The Sky Is Gray," first published in 1963, the lady
is the one wearing a white dress and black sweater; she is first to voice
her concern about the distant cries of a young patient, observing: "I often
wonder why the Lord let a child like that suffer" (94).[1] She goes on to
add: "And look like it's the poor who suffers the most. . . . I don't understand it" (95). In response, a fat man in a black suit and gold chain—the
preacher—counsels against the dangers of the lady's presumptive query.
"Not us to question," he advises and draws on the authority of scripture to
bring her uncertainty to an end: "He works in mysterious ways—wonders
to perform" (95). And so it is the boy, the one carrying a book, who breaks
the silence. The boy assertively disputes the preacher's warning, startling
the room of black men and women in the small Louisiana town. He uses
the preacher's attitude toward the child's suffering to condemn the unex-
amined faith of an entire racial community that has too long been denied
justice and freedom in their own country. "We don't question is exactly
our problem," the boy declares. "We should question and question and

question—question everything." When the preacher asks for an explanation, the conversation continues:

> "I said what I meant," the boy says. "Question everything. Every stripe,
> every star, every word spoken. Everything."
> "It 'pears to me that this young lady and I was talking 'bout God, young
> man," the preacher says.
> "Question Him, too," the boy says.
> "Wait," the preacher says. "Wait now."
> "You heard me right," the boy says. "His existence as well as everything
> else. Everything." (95–96)

This emblematic exchange prefigures the characters and thematic structures that have distinguished Gaines's writing career from his first novel,
*Catherine Carmier* (1964), to *A Lesson before Dying* (1993) and his most recent collection, *Mozart and Leadbelly: Stories and Essays* (2005).[2] "The Sky
Is Gray" contains, perhaps, his most straightforward rendering of the
philosophical debate over the nature of God and the meaning of suffering within the context of African American experience. The heightened
iconic dimensions of the dentist office's conflict, as seen from the point
of view of a child narrator, allow each character to efficiently personify a
constellation of spiritual beliefs and varying approaches to life's challenges.
Assumptions about age, gender, education, political ideology, and the value
of religious tradition further correspond to the maternal compassion and
racial wisdom of the lady, the stubborn self-righteousness of the preacher,
and the antagonistic skepticism of the boy. But what makes "The Sky Is
Gray" especially significant is the process through which the clear-cut distinctions that are evoked by this trio blur and collapse in the world beyond
the waiting room. Once the nurse announces that the dentist will not see
any more patients until one o'clock, the narrator will be forced to make
decisions about how best to manage his suffering (and his toothache) when
answers are simply not forthcoming.

In 1957, six years before Gaines's story appeared in *Negro Digest*, James
Baldwin struck a similar chord in the *Partisan Review* with his short story
"Sonny's Blues."[3] At first glance, Baldwin's account of a Harlem schoolteacher's struggle to reconcile with his younger brother—a recovering drug
addict and jazz musician named Sonny—does not appear to have much in
common with the southern parable of a young boy's journey to the dentist in "The Sky Is Gray." (Their regional differences are suggested rather
ironically in titles that correspond to opposing Civil War military colors

of Union *blue* and Confederate *gray*.) Furthermore, Baldwin has explored issues of spiritual crisis more overtly elsewhere in novels such as the semi-autobiographical *Go Tell it on the Mountain* (1952), *Tell Me How Long the Train's Been Gone* (1968), and *Just Above My Head* (1979), in the drama *The Amen Corner* (1968), and throughout his prolific essays, of which the most widely read is "Down at the Cross: Letter from a Region in My Mind" from *The Fire Next Time* (1963). Yet the two siblings in "Sonny's Blues" disagree over fundamental questions about human existence in a manner not unlike the waiting-room quarrel in Gaines's narrative. And as Sonny's brother, the story's narrator, grapples with the death of his own daughter, we are confronted once again with the Dostoevskian impasse of how to comprehend an innocent child's suffering in a world created by an omni-benevolent God. The father in mourning projects his anxiety onto Sonny and pleads for explanations, apologetic guarantees, or at least some reassurance that his younger brother will not return to heroin when threatened by despair.

> "But there's no way not to suffer—is there, Sonny?"
> "I believe not," he said and smiled, "but that's never stopped anyone from trying." He looked at me. "Has it?" I realized, with this mocking look, that there stood between us, forever, beyond the power of time or forgiveness, the fact that I had held silence—so long!—when he had needed human speech to help him. He turned back to the window. "No, there's no way not to suffer. But you try all kinds of ways to keep from drowning in it, to keep on top of it, and to make it seem—well, like *you*." (66)

"Sonny's Blues" takes seriously the urge to discover the meaning and purpose of human suffering, yet it pointedly seeks to transcend the philosophical dilemma's proclivity for logic and theoretical abstraction through countertexts of subjective experience. Plagued by unbelief, the narrator wonders in the above passage if it isn't better to accept suffering, to simply "take it," since "there's no way not to suffer." Sonny answers his brother with a cogent pragmatism that acknowledges what is inscrutable and unknowable without yielding to material resignation or spiritual quietism. His smile, his "mocking look" invites us to venture beyond speculative logic and recognize our own impulsive, frantic resourcefulness in moments of crisis.

What develops, then, in "Sonny's Blues" and "The Sky Is Gray" are functional theodicies—or, "all kinds of ways to keep from drowning"—that shape the critical thrust of this chapter. Invoking what Cornel West extols as "the tragicomic sense of life" ("Black Strivings," 89), both stories envision an intrinsic urge to stay afloat by drawing on cultural figures of repetition and studied improvisation that can accommodate even the most excruciating ruptures of inexpiable evil. Few of the sufferers in these stories confront God directly, demanding justice as do the wounded characters in Countée Cullen's "The Black Christ" or in Alice Walker's fiction; instead, the protagonists in Baldwin's and Gaines's texts turn to elders who acquire divine purchase through their insight and judicious guidance. And while religious scholars often differentiate moral evils from the calamities of nature, the boundaries are more fluid in these stories as the sting of poverty is likened to a hailstorm and racial violence afflicts black bodies with the same ruthlessness as a terminal disease. Each narrative ultimately conveys the organic sensibilities of a humanist worldview by mitigating unsympathetic images of the physical world, particularly water (i.e., seas, storms) through an ethos of artistic creation (i.e., music, storytelling) that connects the solo performer to a collective audience.

Indeed, it is in his role as musician that Sonny feels empowered to strike out for those deep existential waters. Baldwin explicitly calls forth elements of African American music as a nontheistic response to the reality of suffering, but the story's engagement is not limited to the blues; it is the extemporaneous transcendence of music making in a broad sense that suggests ways of living—a "toughness," to use the author's term—under difficult circumstances ("Uses," 89). In Baldwin's work, Clarence Hardy explains, "music essentially serves to 'invest' black pain with coherence and create a language crucial for the creation of an independent black self that opposes a broader culture steeped in the ideals of white supremacy" (*Baldwin's God*, 51). Women participate in this creative process as well, though it is clear that being able to sing the blues is, for Baldwin, a sign of male development and maturation. Indeed, Sonny's mother, like Sister Margaret from *The Amen Corner* and the maternal figures in Richard Wright's work, often hums and sings religious hymns—a telling difference from the Charlie Parker melodies that Sonny emulates at the piano.

The blues also convey a male-centered engagement with suffering through the lyrical cadence of the young boy's storytelling in "The Sky Is Gray." Indeed, Gaines characterizes his use of repetition and indirection in the story's narrative structure as "blues forms" that are reminiscent of Lightnin' Hopkins and Lester Young (*Mozart*, 147). My reading of Gaines's work further demonstrates the manner in which the simple observations of an eight-year-old boy develop a blues rhythm that moves from critical reflection to lament, and breaks occasionally into a cathartic hum. His voice speaks to the dialectical process that Ralph Ellison so eloquently described as an "impulse" within black folk life "to keep the painful details and episodes of a brutal experience alive in one's aching consciousness, to finger its jagged grain, and to transcend it, not by the consolation of philosophy but by squeezing from it a near-tragic, near-comic lyricism" (*Shadow*, 78).

Likewise, the jazz clarinetist and saxophonist Sidney Bechet offers another way to define the blues by aligning its sacred energy with spirituals:

> And both of them, the spirituals and the blues, they was a prayer. One was praying to God and the other was praying to what's human. It's like one saying, "Oh, God, let me go," and other was saying, "Oh, Mister, let me be." And they were both the same thing in a way; they were both my people's way of praying to be themselves, praying to be let alone so they could be human. The spirituals, they had a kind of trance to them, a kind of forgetting. It was like a man closing his eyes so he can see a light inside him. . . . And the blues, they've got that sob inside, that awful lonesome feeling. It's got so much remembering inside it, so many bad things to remember, so many losses. (*Treat*, 212–13)

This passage from Bechet's memoir acknowledges a cultural kinship between blues music and the spirituals by suggesting how, as Anthony Pinn has stated, both "make use of the same creative and existential material" (*Why Lord?* 121). Yet in distinguishing the blues, Bechet draws upon rhythms of individual and collective remembering that are adopted by both Baldwin and Gaines. Where the spirituals that allow the participant to "forget" worldly concerns ("like a man closing his eyes") and forge metaphysical connections ("so he can see a light inside him"), the blues preserve "that sob inside" and, according to Bechet, gather strength as the eye-opening realities of hardship and loss are shared. Similarly, this "praying to what's human" is how Sonny shares his story when he sits down at the piano in Baldwin's narrative. In "The Sky Is Gray," James sings the blues, too, though his young fingertips do not yet bear the calluses of a guitar player like Monsieur Bayonne. Outside the dentist's office waiting room, where the rain has turned to ice, Gaines's protagonist can only wonder at the philosophical speculations of the lady, the preacher, and the boy; for now, he has more immediate concerns: "The sleet's coming down plenty now. They hit the pave and bounce like rice. Oh, Lord; oh, Lord, I pray. Don't let me die, don't let me die, don't let me die, Lord" (106).

## Good, Evil, and Shades of Gray

> The river is gray. The sky is gray. They have pool-doos on the water.
>
> —Ernest Gaines, "The Sky Is Gray"

To claim that "Sonny's Blues" and "The Sky Is Gray" put forth a *theodicy* suggests that both narratives are engaged in thinking and working through the problem of evil with the aim of offering some sort of defense of God's goodness in light of human suffering. But neither Baldwin nor Gaines is concerned with defending God and the Christian faith in these stories, and their spiritual engagements are not prescriptive enough to satisfy those who may be looking for authoritative religious counsel. Nevertheless, I revisit William R. Jones's treatment of "functional theodicy" here because of his efforts to expand its objectives beyond academic apologia. Jones's contention that theodicy is "defined too narrowly if it is perceived as an abstract and theoretical enterprise executed only by professional philosophers and theologians" is an assertion that soundly guides the course of action and spiritual inquiry in the two short stories (*White Racist?* xxiv).

What is most useful about Jones's discussion of theodicy's functional attributes is his emphasis on the subjective nature of each individual's approach to the problem of evil:

> There is an aspect of [each person's] over-all world view that treats the issue of suffering and relates it to his prevailing beliefs about the nature of ultimate reality and man. It is not difficult, for instance, to demonstrate that each individual makes a fundamental judgment about the character of specific sufferings, whether each is good (positive), bad (negative), or neutral; whether he must endure the suffering he encounters or should annihilate it; whether suffering can be eliminated or whether it is an inevitable part of the human condition. Each person also acts on the basis of some conclusion about the source or cause of suffering. (*White Racist?* xxiv)

Jones points succinctly to the evaluative system that is at the root of humanity's encounter with suffering. As imaginative writers, however, Baldwin and Gaines are uniquely positioned to complicate what Jones describes as a "whether . . . or" process in favor of an even more pliant and ambiguous philosophy of existence. Determinations of positive, negative, and neutral suffering are in flux in their stories; characters are gripped by misery that they can neither endure nor fully annihilate. While the protagonists may not openly theologize, the "nonecclesiastical epiphanies" that prompt their actions are embedded in Judeo-Christian language and metaphor that

invite theological speculation and endow the narratives with ritual qualities (O'Neale, "Fathers," 138). In turn, the difficult choices made by the
characters in "Sonny's Blues" and "The Sky Is Gray" give rise not only to
dynamic functional theodicies, as defined by Jones, but to a kind of "usable
religion"[4] that is often at odds with the binary judgments of a rigid social
and moral order.

In Baldwin's story, binaries of faith/reason, right/wrong, and innocence/
experience are internalized within our narrator, a middle-class algebra teacher
who relies on similar formulas of logic and stable meaning to structure
his worldview.[5] But the reasoned certainties that shape his belief system
are under attack from the very opening line of "Sonny's Blues." Repeated
variations of the phrase "I couldn't believe it" and "I didn't want to believe" convey the difficulty that he has accepting the news that his younger
brother has been caught in a drug raid "for peddling and using heroin" and
jailed (27). That the narrator's struggle for comprehension grows increasingly uncertain is evidenced by the way the semiotic system of signs and
sounds unravels before his eyes. The first paragraph reads as follows:

> I read about it in the paper, in the subway, on my way to work. I read it, and I
> couldn't believe it, and I read it again. Then perhaps I just stared at it, at the
> newsprint spelling out his name, spelling out the story. I stared at it in the
> swinging lights of the subway car, and in the face and bodies of the people,
> and in my own face, trapped in the darkness which roared outside. (26)

After repeatedly failing to "read" the newspaper account, Sonny's brother
stares in vain at the printed words and letters, now empty signifiers devoid
of meaning. He then directs his energies to the subway lights, and despite
its guiding beams, he fails to extract any meaning from these objects before
shifting his attention to the subjective scripts of other bodies. Understanding eludes Sonny's brother even as he stares at his own face in the darkened
subway window. And as he becomes more distressed, the pronoun "it" in
the passage becomes more indefinite: *it* is the reality of Sonny's drug conviction; *it* is his own guilt and shame; *it* is the immediacy of unknown fear.
In expressing this unbelief, the narrator also introduces careful distinctions
between inside and outside and other oppositional structures that are contested throughout the story. Different manifestations of darkness—from
the darkness of subway tunnels and movie theaters to a Platonic darkness
within the human psyche—are contrasted against sunlight, glimmers of
luminous recognition, and, as Donald C. Murray notes, the necessary "glare
of reality" ("Complicated," 354).

But Sonny—his name, an ironic homophone for "Sunny"—defies easy classification. He is one who seems to move in "stillness" (36), and his actions reveal to his brother an unfamiliar world inundated with shades of gray. The schoolteacher is baffled, for instance, by the paradoxical notion that the institutional penal system might not actually be interested in reforming Sonny, releasing him before he can "kick the habit" (33). More significant is the narrator's fundamental misinterpretation of Sonny's behavior as self-destructive. When he asks a friend of Sonny's: "He must want to die, he's killing himself, why does he want to die?" the man, also an addict, responds: "He don't want to die. He wants to live. Don't nobody want to die, ever." Unwilling to forgive or empathize, the narrator cuts short this particular conversation with the words: "Well, I guess it's none of my business" (33). Keith E. Byerman characterizes such fearful and disingenuous comments by the narrator as the "failed communication" and "misreadings" that hinder his personal growth in the story ("Words and Music," 199). In fact, the exchange with Sonny's friend is indicative of the narrator's countless missed opportunities to be his brother's keeper ("How you been keeping?" are Sonny's first words upon returning to New York [36]). Their mother's advice, which will be discussed presently, also makes clear that the narrator will have to ease his strict adherence to certain absolutes in order build a relationship with his brother.

Countée Cullen adopts a similar representational strategy in "The Black Christ." His poem is narrated from the vantage point of the unnamed eldest brother, whose efforts to abide by the values and judgments of the status quo are contrasted against the irreverent autonomy of his younger brother, Jim. Cullen also uses a tragic incident—Jim's lynching—to forge a philosophical reconciliation between siblings. To be sure, the texts ultimately draw different conclusions about God's role in relation to suffering. Baldwin's story emphasizes an existential humanism that disengages itself from the question of God's existence and determinations of God's benevolence or malevolence. Cullen's poem, however, invests every aspect of human activity with God's grace and champions a Christian theodicy of redemptive suffering. Yet the parallels in their characterizations are especially useful for reminding us that within each sibling rivalry, the older brother's concern is fueled by love and profound admiration: the narrator in "The Black Christ" romanticizes Jim's prideful nature and "imperial breed" (line 274), while, in "Sonny's Blues," Baldwin's speaker boastfully describes Sonny on stage in his "kingdom" as bearing "royal blood" (71). In a previous chapter, I examined the manner in which Cullen ascribes Christ-like attributes to the martyred brother, foreshadowing an otherworldly bond in the description of his death. Nevertheless, the notion that Sonny's majesty in Baldwin's story is more "earthbound" by comparison does not restrict the Harlem musician's capacity for compassion and understanding. It makes Sonny arguably more generous with others who have suffered.

The narrator of "Sonny's Blues" witnesses this generosity of spirit when he sees Sonny watching a revival meeting on Seventh Avenue. The schoolteacher had been observing the gathering from the window of his apartment; he is familiar enough with the street to doubt the "holiness" of the singers, and to reflect with pity upon the "sullen, belligerent, battered faces" of the old folks, children, and working people who tolerate these kinds of periodic distractions. He goes on to state that, the hymns of salvation notwithstanding, "not a soul under the sound of their voices was hearing this song for the first time, not one of them had been rescued. Nor had they seen much in the way of rescue work being done around them" (62). In spite of these realities, however, he is also able to recognize that "as the singing filled the air the watching, listening faces underwent a change, the eyes focusing on something within; the music seemed to soothe a poison out of them" (62). This passage, so reminiscent of Sidney Bechet's description of the spirituals, begins to explain why Sonny, who stands "on the edge of the crowd," is so captivated by the performance, mindful of what the songs might add to his own creative work. The notebook that he carries in his hand indicates this posture of learning, and as he leaves an offering of loose change, "looking directly at the woman with a little smile," this intimate moment of recognition during the revival—described by one critic as the story's climactic scene—is a telling contrast to his brother's literal and figurative distance from the event.[6]

After he returns to the apartment, Sonny goes on to affirm his connection with the revival meeting by comparing the hymns to his heroin addiction, in part because both confer upon the helpless a steady sense of control. The always-suspicious narrator interrogates Sonny with a voice "full of contempt and anger" and asks if he, too, needs a narcotic to be productive and to play the piano. "It's not so much to *play*. It's to *stand* it, to be able to make it at all. On any level," replies Sonny (65). Returning to the street corner gathering, he goes on to say: "While I was downstairs before, on my way here, listening to that woman sing, it struck me all of a sudden how much suffering she must have had to go through—to sing like that. It's *repulsive* to think you have to suffer that much" (66). Indeed, it is clear that Sonny, who can describe the woman's singing as both "warm" and "terrible," is capable of thinking beyond the binary oppositions that structure his brother's world and can hear echoes of pain beneath the vibrancy of her music. The narrator, however, is less interested in Sonny's kinship with a fellow sufferer; "I just care how *you* suffer," he insists, and he tries to push his brother into assuring him that he is "safe" (67).

Clearly the question of why and how people suffer sparks a pivotal confrontation between the two siblings. The narrator insists on an approach that emphasizes endurance, fortitude, and "will power" rather than what he insists are Sonny's suicidal tendencies (67). Sonny, on the other hand, encourages his brother to see suffering from a larger perspective as a fundamental part of the human experience.

> "But we just agreed," I said, "that there's no way not to suffer. Isn't it better, then, just to—take it?"
>
> "But nobody just takes it," Sonny cried, "that's what I'm telling you! *Everybody* tries not to. You're just hung up on the *way* some people try—it's not *your* way!" (67)

Sonny's approach is more perceptive and more empathetic than his brother's, yet it is also less definitive, and at times, exasperatingly vague. While this scene represents Sonny's most vocal attempt to express himself, he is initially reluctant to speak from his own point of view, preferring instead the invitational stance of the second person: "and when you finally try to get with it and play it, you realize *nobody's* listening. So *you've* got to listen. You've got to find a way to listen" (67–68). Just as his brother struggles with limitations of language in the story, so too does Sonny's speech falter with stilted, unfocused, rambling words that can only approximate his emotions.[7] To further convey the existential uproar of what Sonny can only seem to describe as "that storm inside," he draws on abstract sensory images of captivity and despair: "Oh well. I can never tell you. I was all by myself at the bottom of something, stinking and sweating and crying and shaking, and I smelled, you know? *my* stink, and I thought I'd die if I couldn't get away from it and yet, all the same, I knew that everything I was doing was just locking me in with it" (69).

Thus reconciliation between brothers begins in the darkening living room of the Harlem apartment, a relatively safe space that is physically, if not psychologically, removed from the dangers of "the avenue." But understanding can only *begin* here; Sonny's lurching explanations are evidence of that. Further suggesting the limits of their conversation and other more formal exchanges are Baldwin's repeated references to Sonny's notebook, which he occasionally opens, handles, and drops to the floor with a sigh. When finally he admits to his brother, "it can come again. . . . I just want you to know that," it is clear that a discursive space has been opened for Sonny to acknowledge his own vulnerability (70). But full understanding—the kind of recognition that is typically described as "listening" and "hearing" in the narrative—must occur elsewhere, in a more fluid landscape that more accurately reflects the indeterminacy of life. So before the conversation ends, Sonny invites his brother to a club in Greenwich Village where he will be playing piano with the band that evening, but only, he tells his brother, "if you can stand it" (64).

## Acts of God and the Manifold Evils of Nature

> It ain't a question of his being a good boy . . . nor of his having good sense. It ain't only the bad ones, nor yet the dumb ones that gets sucked under.
>
> —James Baldwin, "Sonny's Blues"

Baldwin's strategy of using the narrator to embody the fixed boundaries and normative processes of the social order is reenvisioned in "The Sky Is Gray" through the philosophical schisms between the eight-year-old protagonist and the adults around him. Before returning to "Sonny's Blues," an examination of Gaines's story sheds light on another way in which both texts frame their multiple interrogations of the problem of evil. "The Sky Is Gray," set in rural Louisiana during the late 1950s, also makes a special effort to demonstrate how the religious discourse of suffering can be disconnected from the actual experience of unmerited pain, injustice, and personal anguish. Familiar binary oppositions of good/evil, faith/reason and inexperienced youth/aged wisdom are expressed overtly through the debate over the "head" and the "heart" in the dentist's office scene discussed at the start of this chapter. Yet our main character confronts the "either/or" logic of dogmatic religious belief long before his bus trip to the dentist. After his aunt becomes aware of his toothache, for instance, James is sent with his brother, Ty, to visit Monsieur Bayonne, a family friend. Monsieur Bayonne prescribes prayer for the pain and traces the "Sign of the Cross" on James's tender jaw. The young boy states:

> Monsieur Bayonne mashed harder and harder on my jaw. He mashed so hard he almost pushed me over on Ty. But then he stopped.
> "What kind of prayers you praying boy?" he say.

"Baptist," I say.

"Well, I'll be—no wonder that tooth still killing him. I'm going one way and he pulling the other. Boy, don't you know any Catholic prayers?"

"I know 'Hail Mary'," I say.

"Then you better start saying it."

"Yes, sir."

He started mashing on my jaw again, and I could hear him praying at the same time. And, sure enough, after while it stopped hurting me. (85–86)

It is not long before the tooth begins to ache again and James is forced to kneel for more treatment. Even as Monsieur Bayonne quarrels over whether or not the Baptist or Catholic prayers will alleviate the youth's discomfort, the narrative insinuates that the elder's cure is considerably more painful than the toothache itself. The exchange as told conveys a sense of pathos and levity that allows James to cope with the economic reality that necessitates this faith-based solution: "Auntie wanted to tell Mama, but I told her, 'Uh-uh.' 'Cause I knowed we didn't have any money, and it just was go'n to make her mad again" (85). And so we see James begin to modify his actions on the basis of certain conclusions about what kinds of suffering he can and can not endure: the throbbing tooth? Monsieur Bayonne's excruciating "Catholic" prayers? his mother's wrath? Because one choice seems as miserable as the next, James must become more pragmatic and sensitive to the indeterminacy of his world, a place where the river, the sky, and the "pool-doos" on the water are all gray (91).[8]

Significantly, Gaines's use of physical or *natural evil* is central to how the question of suffering is constructed and scrutinized in "The Sky Is Gray." Our world abounds with tragedies of the plant and animal kingdom, environmental disasters, inexplicable disease, and defects that simply defy explanation. As the religious scholar John G. Stackhouse notes, "the inefficiency, wastefulness, suffering, and death of the natural world prompts many to wonder about the goodness and power of God." Even though a life lost to a terminal illness may elicit the same anguish as a death caused by premeditated murder, physical evil is often approached as a category distinct from the suffering caused by humanity: "Natural evil is no one's 'fault' (except maybe God's, as in 'acts of God'), because no moral agent effects it" (*Can God Be Trusted?* 36).

Historically, according to the philosopher Susan Neiman, the separation between natural and moral evil is a modern phenomenon, which can be traced back to the devastating Lisbon earthquake in 1755. While earlier religious leaders and intellectuals rarely troubled the link between sin and suffering, Enlightenment thinkers such as Immanuel Kant responded to the epistemological problem of the earthquake by isolating acts that seemed utterly beyond human control from those for which humans could reasonably assume responsibility: "After Lisbon, the word *evil* was restricted to what was once called moral evil. Modern evil is the product of will. Restricting evil actions to those accompanied by evil intention rids the world of a number of evils in ways that made sense" (*Evil in Modern Thought*, 268). Neiman goes on to cite the mass executions of Auschwitz and the atomic bomb in Hiroshima as events that mark the collapse of natural and moral precincts of evil; believers who once attributed such enormous suffering to God were baffled by humanity's ability to inflict shocking acts of cruelty in an era of technological and intellectual progress.

Perhaps the nation's growing reluctance to differentiate between kinds of catastrophic evil resonated with Gaines, who came of age during World War II. In a story like "The Sky Is Gray," in which moral evil is ever-present via the social, political, and economic brutalities of racial segregation and rural poverty, we must be attentive to the way Gaines chooses, instead, to foreground occurrences of bafflingly unprovoked suffering for which no one *person* or system can be blamed: the bristling cold, rain, and sleet of a Louisiana winter morning as well as the youth's toothache.[9] This is an "odyssey" not only "through the elementals of human experience," as John F. Callahan notes, but through the elements of nature ("Hearing," 98). Clues throughout the narrative suggest that Gaines uses James's encounter with *nature's* brutal indifference to posit more constructive ways of responding to acts of *human* cruelty. In doing so, Gaines's protagonist acquires a wisdom beyond his years that allows him not only to endure his toothache, but to confront greater storms of suffering and social injustice. This metaphorical parallel between moral and natural evil, though not without its dangers, proves to be persuasive and poignant.

With the distinctions between moral and natural evil in mind, we return to the dentist's office in Bayonne, where James and his mother, Octavia, have arrived after a ride on the segregated bus into the town. In the waiting room, the unnamed woman's aforementioned comment—"I often wonder why the Lord let a child like that suffer"—is triggered by the fearful cries of a younger boy named John Lee Williams; it is important to note, however, that when James initially enters the room he hears "hollering like a pig under a gate" from an *adult* patient in the dentist chair. This sufferer is "a big old man," James comments, "and he's wearing overalls and a jumper" (94). The *waiting* room is, itself, an evocative liminal space where the weak and injured gather for treatment of their physical pain. Therefore, James's observations further reinforce the universal actuality of suffering as evidenced by the way in which it inexplicably afflicts both the "big old man" and "little John Lee" alike. Gaines's narrator is learning to evaluate how such a notion of impartiality might shape his understanding of God and the experience of suffering. Yet before he can fully assess what is at stake here, multiple viewpoints are brought to bear on the issue. The woman in the black sweater raises socioeconomic concerns that make her anxieties over the divine purpose of the child's pain all the more urgent. The dialogue between the preacher and the student also underscore this kind of interplay between moral and natural evil as the former insists on God's perfection and immutability, while the latter argues that not even the most sacred principles are beyond scrutiny in a Jim Crow society.

The college student's strategy involves disputing the preacher's fundamental assumptions on several fronts. When the older man's language presumes a collective responsibility for the student's upbringing, as reflected in his query, "Is this what we educating them for?" the young man responds: "You're not educating me. . . . I wash dishes at night so that I can go to school during the day. So even the words you spoke need questioning" (96). He goes on to assert that the preacher's religious beliefs are based on racist indoctrination: "A white man told you to believe in God. And why? To keep you ignorant so he can keep his feet on your neck" (97). But the student also raises broader questions about how meaning is determined in relation to systems of power and authority. To make his point, the youth, like the SNCC activists of the coming decade, reclaims the communal "we" in favor of more revolutionary aims:

> "I'm not mad at the world. I'm questioning the world. I'm questioning it with cold logic, sir. What do words like Freedom, Liberty, God, White, Colored mean? I want to know. That's why *you* are sending us to school, to read and to ask questions. And because we ask these questions, you call us mad."
> "You keep saying 'us'?"
> "'Us.' Yes—us. I'm not alone." (97)

The student goes on divest the physical world of its accepted denotations with statements such as "the wind is pink" and "grass is black" in order to stress the radical reconceptualization that is required to bring about lasting social and political change (100). These claims are not meant to simply meddle with human perception, but to create a new awareness of the interpretive systems that shape our understanding of the world, and more specifically, American society during segregation. The student declares: "Words mean nothing. Action is the only thing. Doing. That's the only thing" (101). Perhaps considering whether or not "the wind is pink" will encourage the black people of Bayonne to interrogate the tacit validation given to a town that prevents them from exercising their constitutional rights as citizens.

The fundamental reassessments that the college student advocates in "The Sky Is Gray" bear striking similarities to the dissociative haze through which Sonny's brother finds himself stumbling at the start of Baldwin's short story, unable to "believe" and fully process the news of Sonny's narcotics arrest. Both stories inaugurate the main character's exploration of life's deepest and most elusive mysteries with questions about belief and the inner workings of faith. Although James may not be fully aware of the political concerns being discussed, the student's attitude clearly has an effect on him as he observes: "When I grow up I want be just like him. I want clothes like that and I want keep a book with me, too" ("Gray," 100). And where James previously described the unnamed woman's attire as a white dress and black sweater, the more discerning youth now notices a green sweater beneath the black one (101). Scenes such as this are what lead Lee Papa to suggest that "Gaines and his characters are creating a new text of religiosity that stands at an opposite pole from traditional Christianity" ("His Feet," 187). This new text underscores human responsibility not only in the face of corporate tribulations, but when wrestling with individual anguish as well.

Important questions are raised in the dentist's office waiting room, but the experiential shortcomings of the debate are also apparent. Just as the pivotal conversation between brothers in "Sonny's Blues" takes place in the highly controlled refuge of the brother's apartment, so does the waiting room in "The Sky Is Gray" represent a contemplative space—or "sanctuary" (Callahan, "Hearing," 97)—where critical inquiry remains within the realm of theoretical speculation and judgment. Consider, for example, that after the student's exchange with the preacher, the older man hits him across the face and leaves the waiting room angry and insulted. If the elder's departure indicates the dwindling relevance of his ministry, Gaines also makes it clear that the youth's social advocacy is impeded by his failure to successfully convey his ideas to people such as the woman, who is curious about, but puzzled by, his nihilistic wordplay. The irresolute and ineffective conclusion of the scene revisits Monsieur Bayonne's disgust with the battle between his Catholic prayer and James's Baptist one; in this instance, it is the preacher who is "going one way" and the student who is "pulling the other" (86).

Even more critically interesting than the intellectual exchange between the preacher, the student, and the woman, I would argue, is James's own *personal encounter* with suffering. While his toothache—unanticipated, agonizing, persistent—evokes the nature of physical pain, the winter storm outside the dentist office further symbolizes the indiscriminate forces of natural evil. "Nature impales men," John Stuart Mill stated in 1874, "breaks them as if on the wheel, casts them to be devoured by wild beasts, burns them to death, crushes them with stones like the first Christian martyr, starves them with hunger, freezes them with cold" (*Three Essays*, 29). Indeed, the existential tempest that Baldwin's Sonny figuratively describes as "that storm inside" is externalized through devastating natural events in Gaines's story. Outside the dentist's office where James and his mother are forced to wait longer than originally expected, the blowing wind and rain are a constant aggravation. Dressed only in a thin coat and cap, he travels through the frigid weather and gazes longingly at every store and café that he passes. His journey into the unknown (and the wearisome known) is a subtle analogue for the human condition, but it also speaks, in particular, to his race's struggle against the absurdity of oppression. Consider James's reflections in the following passage:

> I'm getting cold all over now—my face, my hands, my feet, everything. We pass another little café, but this'n for white people, too, and we can't go in there, either. So we just walk. I'm so cold now I'm 'bout ready to say it. If I knowed where we was going I wouldn't be so cold, but I don't know where we going. We go, we go, we go. We walk clean out of Bayonne. Then we cross the street and we come back. Same thing I seen when I got off the bus this morning. Same old trees, same old walk, same old weeds, same old cracked pave—same old everything. (104)

Racial bigotry intensifies the distress James suffers from the cold weather in this passage. Through the candid observations of what Mary Ellen Doyle calls "camcorder narration" (*Voices*, 52), James treats the segregation laws as "natural" or established reality, almost as if "no moral agent effects it," yet surprisingly he appears to have within his grasp the power to control the weather—or at least, his response to it, as in: "If I knowed where we was going I wouldn't be so cold." But is there more at stake in this analogy? I have argued that Gaines's relentless descriptions of the "manifold evils in nature" point to the youth's capacity to confront human misdeeds and cruelties. Provocative reversals such as the one quoted above, however, call attention to the risks embedded in this claim. If segregation is seen as a natural way of life, will James cultivate a kind of spiritual and political deference that assures that the "same old everything" will remain so? Is Gaines's text, in effect, *naturalizing* moral evil by suggesting that social injustice can only be alleviated through the same strategies of endurance used to lessen (without entirely eliminating) the numbness of cold hands and feet?

A number of factors indicate otherwise, that James is equipping himself to use both his "head" and his "heart" to actively engage moral evil and not simply endure it. His inquisitiveness and deductive observations are easily attributed to the curiosity of an eight-year-old child, but through these reflections Gaines also presents a boy who refuses to internalize notions of inferiority based on race, socioeconomic status, or age. While he is alert to his family's dependence on money, he conducts himself as if it is within his means to meet their needs, defiantly anticipating the red coat he plans to buy his mother, for example. The way he scrutinizes his surroundings demonstrates that even the notion that God "sends rain on the just and on the unjust" (Matt. 5:45) does not encumber the sense of inventiveness that James brings to his personal struggle against suffering. During the walk through town, James explains: "When we come to a store we stand there and look at the dummies. I look at a little boy wearing a brown overcoat. He's got on brown shoes, too. I look at my old shoes and look at his'n again. You wait till summer, I say" (103). Although he may be too young to change the laws that prevent him and his mother from entering the segregated café or the labor conditions that provide scant wages, I would argue that James's aspirations to conquer the inexplicable weather points to a similar desire to challenge unmerited oppression and fight social and economic inequality.

NATURAL EVIL generates a comparable mode of existential wakefulness in the characters of "Sonny's Blues." A critical look back at Baldwin's story reveals how the suffering caused by accountable human agents intersects with nature's propensity for extinguishing human lives "with the most supercilious disregard both of mercy and of justice, emptying her shafts upon the best and noblest indifferently with the meanest and the worst" (Mill, *Three Essays*, 29). The narrator's mother offers crucial guidance to prepare her son for these inexplicable moments, while Sonny's music serves as a vessel of sorts, navigating through crisis with creativity and cultural vigor. Such a reading reminds us that it is the story's unnamed algebra teacher, and not the title character, who is most in danger of "shaking to pieces" (65). Convinced that he has failed Sonny, the narrator's guilt drives the story's plot as he seeks to establish a meaningful relationship with his younger brother. I would also argue, however, that the tragic death of the narrator's two-year-old daughter, Grace, is what fuels the most tortured moments of introspection in the story; in reaching out to Sonny, the narrator is forced *to listen* in deeper, more profound ways to his wife's sorrow and his own feelings of helplessness in the face of evil. Surprisingly, the impact of Grace's death has been largely overlooked by critics who consistently set the middle-class sensibilities of one brother against the artistic bohemianism of the other, or are too concerned with the narrator's disengagement from a racial community to attend the sense of estrangement and existential terror brought about by the story's moments of unforeseen loss.[10]

We are made aware of Grace's death through the written correspondence exchanged between the two brothers during Sonny's incarceration, but no further details are given until considerably later in the story. The narrator begins simply with "she died of polio and she suffered" before going on to recount the day she collapsed soundlessly on the floor during play. Her death was particularly unexpected, since Grace had just recovered from a fever that was thought to have been a result of a common cold. The narrator details the painful scene as described by his wife: "And when [Grace] did scream, it was the worst sound, Isabel says, that she'd ever heard in all her life, and she still hears it sometimes in her dreams" (59). Clearly Baldwin is placing before his readers, through an even more chilling and devastating image, the question raised in "The Sky Is Gray" of "why the Lord let a child like that suffer." The narrator does not explicitly voice the philosophical dilemma in this manner, but it is evident that an agonizing spiritual crisis is embedded within his thoughts of his daughter's death as well as his concerns for Sonny.[11]

Significantly, Grace and Sonny are discussed in tandem throughout the story, as in parallel configurations such as, "I read about Sonny's trouble in the spring. Little Grace died in the fall" (59). He refuses to communicate with Sonny after the drug raid, but his child's death compels him to reach out to his brother by writing a letter. Of course, we can not overlook the symbolic significance of the little girl's name, particularly when it is the loss of "Grace" that makes the father in mourning more attentive not only to the question of God's mercy, but to his own selfish denial of his brother.

Later, when reflecting on the day of Grace's burial, the narrator states: "I was sitting in the living room in the dark, by myself, and I suddenly thought of Sonny. My trouble made his real" (60). And so the narrator's effort to truly understanding Sonny's plight transpires on multiple registers, for it also represents his attempt to reconcile his ideas about ultimate reality with his experience of evil as an "act of God." Baldwin suggests that working through this religious problem requires that the narrator make deeper connections with others who, like the revival meeting singers, have themselves suffered great pain. In other words, he can no longer sit "by himself" if he is to move out of the dark. Sonny's written condolences are especially significant in this regard: "I was sure sorry to hear about little Gracie. I wish I could be like Mama and say the Lord's will be done, but I don't know it seems to me that trouble is the one thing that never does get stopped and I don't know what good it does to blame it on the Lord. But maybe it does some good if you believe it" (36–37).

Another sudden, tragic death affirms Sonny's observations about the persistent nature of "trouble." The narrator recalls a conversation with his mother in which she shared a detailed account of the murder of his father's brother. This uncle was a guitar player who enjoyed drinking and singing on Saturday nights after working at the local mill. "He was maybe a little full of the devil," the mother notes, "but he didn't mean nobody no harm" (45). She goes on to describe the late night long ago when the two brothers were walking home through the country. The narrator's father heard a car approaching as his uncle, a guitar slung over his back, began to cross a moonlit road at the bottom of a hill. The story continues as follows:

> This car was full of white men. They was all drunk, and when they seen your father's brother they let out a great whoop and holler and they aimed the car straight at him. They was having fun, they just wanted to scare him, the way they do sometimes, you know. But they was drunk. And I guess the boy, being drunk, too, and scared, kind of lost his head. By the time he jumped it was too late. Your father says he heard his brother scream when the car rolled over him, and he heard the wood of that guitar give, and he heard them strings go flying, and he heard them white men shouting, and the car kept on a-going and it ain't stopped till this day. And, time your father got down the hill, his brother weren't nothing but blood and pulp. (46)

The car crash is made all the more horrific by the ugly racism of white men "having fun" in such a reckless manner. The death of the narrator's uncle, like that of his little girl, invokes the senseless and indiscriminate qualities of suffering that compel classic considerations of the problem of evil.

In contrast to the viral disease that ended Grace's life, however, there are clearly human agents that can be held responsible for the uncle's murder. But none are, and where hegemonic white power structures brandish such "godlike" authority, it is unlikely that black life so devalued will receive justice in this society. Moral evil has, once again, become a "natural" way of life. The possibility of divine abandonment and the base actuality of human negligence intersect in the darkness of the road after the car speeds away ("weren't nothing, weren't nobody on that road") and linger in the frustration that the narrator's father suffered from then on, according to the mother's account: "Till the day he died he weren't sure but that every white man he saw was the man that killed his brother" (46–47).

Even so, the mother maintains a strong faith in her "Redeemer" (47). The benevolent, personal Christian God of the spirituals is the foundation of her belief system, one that pointedly balances otherworldly hope with a clear-eyed awareness of black people's experience in America. Having wiped her tears away, she looks at her oldest son and says: "I ain't telling you all this . . . to make you scared or bitter or to make you hate nobody. I'm telling you this because you got a brother. And the world ain't changed" (47). For the narrator, the pedagogical aims of her story seem clear enough: he, too, must "look out" for his brother, watch over Sonny after she is gone. But his mother is preparing him for a truth more sobering and resonant than the platitudinous charge of fraternal responsibility. She knows, to use Sonny's words, that "trouble is the one thing that never does get stopped" (36)—much like the car that "kept on a-going" down the dark road that night—and so his mother is careful to emphasize the unique spiritual and psychological resources that must be brought to bear on such inexplicable moments of suffering.

> "You got to hold on to your brother," she said, "and don't let him fall, no matter what it looks like is happening to him and no matter how evil you gets with him. You going to be evil with him many a time. But don't forget what I told you, you hear?"
>
> "I won't forget," I said. "Don't you worry, I won't forget. I won't let nothing happen to Sonny."
>
> My mother smiled as though she were amused at something she saw in my face. Then, "You may not be able to stop nothing from happening. But you got to let him know you's *there*." (47–48)

In this moving exchange, the mother's insistence on "letting him know you's *there*" requires the narrator to leave his hasty opinions about Sonny's character and behavior aside. To be *there* suggests an unmediated human connection in which the experience of suffering is shared with others who do not judge or control, but take the time to listen. Between the uncle's murder, Sonny's trouble, and little Gracie's death, Baldwin draws our attention again and again to the debilitating moments when "you may not be able to stop nothing from happening." The narrative blurs the division between moral and natural evil and clearly demonstrates, in the mother's words, that "it ain't only the bad ones, nor yet the dumb ones that gets sucked under" (44). More important, however, is the way in which Baldwin uses the notion of "being there" to move beyond the question of *why* and elaborate on *how* one can respond to such awful misery.

## Repetition, Rupture, and Healing "Cuts"

> And I want to suggest that the acceptance of this anguish one finds
> in the blues, and the expression of it, creates, also, however odd this may
> sound, a kind of joy.
>
> —James Baldwin, "The Uses of the Blues"

In spite of the promise made to his mother, Baldwin's narrator does "forget" her advice concerning Sonny and willfully so. Forgetting takes shape through fresh and inventive forms of denial as the schoolteacher initially refuses to confront the reality of Sonny's problems and the "hidden menace" that threatens his own sense of security. Actively processing misery, loss, and regret requires, then, a mode of remembering that the story conveys through listening—to "clear a way" and "find a space" to engage your own story, even when no one else will (68, 69). To develop this idea, Baldwin employs music in a way that returns us to Sidney Bechet's ruminations on the blues: "they've got that sob inside, that awful lonesome feeling. It's got so much remembering inside it, so many bad things to remember, so many losses" (*Treat*, 213). Indeed, the narrator's changing response to music gauges his growth and development throughout the story; where he once dismissed jazz musicians as "good-time people" (50), he learns to respect music making and discern the grueling struggle that takes place through nuances of sound. In the end, he admits:

> All I know about music is that not many people ever really hear it. And even then, on the rare occasions when something opens within, and the music enters, what we mainly hear, or hear corroborated are personal, private, vanishing evocations. But the man who creates the music is hearing something

else, is dealing with the roar rising from the void and imposing order on it as it hits the air. What is evoked in him, then, is of another order, more terrible because it has no words, and triumphant, too, for that same reason. And his triumph, when he triumphs, is ours. (73)

The music Sonny creates from the "roar rising from the void" originates in the fluid, kinetic, and reflexive network of African American experience that Houston Baker refers to as the *blues matrix* (*Blues,* 3). As a prototypical vernacular trope that enables black subjectivity, blues forms also function as a way of negotiating the problem of evil in Baldwin's story and, as we shall see, in "The Sky Is Gray." These narratives further convey the music's distinct qualities through key motifs of repetition, rupture, and the triumph of improvisational joy over human suffering.

Baldwin's most pointed discussion of the blues as an existential and spiritual force takes place during Sonny's performance at the nightclub in the concluding scene. It is important to note, however, that the band's rhythmic orchestrations—from the nurturing dialogue between instruments to the intrepid solo acts and the cacophonous surges of the collective group—have all been in play from the very beginning of Baldwin's narrative. Consider the many scenes in which the algebra teacher observes one musician after another. Early in the story, the narrator sees Sonny in the faces of his students and hears him in their "disenchanted" laughter, repeating a vicious cycle of resignation and failure. Yet as an icy dread threatens to consume him, he hears a boy "whistling a tune, at once very complicated and very simple." He goes on to note that the tune "seemed to be pouring out of him as though he were a bird, and it sounded very cool and moving through all that harsh, bright air, only just holding its own through all those other sounds" (28). When the whistling student appears, the natural sense of control that his tune sustains in an antagonistic atmosphere is highly suggestive of the way the narrator, like his brother Sonny, must also learn to hold his own "through all those other sounds."

In another instance, the narrator watches through the doorway of a bar as a woman dances in front of a juke box, "blasting away with something black and bouncy" (31). She smiles and engages her customers in the bar while "still keeping time to the music," but the narrator detects a deeper, harsher truth within her laughter: "When she smiled one saw the little girl, one sensed the doomed, still-struggling woman beneath the battered face of a semi-whore" (32). Still unprepared to linger with people for whom "this menace was their reality," the narrator projects a vulgar mask onto the dancing barmaid in a way that associates his own unresolved troubles with her "battered face." Likewise, in later scenes, his mother's humming and the tambourine-accompanied hymns at the Seventh Avenue revival meeting prove to be further demonstration of what Hardy calls an "aristocracy of sufferers" who are able to express their pain and still "keep time" with the music (*Baldwin's God*, 50). In each of these cases, music negotiates difficulties in a manner that does not ignore or surrender to the hurt, but translates the experience into a stirring and cathartic new idiom.

Sonny is clearly more attuned to this language, but as the narrative illustrates, he was not always proficient enough to master it. As a teenager after their mother's funeral, he informed his older brother of his intention to become a jazz musician. He was obliged, as a minor at the time, to live with the narrator's wife, Isabel, and her family, while his brother returned to his military post overseas. Isabel's letters speak of Sonny's relentless piano playing during those most vulnerable years. Especially significant are Sonny's dogged efforts to imitate, then improvise from, the music of others, as in the following passage:

> As soon as he came in from school, or wherever he had been when he was supposed to be at school, he went straight to that piano and stayed there until suppertime. And, after supper, he went back to the piano and stayed there until everybody went to bed. He was at the piano all day Saturday and all day Sunday. Then he bought a record player and started playing records. He'd play one record over and over again, all day long sometimes, and he'd improvise along with it on the piano. Or he'd play one section of the record, one chord, one change, one progression, then he'd do it on the piano. Then back to the record. Then back to the piano. (55)

The narrator goes on to state that Isabel and her family "dimly sensed, as I sensed, from so many thousands of miles away, that Sonny was at that piano playing for his life" (56). Unable to escape his suffocating existence in Harlem, the piano becomes Sonny's way of breathing. In learning how to play the music, he simultaneously engages a creative process that parallels a search for self.

One of the most critical elements of Baldwin's depiction of Sonny's playing is *repetition*, or his repeated efforts to strengthen and modify his sound—efforts that are highlighted by the frequent references to music making in the narrative itself. Such recurrences are essential to elaborating how jazz and blues music operates as a cultural mode of processing experience. In his essay "Repetition as a Figure of Black Culture," James A. Snead examines the ways in which black culture anticipates the "inevitability of repetition" and vividly expresses life cycles through music as well as story-telling, art, ceremonial rituals, and labor practices (67). Western views of culture privilege linear thinking and work to maintain carefully delineated representational boundaries, Snead argues, while insisting that "there is *no* repetition in culture but only a difference, defined as progress and growth" (63). Snead draws on the philosophical projects of Hegel to further document the way European thought assumes that cultural cycles must be goal-oriented and characterized by quantifiable change. Yet African-based approaches to culture do not rely on "illusions of progression and control" to shape meaning. Where Hegel regarded African consciousness as incapable of self-awareness, Snead asserts that black culture embraces repetition as an organizing principle that is attentive to patterns and cyclical rhythms, anticipating joy and sorrow as one anticipates the seasonal changes of nature or a folk song's call and response.[12]

But unexpected ruptures and mishaps are also a part of human experience. Snead uses jazz allusions to facilitate his discussion of how black culture comes to terms with the unforeseen, noting, for example, the ways in which accidents are mirrored in musical play. "Black music sets up expectations and disturbs them at irregular intervals," Snead states; "that it will do this, however, is itself an expectation" (72). Particularly instructive are his references to the "cut": the "abrupt, seemingly unmotivated break (an accidental *da capo*) with a series already in progress and a willed return to a prior series" (69). Improvisation becomes a guiding force in determining when and how the "cut" is used. In moments of chaos, a musician may break and return to the background beat, invoking a welcoming sense of recognition, remembrance, and continuity—but only, that is, until the next *da capo*. Likewise, Snead contends that "black culture, in the 'cut,' builds 'accidents' into its coverage, almost as if to control their unpredictability. Itself a kind of cultural coverage, this magic of the 'cut' attempts to confront accident and rupture not by covering them over but by making room for them inside the system itself" (70). Black music contains a sense of pliancy against the back beat that expands to accommodate ruptures and breaks.

Snead's theory provides a useful framework for evaluating "Sonny's Blues." Could human existence, with its recurring joys and trials, figuratively constitute the structuring apparatus known as the background beat in this story? Baldwin fills his narrative with musicians and dancers—the whistling boy, the barmaid, the revival singers, and even the narrator's uncle with his precious guitar—who each rely on those inevitable cycles of life to improvise subjective truths and develop a meaningful view of the world. As a young Sonny remains at the piano, replaying the same chords and melodies again and again, he may irritate Isabel and her family, but he is also developing a sense of hearing that is attentive to the guiding rhythms of existence. He is learning the basics of piano playing and the power of repetition so as to demonstrate his own individual skill and creativity through improvisational *responsiveness.* As Snead points out, "without an organizing principle of repetition, true improvisation would be impossible, since an improviser relies upon the ongoing recurrence of the beat" (70). Sonny's trip back to Harlem, his attempts to reconcile with his brother, and finally, his homecoming at the club in Greenwich Village are all examples of "willed return[s] to a prior series" that allow him to come to grips with his suffering and take responsibility for the hurt he may have caused others.

To extend the metaphor further, I maintain that the presence of moral and natural evil constitutes the unpredictable ruptures that are transformed through healing "cuts" in Baldwin's story. As the narrator attempts to cope with Grace's death, he experiences other moments of anguish—the pain evoked by Sonny's trouble and the senseless murder of his uncle—that break and skip the narrative back to the recurrent theme of suffering, or "back to another beginning which we have already heard" (Snead, "Repetition," 71). Even the moments of musical improvisation that appear throughout the tale offer pragmatic alternatives to the narrator's desperate efforts to keep Sonny safe. Although his father once declared, "Ain't no place safe for kids, nor nobody" (41), and his mother warned him that the car that killed his uncle "kept on a-going and it ain't stopped till this day" (47), the narrator refuses to see how being alert to unforeseen ruptures (learning to expect the unexpected, so to speak) can provide him with the inner resources to survive. To deny "the reality of pain, of anguish, of ambiguity, of death" is more self-destructive than any narcotic addiction, for as Baldwin once stated, "it means that if your son dies, you won't survive it on your own. If you don't survive your trouble out of your own resources, you have not really survived it; you have merely closed yourself against it" ("Uses," 96–97).

One last example of the narrative's blues structures is represented through wry smiles and laughter—another figurative expression of the "cut." It is hard to overlook the protean smiles of the dancers and musicians in the story, or how often the narrator expresses confusion and takes insult at their strange amusement. The "disenchanted" laughter of the high school boys (28), the "repulsive" grin of Sonny's friend outside the subway station (30), the smiles of the "dark, quick-silver barmaid" (32), or his mother, who "smiled in a way that made me feel she was in pain" (44)—in each instance, the narrative complicates ostensible expressions of happiness by placing them in concert with sorrow and pain. Of course, Sonny, who grins and laughs easily at his brother's earnestness, embodies this tragicomic mode, most notably when he announces his plans to be a musician.

> "Be *serious*," I said.
> He laughed, throwing his head back, and then looked at me. "I *am* serious."
> "Well, then, for Christ's sake, stop kidding around and answer a serious question. I mean, do you want to be a concert pianist, you want to play classical music and all that, or—or what?" Long before I finished he was laughing again. "For Christ's *sake*, Sonny!"
> He sobered, but with difficulty. "I'm sorry. But you sound so—*scared*!" and he was off again.
> "Well, you may think it's funny now, baby, but it's not going to be so funny when you have to make your living at it, let me tell you *that*." I was furious because I knew he was laughing at me and I didn't know why. (49)

Sonny, who walks with "his own half-beat" (63), personifies the rehearsed spontaneity of jazz improvisation; his self-assured laughter, so easily mistaken for anxiety or youthful naïveté, is actually a reflection of this experiential limberness. His adventurous nature extends to matters of the spirit, as evident not only by his passing interest in visiting India and learning about Hinduism (with its own cycles of reincarnation and *karma*) but also through his connection with the revival singers, and his metaphorical plunge "in the water" during his solo performance at the end of the story. Believing that Sonny's troubles are a sign that he wants to die, the narrator has yet to realize what his younger brother and the members of his band already know—that "the ensuing rupture does not cause dissolution of the rhythm," as Snead states; "quite to the contrary, it strengthens it, given that it is already incorporated into the format of the rhythm" ("Repetition," 71). Indeed, during his pivotal conversation with his brother, Sonny insists that he can't forget "where" and "what" he has been. The knowledge of his painful experience has become incorporated into "the format of [his] rhythm," resulting in a hard-won wisdom that he conveys to his brother in an exchange abounding with figures of repetition:

"It can come again," he said, almost as though speaking to himself. Then he turned to me. "It can come again," he repeated. "I just want you to know that."

"All right," I said at last. "So it can come again. All right."

He smiled, but the smile was sorrowful. "I had to try to tell you," he said.

"Yes," I said. "I understand that."

"You're my brother," he said, looking straight at me, and not smiling at all.

"Yes," I repeated, "yes. I understand that."

He turned back to the window, looking out. "All that hatred down there," he said, "all that hatred and misery and love. It's a wonder it doesn't blow the avenue apart." (70)

Considering this study's principal concern, however, the question remains: How is the nature of God shaped by the existential import of repetition as an organizing principle in Baldwin's narrative? If unexpected pain and suffering are treated as an inevitable part of life, is divine power understood as benevolent, malevolent, or indifferent—that is, if God exists at all? For the narrator's mother, and for the church community in which he and Sonny were raised, God's comforting presence adheres to more traditional understandings of religious faith in evangelical Protestant black communities. But neither brother seems to accept the idea of God's goodness and omnipotence as willingly; each tacitly grants a humble respect for the mother's belief system without fully embracing it as their own. Recall Sonny's remark to his brother, for example: "I wish I could be like Mama and say the Lord's will be done, but I don't know" (35). And certainly, the grieving narrator's theological concerns about the nature of God and the problem of evil are couched within the process of mourning his daughter's death. But here again, Sonny's actions serve as a model. Not only is Sonny open to learning about alternative concepts of the divine, but Baldwin portrays the title character as a seeker who is concerned with maintaining a sense of spiritual health in a manner all his own.

By the conclusion of the narrative, a vision of God does emerge, one that strongly resembles the sagacious bass fiddler who leads Sonny's musical band. Directing the group of musicians in the Village nightclub is Creole, an "enormous black man, much older than Sonny," with "a big voice." A fatherly character whose name encompasses multiple cultures and languages, Creole has a voice that "erupts" out of the "atmospheric lighting" of the club, and after embracing Sonny, he remarks, "I been sitting right here . . . waiting for you" (71). Donald C. Murray, who reads the nightclub as a "womblike room," describes Creole as a "quasi-midwife" who facilitates the title character's rebirth ("Complicated," 356). Creole certainly functions as an important elder or "ancestor figure"[13] in Sonny's life, a guide who literally and figuratively, "took Sonny by the arm and led him to the piano" (72). Yet, related from the perspective of Sonny's brother, who continually shapes the reader's perception through his telling of the tale, Creole is even more important in that he is capable of initiating a restorative spiritual dialogue with Sonny as they play *together*. With his fiddle, Creole clearly holds the "reins" of the band, but his concern and compassion is unintrusive and yields easily to the other musicians as the quartet attends to Sonny and "push[es] him along" (73). At first, Sonny has difficulty performing, and we are told that "his face was troubled, he was working hard, but he wasn't with it" (73). But with Creole keeping the background beat, Sonny begins to develop a rhythm that complements his fellow musicians and speaks to his own personality.

The most gripping moments of this concluding scene are expressed through water, with its rich symbolic imagery that can be expanded to include religious allusions to the flood, Moses's river rescue, and other Hebraic watery crossings, as well as to baptism and sanctification in the New Testament.[14] Accordingly, the verses of African American spirituals frequently cite the rolling River Jordan, Jesus waiting by the riverside, the rescuing ship of Zion, and "one more river to cross" before reaching heaven. Historical references to the transatlantic slave trade and the Middle Passage must also be taken into account when discussing the journeys of people of African descent. So in comparing Sonny's efforts to play the piano to an intrepid swimmer wading in the water, the narrator endows his younger brother's performance with a sacred quality that carries particular cultural and historical resonance. Again, the elder musician serves as a guide:

> [Creole] was having a dialogue with Sonny. He wanted Sonny to leave the shoreline and strike out for the deep water. He was Sonny's witness that deep water and drowning were not the same thing—he had been there, and he knew. And he wanted Sonny to know. He was waiting for Sonny to do the thing on the keys which would let Creole know that Sonny was in the water.
>
> And, while Creole listened, Sonny moved, deep within, exactly like someone in torment. (73–74)

He and Creole emerge breathless from this baptism, significantly enough, "soaking wet, and grinning" (77). Although Sonny must ultimately play at the piano alone, it is important that his extemporaneous transformation takes place on stage in a public venue among his friends and family. And Baldwin's language is particularly salient. Sonny does not attempt to traverse *across* the troubled seas; Creole guides him *into* the water, encourages him to move into the pain and pass through it, so that he may know that crucial, lifesaving distinction between "deep water and drowning." Just as important, as Hardy aptly notes, is Baldwin's reluctance to assign negative or positive values to this kind of suffering: "Pain and suffering, instead, are fitted however inequitably among us into the very fabric of human existence. . . . And since suffering cannot be avoided, it can provide some context for a response that harnesses that human adaptability that sometimes surfaces in the midst of hardship" (Hardy, *Baldwin's God*, 51–52). The existential metaphors of the bandstand are further intensified as the narrator marvels at the way his brother confronts this self-creative task and actively works to fill the piano "with the breath of life, his own" (74).

In considering what it means to make music, the narrator reflects on Sonny's piano in a way that harkens back to the jukebox in the bar and the tambourine on the street corner revival. All are instruments—tools and materials dependent on the musicians to create sound. Baldwin likens them to the human body, which also operates instrumentally through the agency of human will, power, and spirit. Indeed, the narrator admits: "I had never before thought of how awful the relationship must be between the musician and his instrument. He has to fill it, this instrument, with the breath of his life, his own. He has to make it do what he wants it to do. And a piano is just a piano. It's made out of so much wood and wires and little hammers and big ones, and ivory. While there's only so much you can do with it, the only way to find this out is to try, to try and make it do everything" (74). The narrator anatomizes Sonny's piano in a way that underscores just how fragile and vulnerable is his own body, as well as his brother's, his infant daughter's, and that of his uncle—whose guitar, we may recall, was as broken as his flesh (46). The limitations of the material instrument are unmistakable, but the music that it can produce contains a timeless, metaphysical quality which, in turn, fuels the desire to push beyond socially constructed boundaries of reason and "try and make [the piano] do everything."[15] With his newfound respect for bluesmen like Sonny, the narrator is able to appreciate the creative impulse that thrives in the midst of moral and natural evil.

Sonny's brother is also able, at last, to listen. As he witnesses the unspoken tumult taking place between the musicians and their instruments on the bandstand, he becomes more attuned to Sonny's "way" (67). Where

Sonny is liberated through Creole's experienced guidance, our narrator is buoyed by his mother's prophetic advice. He relinquishes his preconceived ideas about Sonny and learns to "be *there*"; Sonny reciprocates the deed by providing unspoken reassurance to his grieving brother. As a result, the narrator develops a deeper awareness of life's recurrent cycles and rhythms, making him better equipped to understand Sonny's pain and improvise his own subjective response to evil. Under Creole's numinous influence, blues improvisations such as these acquire spiritual dimension as well as cultural purchase:

> Then Creole stepped forward to remind them that what they were playing was the blues. He hit something in all of them, he hit something in me, myself, and the music tightened and deepened, apprehension began to beat the air. Creole began to tell us what the blues were all about. They were not about anything very new. He and his boys up there were keeping it new, at the risk of ruin, destruction, madness, and death, in order to find new ways to make us listen. For, while the tale of how we suffer, and how we are delighted, and how we may triumph is never new, it always must be heard. (76)

The experience signals a potent break, the cathartic musical "cut" that allows both Sonny and his brother to integrate painful rupturing experiences into the rhythmic structures of their lives. The narrator can hear how Sonny "had made it his: that long line, of which we knew only Mama and Daddy" (77). And this cathartic recognition of recurrence allows the narrator to view his own loss in a greater context as well: "I saw my little girl again and felt Isabel's tears again, and I felt my own tears begin to rise. And I was yet aware that this was only a moment, that the world waited outside, as hungry as a tiger, and that trouble stretched above us, longer than the sky" (77). In other words, the background beat continues, although now the narrator is spiritually and psychologically stronger, having "made room" inside himself for Sonny and the inexplicable loss of his child (Snead, "Repetition," 70).

The narrator's final act of delivering a mixed drink of Scotch and milk to the piano suggests a repudiation of simplistic reasoning and the illusive boundaries of safety. After a sip and a nod, Sonny places the drink on the piano, which prompts his brother to state: "For me, then, as they began to play again, it glowed and shook above my brother's head like the very cup of trembling" (77). Baldwin's concluding line not only reminds us of the self-reflexive nature of the narrative ("For me . . ."), but it yields to the necessity of cultural repetition (". . . as they began to play *again*") in negotiating the reality of human suffering. The glass "glows and shakes" above Sonny's head, and we are reminded of how evil can be elusive, yet haunting and kinetic in its power.

There are, of course, many references in the Bible to cups with contents that convey their importance, from cups filled with blessings that "runneth over" (Ps. 23:5; 1 Cor. 10:16) to the cup of the new covenant that Jesus offers to his disciples in Matthew 26:27–29. The cup of trembling, however, carries the essence of misery and wretchedness as those who face God's judgment become intoxicated by its heady dregs.[16] It is important to note that the prideful and the rebellious are sometimes portrayed as *intentionally* drinking from this cup, unwittingly bringing about their own afflictions; while on other occasions, "God is seen personally handing sinners their destruction and forcing them to drink"[17] as in Jeremiah 25:27. Still others place their hope in the promises of a God that "pleadeth the cause of his people" in Isaiah 51:22: "Behold, I have taken out of thine hand the cup of trembling, even the dregs of the cup of my fury; thou shalt no more drink it again."

Keith E. Byerman's reading of Baldwin's final scene points out the contradictory meanings of "destruction and nurture" suggested by the Scotch and milk, and goes on to argue that the interpretation of the cup depends on whether or not the drink is being given to Sonny or taken away (see Byerman, "Words and Music," 202–3). Yet the ambiguity that the perched cup generates is central to Baldwin's keen understanding of the elusive nature of suffering itself. The nod exchanged between the two brothers goes beyond fraternal reconciliation to acknowledge the complex potential of human suffering to act dialectically as both "poison" and "nourishment" (Byerman, "Words and Music," 202). Suffering is the ever-present reality that Sonny confronts in this story not only by taking a sip, but by setting the glass back down on his piano and continuing to play.

## "Praying to What's Human": Blues as Usable Religion

> I got to keep movin'
>     blues fallin' down like hail
>
> —Robert Johnson, "Hellhound on My Trail" (1937)

Ralph Ellison has stated that, "as a form, the blues is an autobiographical chronicle of personal catastrophe expressed lyrically" (*Shadow*, 79). Just as Sonny's struggle on the piano keys sounds the depths of his catastrophic troubles, so do the moving recitations in Gaines's "The Sky Is Gray" express the protagonist's personal encounters with misery, physical pain, and the unexpected joy of discovery through the blues. Consider, for instance, the speakerly narration of the story's first section, so replete with repetitive phrases and rhetorical devices such as anaphora and epistrophe that the eight-year-old boy's unembellished observations acquire a keen musical pacing. Even the familiar subjects of mobility and the expectant freedom of railway cars in southern blues songs can be found in James's anticipation of the bus trip into town. I quote Gaines's opening paragraphs here at length, to be read aloud as a way of emphasizing the blues themes and parallel constructions, the melodic rolling *o* (as in "round" and "down" and "out"), the rhythmic beat of the hard *g* ("go'n" and "got"), and the recurring "if" that keeps time in the passage.

> Go'n be coming in a few minutes. Coming round that bend down there full speed. And I'm go'n get out my handkerchief and wave it down, and we go'n get on it and go.
> I keep on looking for it, but Mama don't look that way no more. She's looking down the road where we just come from. It's a long old road, and far's you can see you don't see nothing but gravel. You got dry weeds on both sides, and you got trees on both sides, and fences on both sides, too. And you got cows in the pastures and they standing close together. And when we was coming out here to catch the bus I seen the smoke coming out of the cows's noses.
> I look at my mama and I know what she's thinking. I been with mama so much, just me and her, I know what she's thinking all the time. Right now it's home—Auntie and them. She's thinking if they got enough wood—if she left enough there to keep them warm till we get back. She's thinking if it go'n rain and if any of them go'n have to go out in the rain. She's thinking 'bout the hog—if he go'n get out, and if Ty and Val be able to get him back in. (83)

Evenings spent on the gallery at home listening to Monsieur Bayonne's guitar suggest that James is already accustomed to the sequential patterns and improvisational energy that typically characterize the blues, spirituals, and other black musical forms. Furthermore, in the same way that "one rhythm always defines another in black music" (Snead, "Repetition," 71), James's voice unfolds in relation to the narrative rhythms of other blues figures in the story such as his cranky younger brother, Ty, who laments the family's meager breakfast offerings in a lyrical fashion: "I'm getting tired of this old syrup. Syrup, syrup, syrup. I'm go'n take with the sugar diabetes. I want me some bacon sometime" (88).

More important than James's ability to incorporate musical compositions into his storytelling, however, is his awareness of the blues as a means of processing painful personal experiences. Gaines, like Baldwin, knows that a "series of disasters" is what drives the blues impulse, but more important than this is the sufferer's ability to watch with "eyes wide open" (Baldwin, "Uses," 91). In working through his troubles, James begins to grapple with the Big Questions—about God and religion, about racism and poverty, and about love for his family and the responsibilities of manhood as defined by his community. With the absence of his father, who has not yet returned from the army, he is also aware of his responsibility to set a good example for his younger brother. He learns, through his mother's direction, the vital difference between "deep water and drowning" as he experiences his own version of Bessie Smith's "Backwater Blues." And like the Mississippi Delta bluesman Robert Johnson, quoted at the start of this section, James develops the gritty determination to keep his body and his spirit *moving* when "blues fallin' down like hail" on the cold sidewalks of Bayonne.

James's mother, Octavia, is central to understanding his response to suffering and the problem of evil through blues narration. Like the mother from "Sonny's Blues," Octavia is James's moral and spiritual guide. She leads her son through the storm in a way that does not necessarily shield him from harm, but shows him how best to confront inexplicable and unforeseen suffering so that he will be prepared to "improvise" on his own. In her study of black maternal literary figures, Trudier Harris effectively scrutinizes mothers like Octavia, who in spite of their good intentions, are known to use violence and emotional intimidation to silence opposing opinions. Where the black mother's strength and "suprahuman" qualities are often viewed as beneficial, Harris aptly notes that "these representations of tyranny between mother and child, pictured as almost biologically determined, gain ongoing credibility from religious forbearance and personal sacrifices these women make for their kin. In such cases, these mothers may inadvertently replicate the power dynamics of masters over enslaved persons, for they seldom allow anyone to challenge their authority" (*Saints*, 11).

In "The Sky Is Gray," I would argue that the "tyrannical" relationship between James and his mother also opens up a discursive space for exploring how these same power dynamics operate in the youth's understanding of spiritual matters. When considered from her son's adoring perspective, many of Octavia's character traits, including what Harris describes as "pervasive taciturnity" (11) are, indeed, *godlike*. James deifies her place in his world. Octavia conveys an image of God's nature that is stern, attentive, and compassionate (though not necessarily affectionate) and one that James finds preferable to any other divine image suggested in the story. For "The Sky Is Gray" imagines God in a number of different ways: as a fickle deity whose favor can be incurred only through specific beliefs and practices such as Monsieur Bayonne's "Catholic prayers"; as an indifferent, unseen practitioner who, like the dentist, heals and brings forth good, but only through tortured cries of pain; as a mystery too great to question, in the preacher's view; and, finally, as an illusion, according to the student, that was created by white society to oppress those deemed inferior. James is made aware of all these perspectives, and although he doesn't comment on them directly, his posture toward his mother is instructive. The fear, admiration, and protective love that he feels toward her parallels a kind of spiritual reverence. At times, Octavia seems unforgiving in her efforts to raise her oldest son, to teach him the kind of responsibility that she associates with "being a man." Evidence of this can be found in the painful beating James receives from his mother after refusing to kill a redbird for dinner (90). In other instances, she seems unsure of the best path to take—"walking real slow"—as she decides what is best for her family (103). Nevertheless, as Octavia guides him against the fierce wind, James remembers her lessons "to carry on" (90) and "to stand for yourself, by yourself" (106) as he braves the outdoors. Indeed, like Creole and Sonny on the bandstand in Baldwin's tale, the journey that James and his mother take together in "The Sky Is Gray" intimates a philosophical allegory of the relationship between humanity and the divine.

One significant way in which Octavia imparts critical life lessons is through language, where both speech and silence are employed assiduously to achieve specific aims. James tells us early on that his mother "don't like for you to say something just for nothing" (88), and so, in contrast to the fluid lyricism of his inner thoughts, James's spoken words are brief, respectful, and carefully considered. The practice appears to heighten his powers of observation, but it also allows him to reflect on how certain social and cultural patterns are determined by a variety of linguistic tools. Much like the preacher and the student who engage in interpretive verbal wordplay or "signifyin(g)" over the value of religion, Octavia plays an instrumental role in teaching James how to use black vernacular "double-voicedness" and other rhetorical strategies as a measure of control and protection (Gates, *Signifying Monkey*, 51). She leads her son into a white-owned hardware store, for instance, so that he can discreetly warm himself by the heater while she feigns interest in axe handles. Particularly telling is the way in which she examines the axe handles and "shakes her head and says something to the white man." Afterward, "the white man just looks at his pile of axe handles, and when Mama pass him to come to the front, the white man just scratch his head." The two exit the store without making a purchase (105).

Contrasted against the hardware store scene is Octavia's behavior later in a café at the "back of town where the colored people eat" (107). Once the two warm themselves in front of the heater in the café, she studies the remaining change in her hand, and, though James insists that he isn't hungry, she states: "Got to pay them something for they heat" (109). Octavia's actions express what her words do not explicitly convey—a sense of responsibility to the black community, but also a caution toward white authority.[18] Her actions also indicate her awareness of just how hungry her son really is that afternoon in spite of James's valiant performance (he later admits to himself, "I'm almost starving I'm so hungry" [110]). My view of Octavia, in this respect, diverges from the readings of critics such as John Roberts who see her behavior as an obstacle to James's participation in the "human community" ("Individual," 112). Where Roberts considers Octavia to be too individualistic and uncompromising—similar to the student in the dentist's office—I would argue that her actions contain instructive codes and subtle meanings that result in critical learning moments for our perceptive narrator. His mother's inventiveness, acuity, and linguistic dexterity as illustrated in the hardware store and café are resources James will need to survive in the South. These same skills are key to the young boy's blues narration as he follows his mother's lead and draws on similar improvisational talents when he is, indeed, compelled to manage his discomfort *on his own*.

It is clear, however, that James must accept that there are some things that are beyond even his mother's control, whether we regard Octavia's deeds as spiritually emblematic or simply as the actions of a concerned parent. The sleet and icy winds represent the most immediate and devastating threat to his well-being in the story, and his mother's ingenuity, as she guides him from one heater to another, offers only temporary relief. The cold grips his limbs, aggravates his runny nose and toothache. As the weather worsens, he comments to himself: "I'm so hungry and cold I want to cry. And look like I'm getting colder and colder. My feet done got numb. I try to work my toes, but I don't even feel them. Look like I'm go'n die. Look like I'm go'n stand right here and freeze to death" (106). On the brink of despair, James uses familiar figures of repetition to negotiate his suffering by reiterating phrases—"Don't let me die, don't let me die, don't let me die, Lord" (106)—and allowing his thoughts to wander occasionally to the warmth of summer, a ringing church bell, and Ty "making jokes." At one point during their journey, James states: "They say think and you won't get cold. I think of that poem 'Annabel Lee.' I ain't been to school in so long—this bad weather—I reckon they done passed 'Annabel Lee' by now." And later he continues: "I'm still getting cold. 'Annabel Lee' or no 'Annabel Lee,' I'm still getting cold. But I can see we getting closer. *We getting there gradually*" (112; my emphasis).

It is in these moments when James is able to maintain an optimistic outlook in the midst of the storm that his narration acquires a transcendent energy that can be favorably compared to the spirituals and the blues. For the purposes of my argument, I am singling out Robert Johnson's song "Hellhound on my Trail," recorded in 1937, for its delightful similarities to Gaines's story in theme, lyrical diction, and patterns of repetition. Clearly the vision of "blues fallin' down like hail" has both denotative and connotative significance for the short story's winter setting. James even signifies on the musical "Umm mmm mmm mmm" of Johnson's song in his reflections on his toothache: "But, Lord, it been hurting me. And look like it wouldn't start till at night when you was trying to get yourself little sleep. Then soon's you shut your eyes—ummm-ummm, Lord, look like it go right down to your heartstring" (84). More significant, though, is how the unwavering grit of Johnson's opening couplet, "I got to keep movin'/I got to keep movin'," carries over into the distinctive blues voice and sentiment of Gaines's story. So with the hope of the warm café in mind, James tells us:

> My hands numb in my pockets and my feet numb, too, but if I keep moving I can hold out. Just don't stop no more, that's all.
>
> The sky's gray. The sleet keeps on falling. Falling like rain now—plenty, plenty. You can hear it hitting the pave. You can see it bouncing. Sometimes it bounces two times 'fore it settles.
>
> We keep on going. We don't say nothing. We just keep on going, keep on going. (107)

The young protagonist continues to remark on the indeterminate gray of the sky in this passage, yet his dogged refusal to give up (or slow down) suggests that he is learning how to navigate through life's troubles in a manner similar to Sonny's metaphorical plunge on the piano. Furthermore, during the process of telling his story, James practices strategies for "holding out" and coping with unpredictable physical, emotional, and social ruptures by invoking small improvisational breaks or "cuts"—such as his brief meditation on "Annabel Lee" or the bouncing sleet—before returning to the familiar verse: "We just keep on going, keep on going."[19]

James studiously observes the world around him, constantly evaluating, questioning, and struggling to find an appropriate response to the moral and natural evil that afflicts him and his family. In keeping with the theology of the black preacher in the waiting room, James *is* humbled by God's mysterious ways. But his behavior also reflects the student's insistence that "words mean nothing. Action is the only thing. Doing. That's the only thing" (101). Being able to recognize the merits of each perspective is what constitutes the difference, in his mother's view, between being "a bum" and "a man" (177). Furthermore, his encounter with a concerned elderly white couple at the end of the narrative reminds us that just as suffering can be inexplicable and unexpected, so are kindness and compassion. Although the story ends with James and his mother venturing back out into a storm in which "the sleet's coming down heavy, heavy now" (117), the calculated ambiguity of Gaines's conclusion invites a cautiously optimistic reading. His narrator joins a long tradition of blues singers who, as Baldwin observes, "in some sense know [that] who they are can't change the world always, but they can do something to make it a little more, to make life a little more human. Human in the best sense. Human in terms of joy, freedom, which is always private respect, respect for one another" ("Uses," 97).

Surely the experience of suffering *feels* different to the child who sits in the waiting room of a dentist's office than to the one who trembles in the dentist's chair. And the woman who sings and shakes the tambourine on a Harlem street corner *hears* the problem in a way that the man who listens from a distant window does not. It is this experiential distinction that both "The Sky Is Gray" and "Sonny's Blues" seek to uncover. Amidst storms inside and out, the seekers in these stories may never know why the Lord allows them to suffer so, yet their wide-eyed awareness of the inexplicable compels them to improvise strategies for survival. At the same time, each holds human beings accountable for perpetuating "naturalized" moral evils such as racial prejudice. These texts offer a careful reconsideration of divine justice and the problem of evil as a strictly academic pursuit with the tragicomic nature of the blues acting as the existential and spiritual force behind narrative structures of repetition, rupture, and improvisation. "[The minister's] there to save the soul," Gaines once stated, "but what about the everyday life? And that's what the artist must deal with. He must deal not only with the soul but with both" (*Mozart,* 137).

# 5

## "But God Is Not a Mystery. We Are."

### Toni Morrison and the Problem of Paradise

> Sometimes good looks like evil; sometimes evil looks like good—you
> never really know what it is. It depends on what uses you put it to.
>
> —Toni Morrison

> The question of whether an omnipotent Creator might have done better
> is an incomplete question. Better for what? We have to specify the gen-
> eral aim or purpose which has motivated the act of creation, and then ask
> whether the world could have been better in relation to that purpose.
>
> —John Hick, *Evil and the God of Love*

THE RELIGIOUS philosopher John Hick invites us to explore the problem of evil by imagining what might happen if God had created a world
blissfully free from pain and human suffering. Bullets could dissolve in the
air, stolen valuables would reappear in an instant, and in an environment
where happiness and safety are assured, gravity could adjust at will so that
individuals would rise uninjured from an accidental fall. Perhaps with the
risk of deprivation and death removed, we would not have to fear our fellow man at all, nor be concerned for our children as they venture out into
the unknown.

Hick's "counterfactual hypothesis" goes on to suggest more sobering
ramifications once he considers how humanity's growth and development
might fare in an earthly paradise. The consequences, he speculates, may
be such that "human existence would involve no need for exertion, no
kind of challenge, no problems to be solved or difficulties to overcome,
no demand of the environment for human skill or inventiveness." It would
become more difficult to uphold the moral and ethical qualities that now
determine how we value human life when the obstacles that often cultivate
these qualities no longer exist. Men and women could run the risk of losing

"the dignity of real responsibilities, tasks, and achievements" (Hick, *Evil*, 343). He weighs such deficiencies against the gains of a painless utopia to focus critical attention on the aspects of our world that drive the human quest for knowledge and innovation, and foster our sense of compassion, virtue, and strength. Further, if humanity's fundamental understanding of evil changes, Hick reasons that it is just as likely that we would discover different ways to distinguish what pleases us *more* from what pleases us *less*, possibly creating fresh iterations of "evil" even in supposedly better, idealized surroundings. And to the extent that God, as understood by Christian faith, could systematically obliterate one evil after another, would this not also curb humanity's cherished ability to freely make choices between right and wrong? Is it possible, as Hick goes on to state, that in the end, "a soft, unchallenging world would be inhabited by a soft, unchallenging race of men" (343)?

These are the kinds of questions that Toni Morrison invites readers to contemplate in her seventh novel, *Paradise* (1998). She probes the spiritual and existential dilemmas arising from the problem of evil through an experimental rendering of a black utopia that spans from Emancipation to the post–civil rights era. Figuring prominently in the narrative's cultural mythology is a group of former slaves who, in the declining years of the nineteenth century, discover their own Promised Land in the Oklahoma wilderness where they establish the town of Haven. Paradise takes root in the enduring faith and pride of this community as they work to create an ideal home among a close(d) network of black families—a society modeled after Old Testament patriarchy and African traditions, and physically removed from present-day racial atrocities. What's more, because the town's most prominent founder, Zechariah Morgan, views the potential "scattering" of his people through the lens of Deuteronomic law as a curse, Haven's willful isolation also represents an attempt on the part of its founding fathers to uphold high moral standards and keep their bloodlines "pure." By the mid-1970s, however, the descendants of Haven's families find their idealistic way of life—newly relocated to a town named Ruby—desecrated by paranoia, internal social strife, and religious discontent. The civil rights movement, for instance, is perceived by the conservative residents as an intrusive waste of time and a distraction for irreverent black youth, rather than as an opportunity for social change. Most shocking of all, though, is the way in which Ruby's self-appointed leaders attempt to protect the paradise their ancestors created by wielding their own murderous form of divine justice against a group of female "outsiders."

Morrison weaves into the triumph and tragedy of the Oklahoma town the story of these five women, unidentified by race, who find their way to an abandoned Catholic school seventeen miles outside of Ruby. The reader learns during the course of the narrative of each woman's aimless pilgrimage to the school—known as "the Convent"—and of their more grueling journeys to self-discovery and spiritual contentment. Over time, disapproval of their attitude, independence, dress, and other arbitrary denunciations by the "New Fathers" of Ruby lead the women to be branded as outcasts. Eventually they become scapegoats too, implicated by Ruby's ministers and businessmen in the turmoil taking place in town. The women are killed as a way to restore order and ensure that "nothing inside or out rots the one all-black town worth the pain" (*Paradise*, 5). In the aftermath of the bloodshed, we are told that the people of Ruby "think they have outfoxed the whiteman when in fact they imitate him. They think they are protecting their wives and children, when in fact they are maiming them" (306). As a result, *Paradise* demonstrates that even a community formed with "so clean and blessed a mission" (292) can collapse when the brittle comforts of rigidly prescribed social and spiritual identities are unable to withstand change, risk, or adventure.

This peculiar "problem of paradise" is the primary focus of my analysis in this chapter. Morrison's fiction as a whole tends to linger in the nebulous moments when, as she once stated in a 1976 interview, "sometimes good looks like evil; sometimes evil looks like good" (Stepto, "Intimate Things," 381). Well-discussed are children like Pecola Breedlove from *The Bluest Eye* who are mentally shattered by the unspeakable horrors of abuse and neglect; the "too thick" love of mothers like Sethe in *Beloved* who struggle to exorcise the suffering of the past made into flesh; and orphaned rebels like the title character of *Sula* who are themselves forced to endure accusations of wickedness.[1] *Paradise* complements these stories and their exploration of "evil" by relocating the discursive horizon of black spiritual struggle to the amorphous existence and meaning of "good." In the larger context of this study, Morrison's creative inquest raises a host of new questions: How does the subjective knowledge of happiness, satisfaction, and fulfillment shape humanity's purpose and affect our understanding of God? Can good be scrutinized in a manner similar to evil in terms of quantity, distribution, value, or intent? And what are the repercussions of such efforts to define goodness in black life and culture? In addressing these questions, the present chapter investigates Morrison's approach not only to the conceptual processes of paradise, but to the real-life consequences of attitudes about goodness for individuals and communities that have endured tremendous suffering. And considering the many symbolic names, numbers, intricate genealogies, and magical interventions through which the narrative's paradisiacal visions are rehearsed, my analysis also scrutinizes Morrison's efforts to deconstruct the way sacred stories and signs are read (and misread) to convey essential truths about humanity's purpose.

Concluding this book with a discussion of *Paradise* is especially fitting since Morrison's novel nimbly incorporates many of the figurative concepts, characters, and narrative strategies that I have analyzed in previous chapters. *Paradise* invokes ideas such as the black Christ and the racialized discourse of redemptive suffering, and reveals the cultural and political implications of religious belief by explicating sacred covenants and conversion experiences. Familiar charges of blasphemy ricochet between the generations. Characters also give voice to systematic critiques of patriarchal religious domination and raise questions about the meaning of undeserved suffering through the death of a child. This is not to suggest that Morrison's text should stand as the final and definitive word, but to reinforce the persistence of the aforementioned critical approaches in African American literary engagements with religion while calling attention to the fresh aspects of Morrison's contribution. Indeed, *Paradise* distinguishes itself by more than simply one town's failure to attain perfection; Ruby's degeneration is analogous to any society that relies on violent and oppressive means to satisfy "the wish for permanent happiness" (*Paradise*, 306). Universal implications notwithstanding, this correlation reveals profound insight into the nature of black suffering as a moral evil. For what is the New World if not a cataclysmic utopian experiment? The analogy poses critical spiritual and existential questions that shape (and are shaped by) the reality of the African Diaspora. And it condemns those who use slave ships, lynch ropes, and even gated communities to create their own *pairidaeza*, or "walled enclosure"—the Avestan term from which the title of Morrison's novel is derived.[2] In the end, such destructive impulses, so readily attributed by some to a divine power, are revealed as little more than the offspring of human frailty, antithetical to a God that is "generosity itself" (306). The realization prompts the narrative's Reverend Richard Misner to observe: "Belief is mysterious; faith is mysterious. But God is not a mystery. We are" (304).

In affirming the "mystery" of humanity, *Paradise* continues the intellectual work that Morrison began over three decades earlier in her 1973 novel *Sula*. I would assert that the story of Sula Peace and her best friend, Nel Wright, raises similar conflicts over the nature of good and evil, particularly as it pertains to the effects that Sula's lively and audacious character has on a small black community in Ohio. The thorough and evocative portrayal of Ruby, Oklahoma, in *Paradise* is arguably anticipated by Morrison's development of the town's literary sibling—the hilltop enclave in *Sula* called "the Bottom." This small area in which the black Ohioans are segregated received its nickname from a "nigger joke" in which a white master tried to convince his black slave that the hilly area was "the Bottom of Heaven" (*Sula*, 5). (Interestingly, where the black people in *Sula* struggle to find solace "*up* there in the Bottom," the residents of Ruby must learn to thrive and flourish "*down* here in paradise.")³ Both fictional towns share a weakness in their need to scapegoat the community's fears and failings onto insubordinate women in a way that maligns self-willed movement, experimentation, and difference as heretical. The same people who accuse Sula of "laughing at their God" grumble in *Paradise* about the Convent women who presumably "don't need God" at all.⁴

Key differences emerge, however, in each community's philosophical approach to the presence of suffering. A sense of inevitability accompanies the Bottom's attitude toward evil and oppression as the inhabitants in *Sula* take "precautions" but, nevertheless, "let it run its course" (*Sula*, 89–90). Morrison explains this stance in terms of the town's "full recognition of the legitimacy of forces other than good ones" (90) so as to draw the reader's attention to the acute spiritual processes of collective survival among black communities. As I have argued in the previous chapter, the idea that "the purpose of evil was to survive it" can be problematic as it has the potential to naturalize moral evils for which humanity is responsible, implying that certain forms of suffering are simply a part of life and can never truly be obliterated. Yet, as is common in twentieth-century African American fiction, *Sula* attempts to supersede the dangers of quietism and "blind faith" by demonstrating how the reality of oppression has required black people to prepare themselves emotionally and spiritually for the unavoidable moments when, to recall the mother in Baldwin's "Sonny's Blues," "you may not be able to stop nothing from happening" (47).⁵

Likewise, when Sula's return is likened to an unusual plague of robins, Morrison's narrator entwines the consequences of moral and natural evil by describing the belief system of the Bottom as follows:

> In their world, aberrations were as much a part of nature as grace. It was not for them to expel or annihilate it. They would no more run Sula out of town than they would kill the robins that brought her back, for in their secret awareness of Him, He was not the God of three faces they sang about. They

knew quite well that He had four, and that the fourth explained Sula. They
had lived with various forms of evil all their days, and it wasn't that they believed God would take care of them. It was rather that they knew God had
a brother and that brother hadn't spared God's son, so why should he spare
them? (*Sula*, 118)

The critic Allen Alexander astutely argues that Morrison's observations in
this passage "humanize God" by giving him a "fourth face." He explains
that "God for her characters is not the characteristically ethereal God of
traditional Western religion but a God who, while retaining certain Western characteristics, has much in common with the deities of traditional
African religion and legend" ("Fourth Face," 293). In contrast, the patri-
archs in *Paradise* depart from this view somewhat by structuring their lives
around more traditional interpretations of God's supreme power and unquestioned goodness. Convinced of their exceptionality, they *do* attempt to
forcibly "expel" and "annihilate" anything or anyone who interferes with
their utopian experiment. The descendants of Zechariah Morgan see "ab-
errations" not as part of nature, but as unmistakable signs of God's disfavor.
In contrast to the Bottom, where the black residents "never invented ways
either to alter [evil], to annihilate it or to prevent its happening again"
(*Sula*, 89–90), such aggressive inventions are at the heart of the conflict
in *Paradise*. Also worth noting is Morrison's decision in *Sula* to use the
title character as the narrative's most prominent symbol of dissent. Sula's
autonomy defies the neighbors who regard her unrestrained quest for identity as heresy, and on the surface at least, she serves as an easy counterpoint
to Nel's conventionality and self-righteousness. But the critiques that are
embedded in Sula's choices (or in the shell-shocked madness of the World
War I veteran Shadrack) are given wider berth in *Paradise*, where Morrison
offers a chorus of dissenting voices that know how illusive are the boundaries between good and evil, life and death.

   Of these voices, my analysis closely scrutinizes Consolata Sosa, Reverend Richard Misner, and Lone DuPres—three characters whose pragmatic
spiritual wisdom and worldly insight provide a compelling alternative to
the constraints of the New Fathers' theodicy. Each figure emerges as a
harbinger of unconventional holiness in the narrative with the matrilineal
mysticism of "Sister" Connie positioned among the Convent women, Reverend Misner's black liberation theology focused on Ruby, and the midwife
and conjure woman Lone negotiating the spiritual road in between. All
uphold the notion of a transcendent force, a God that empowers human
activity by creating a world to foster, recalling John Hick, "human skill or

inventiveness." For these prophetic figures, paradise is not found in impenetrable seclusion, or even in the promise of mindless ease and prosperity, but in the response/ability that comes from answering God's call to existential wakefulness. The divine challenge—described in the narrative as "endless work" and activated by "intelligence", "in sight," and learning how to "pay attention"—generates a deep mode of awareness that unites body and spirit, and makes every human being beholden to one another. My analysis demonstrates that this humanocentric theism, when combined with the subjective experiencing of good and evil, allows Morrison to argue that humanity's God-given capacity to critically reflect, question, and interpret is central to developing a fulfilling spiritual identity.

Of course, an "ancestor figure"[6] like Lone DuPres may be familiar to Morrison's readers. Reverend Richard Misner, however, represents a new and significant undertaking. Holy places and holy people abound in Morrison's fiction, but the author seldom lingers within the walls of a traditional church. (Notable scenes include Chicken Little's funeral in *Sula* and the clearing where Baby Suggs gathered her community for worship and celebration in *Beloved*.) We rarely get more than an occasional glimpse of a minister, and yet *Paradise* features three: in addition to Misner, who leads the largest congregation in Mount Calvary Baptist, there are two older, more conservative preachers, Senior Pulliam at New Zion Methodist and Simon Cary at Holy Redeemer Pentecostal. The unique station of the black preacher in life and, significantly, in cultural representations, is illustrated by these ministers and articulated mostly explicitly by Misner in the following passage, quoted at length:

> For centuries they had held on. Preaching, shouting, dancing, singing, absorbing, arguing, counseling, pleading, commanding. Their passion burned or smoldered like lava over a land that had waged war against them and their flock without surcease. . . . On stage and in print he and his brethren had been the heart of comedy, the chosen backs for parody's knife. They were cursed by death row inmates, derided by pimps. Begrudged even miserly collection plates. Yet through all of that, if the Spirit seemed to be slipping away they had held on to it with their teeth if they had to, grabbed it in their fists if need be. They took it to the buildings ready to be condemned, to churches from which white congregations had fled, to quilt tents, to ravines and logs in clearings. Whispered it in cabins lit by moonlight lest the Law see. Prayed for it behind trees and in sod houses, their voices undaunted by roaring winds. . . . Rocked as they were by the sight of evil, its snout was familiar to them. Real wonder, however, lay in the amazing shapes and substances

> God's grace took: gospel in times of persecution; the exquisite wins of people
> forbidden to compete; the upright righteousness of those who let no boot
> hold them down—people who made Job's patience look like restlessness.
> Elegance when all around was shabby. (159–60)

In his recognition of the "elegance" of the ministry, Misner embodies an
attempt on the part of the author to portray a fuller, more multidimensional characterization of the black preacher. Misner's reflections here also
represent his effort to understand why his conservative colleagues are so
adamant in their refusal to couple their otherworldly aspirations with the
pressing social and political concerns of the day. The young minister, who
was hired to lead Mount Calvary in 1970, is set apart from Pulliam and
Cary by his experience outside the town as a civil rights activist—one who
has the reputation for being willing to "stir folks up" in the fight against
injustice (56). He openly favors what he calls "Du Bois problems" over
"Booker T. solutions." (212).

But Misner is also wise enough to acknowledge that in the wake of Martin
Luther King's death, many of the civil reforms across the country have become merely "decorative: statues, street names, speeches" (117), and so
the minister further allies himself with young people who are longing for
more substantive change in Ruby. Where Reverend Pulliam is said to have
"history on his side" in his steadfast observance of tradition, Misner has
"the future on his" (150), and he continually encourages the community to
move beyond its isolation and distrust. He even laments at one point that
"seven years after the murder of the man in whose stead he would happily
have taken the sword, he was herding a flock which believed not only that it
had created the pasture it grazed but that grass from any other meadow was
toxic" (212). Yet what is particularly significant about the young minister is
his resolve to remain in Ruby following the Convent murders and to argue
for a way of thinking and believing that can prevent this community of sufferers from succumbing to despair. More than any other character in this
study, Reverend Misner explicitly interrogates the problem of evil in both its
theoretical and existential dimensions. And speaking both to Ruby and the
society-at-large, he joins Lone and Consolata in urging those in anguish to
think, hope, and act beyond survival to a renewed reality.

## The Old and New Testaments of Haven

The sacred history of Haven that is inherited by Ruby's citizens is explicitly shaped by Judeo-Christian discourse and structured, more subtly, on

African and Greek oral traditions. But it is the fierce and unremitting search for a home—what Reverend Misner describes as "a real earthly home" (213)—that gives rise to the community's elaborate creation myth, a story that is created and re-created with each new storyteller. In his discussion of the novel, the critic Philip Page emphasizes the considerable obligations that each new version places on the reader, who, much like Morrison's fictional characters, is compelled to participate as an "active agent" in rigorous acts of interpretation in order to "enter into the text" ("Furrowing," 638, 640). *Paradise* is heavily invested in this kind of interpretive multiplicity for what it reveals about how the people of Ruby, and African Americans more generally, engage the past and attempt to construct a worldview that is in accordance with the (re)visions of their ancestors. Of special interest to my analysis are the ways in which such demanding "hermeneutic concentration" manages to both clarify and obscure religious matters in the novel, especially since "no single text, version, or interpretation is adequate" (Page, "Furrowing," 640). Various readings of Haven's covenanted creation, each offering a relative glimpse into the community's formative cultural moments, convey a range of contested spiritual beliefs and moral principles.

Steward and Deacon Morgan command what is considered to be the "official" version of Haven's creation. They use their privileged birthright as twin grandsons of Zachariah "Big Papa" Morgan to wield the details of the story like sacred scripture and legitimize their own patriarchal authority in Ruby. It is through Steward that we learn of the nineteenth-century settlement that was founded by Zachariah and other former slaves from Mississippi and Louisiana after the crushing failures of Reconstruction. Beginning around the 1880s, the small but significant social, political, and economic developments made by blacks after Emancipation were aggressively eradicated throughout the former Confederate states by voting disenfranchisement, black codes, and escalating racial terrorism. To escape ills such as these, black migrants traveled west to areas including the Oklahoma Territory that began offering land grants to new settlers in 1889. Twenty-five black towns were founded in Oklahoma between 1890 and 1910, according to the historian Barbara Bair, who explains that "these were places where African Americans could form their own municipal governments and protect one another from white incursions and violence" ("Justice Sleeps," 7). Nevertheless, as Morrison discovered in her own research of similar frontier communities, it was not unusual for families who "arrived after difficult journeys, impoverished, undernourished, and

in need of help" to be turned away for failing to meet the social and economic criteria for residency (Bair, "Justice Sleeps," 8).

In *Paradise*, a group made up mostly of nine large families are enticed
by a newspaper advertisement from one of the newly formed black towns
that declares, "Come Prepared or Not at All" (13). Some of the former
slaves had served in prominent political positions or operated thriving
businesses during Reconstruction, and so they believed themselves fully
prepared to become citizens of these new settlements. The nine families were
said to have cherished, in particular, the dark "blue-black" color of their
skin as a sign of superiority and strong bloodlines uncontaminated by the
physical and psychological assaults of the New World (193). But they are
shocked to find their progress hindered by more than the anticipated ran-
cor and aggression of white racism. When a group of light-skinned black
residents from Fairly, Oklahoma, are unwilling to welcome the traveling
families, Zachariah concludes that "the sign of racial purity they had taken
for granted had become a stain" (194). This rejection by people who had
also been "slave like them" elicits fresh shame and outrage that over time
becomes remembered as the Disallowing (14). The humiliation drives the
group's leaders—referred to collectively as the Old Fathers—deeper into
the western wilderness. Once hunger and exhaustion render the families
in Zechariah's charge utterly hopeless, "on foot and completely lost" (95),
he follows his biblical namesake in experiencing a miraculous encounter
with an apparition known as "the walking man" (97). Described as small in
stature, but with footsteps "like a giant's tread," the man guides the travelers across the state through Zechariah's visions. He walks with a satchel by
his side for twenty-nine days before placing it down and unpacking it on
the spot that would become Haven and swell from 158 travelers in 1890 to
1,000 citizens two decades later.

As the description of this westward journey becomes richer and more
complex, it clearly invites comparisons with the Old Testament account
of the Exodus, a story already well known as an "archetypal myth" for
enslaved African Americans (Raboteau, *Fire*, 33). The wilderness wanderings of Israel are especially relevant because of its portrayal of God's people
as lost desert travelers who have been disallowed from entering Canaan.
Likewise, the mysterious walking man transforms the ex-slave's struggle
for communal survival after Emancipation into a divine charge. Culturally,
as Katrine Dalsgard points out, the interpretation allows Haven to "live its
own version of the exceptionalist narrative" so commonly associated with
the Puritan "city upon a hill" ("All-Black Town," 236). The supernatural

guide further corroborates the group's belief in their uniqueness as a kind of chosen people who have been carefully selected and, perhaps more importantly, carefully tested, by God to serve as examples of his power and righteousness.

As a reminder of their special covenant with God and to one another, a "huge, flawlessly designed" brick oven glows at the center of the Haven's communal kitchen. It is a defining symbol, a sacred womblike icon of their rebirth and well-being as freed people (6). The Oven acts as the symbolic face of the community's creation myth and is brought to life through descriptions of its breath, mouth, and lip (14–15). It is considered by many to be sacrosanct, much like the legendary Ark of the Covenant—a container built by the Israelites at God's command to house the stone tablets of the Ten Commandments and other sacred objects (Exod. 25:10–22). The act of divine recognition embodied by the Oven—a term nestled within the word "covenant" itself—aligns the structure's spiritual import with unique cultural and historical significance.[7]

One boon of Haven's relationship with God is material redress for the physical and psychological wounds inflicted upon black families during slavery and its aftermath. The Old Fathers built the Oven as a place for black women to prepare food collectively and, in Steward's telling of the story, as a proud reminder that "none of their women had ever worked in a whiteman's kitchen or nursed a white child" (99). Maternal allusions surround the Oven as one might expect, and yet the discourse is configured in a way that virtually removes women from the creative process, or renders them as objects in the community's reproductive machinery. When viewed from this perspective, the Oven represents a strikingly paternal mode of procreation enacted by generations of "founding fathers." So it comes as no surprise that when Haven's population plunges after World War II, the returning veterans and their families respond by moving the Oven, brick by brick. It is transported 240 miles farther west to serve as the foundation (a new "testament," as it were) for a reconstituted utopia called Ruby.

As we shall see, the terms of this new covenant are expanded to include immortality and everlasting peace for its residents. What the Oven stands for as a historical emblem is further suggested by the fact that in spite of Ruby's three different churches, "the Oven didn't belong to any one denomination; it belonged to all" (83). It is cherished as a communal center—a place to gather after baptisms in the nearby stream, for instance, and to discuss town business. Not everyone, however, is convinced that what one character refers to simply as "the barbecue thing" is so valuable

(67). Deacon Morgan's wife, Soane, recalls: "The women nodded when the men took the Oven apart, packed, moved and reassembled it. But privately they resented the truck space given over to it—rather than a few more sacks of seed, rather than shoats or even a child's crib" (102).

The Oven and the cosmological and soteriological myths that endow it with meaning undoubtedly link the towns of Haven and Ruby. More precisely, though, it is the experience of suffering that acts as a kind of umbilical cord between the "Old" and "New" Fathers in their longing for an earthly paradise. Each reluctant move—whether by ex-slaves in 1890 or ex-soldiers in 1949—is marked by rejection and mortal fears that give rise to a distinct functional theodicy, one that seeks to reconcile God's power with the reality of both moral and natural evil. In addition to the Exodus story, the guiding principles of other Old Testament literatures such as the Book of Job have clearly influenced the account of Haven's creation; the freed people interpret life's challenges, particularly those that occur inexplicably and without warning, as moral and physical "tests" that are evaluated under God's watchful eye. Against the unknown dangers of Oklahoma, the Old Fathers determine: "Here freedom was not entertainment, like a carnival or a hoedown that you can count on once a year. Nor was it the table droppings from the entitled. Here freedom was a test administered by the natural world that a man had to take for himself every day. And if he passed enough tests long enough, he was king" (99). If we recall how the narrator of Countée Cullen's "The Black Christ" speaks of God as a Holy Father that remains ready to reenact "the world's greatest tragedy" (line 13) for the benefit of skeptics and sinners, then a similar argument can be made for Haven's residents, who regard the experience of pain and suffering as God's way of correcting their behavior and restoring their faith. Steward and Deacon cite, as evidence that the "the mystery of God's justice" works in their favor, the growth and prosperity of Haven, and the demise of other black towns across the region due to years of drought, the Great Depression, and racial violence (109). The twins believe that their forebearers have, indeed, "outfoxed" evil and passed the natural world's tests, and so neither brother feels inclined to scrutinize too closely the logic of the fiercely antagonistic freedom they have inherited (6).

When time and circumstance lead more and more people to abandon Haven, however, the Morgan twins and thirteen other men attempt to duplicate the survival strategies of the Old Fathers by founding a new town. ("New" in this context is somewhat misleading, since Morrison makes clear that neither the town nor its ideas are created *ex nihilo*.) The fifteen families, startled by Haven's postwar decline, are determined to lengthen the lifespan of their community indefinitely. Symbolically they name their town Ruby in honor of Deacon and Steward's sister, who died after being denied medical care by whites. Out of tragedy and mistrust, then, emerges a community that cherishes isolation as one of the defining characteristics of their happiness. Morrison continues to play on the discourse of space to convey the town's anxieties over the slippery boundaries of goodness and evil:

> Ten generations had known what lay Out There: space, once beckoning and free, became unmonitored and seething; became a void where random and organized evil erupted when and where it chose—behind any standing tree, behind the door any house, humble or grand. Out There where your children were sport, your women quarry, and where your very person could be annulled; where congregations carried arms to church and ropes coiled in every saddle. Out There where every cluster of whitemen looked like a posse, being alone was being dead. But lessons had been learned and relearned in the last three generations about how to protect a town. (16)

The New Fathers of Ruby believe that they can protect their families from "what lay Out There" by combining physical seclusion with governing belief systems that are just as carefully guarded. Strangers are ignored; untried ideas are avoided; and swiftly suppressed are the initiatives that challenge Ruby's cultural traditions, spiritual beliefs, and collective sensibilities. And where Haven was formed around a particular interpretation of freedom as a test, Ruby is shaped by a comparable understanding of love. It is during a wedding ceremony that Reverend Pulliam warns the church that "love is divine only and difficult always. If you think it is easy you are a fool. If you think it is natural you are blind" (141). Once again, the minister goes on to replace the notion of love as "silly" and "benign" with the weight of God's merciless tests (141). His final decree to the newlyweds, and the audience, that "God is not interested in you" (142) seeks to fix humanity permanently in a state of contrition that accepts suffering as intrinsically punitive and always purposeful. This stance is central to understanding how values are created *and* corrupted in Ruby. We shall explore opposing responses to the minister's diatribe from Richard Misner and Lone DuPres presently, but for now it is important to note that Pulliam's "difficult love" is one of the main driving forces behind Ruby's cultural and spiritual cloistering.

It would appear, then, that the isolated Oklahoma town more closely resembles a "convent" than the abandoned Catholic school up the road.

Ironically enough, there are many such points of convergence between the two areas. We have seen how Haven's history takes on mythic value and the legitimacy of collective remembering in Ruby, but the women who journey to the Convent each have their own personal "creation story" as well. Their stories reveal the people and circumstances that have contributed to their self-image, revealing, in the process, how they came to be. We learn of Mavis Albright, a remorseful mother who abandons (flees?) her unsympathetic husband and children after the accidental death of twin infants in her care; the outspoken Grace "Gigi" Gibson, who, numbed by the violence of a race riot, sets out in search of the existence of natural beauty in a fabled rock formation; Pallas Truelove, a pregnant teenager from a wealthy home, who runs, penniless, into the unknown after discovering her boyfriend and mother making love; and finally, the agreeable Seneca, who endeavors to escape memories of sexual trauma and abuse in her wanderings to the Convent.

Consolata Sosa, the oldest and last remaining resident of the Christ the King School for Native Girls, is the only woman who did not travel to the Convent on her own accord. Consolata was rescued (stolen?) from the streets of a South American country as a child by Mother Mary Magna, a woman whose faith she later came to adore and idolize in the Oklahoma school. There are two regrets that haunt Consolata, however: her brief love affair with Deacon Morgan—a moment in which, she initially believes, she abandoned God for the pleasures of the flesh—and her hidden magical talent for reviving the sick and dying. While Consolata struggles with doubts about her own salvation, she refuses none of the fugitive women (or those from Ruby in need of temporary sanctuary) who arrive at her door. It is she who welcomes them without judgment and listens to their stories, her only requirement being that "lies not allowed in this place. In this place every true thing is okay" (38). And it is Consolata—described by one reviewer as "the embodiment of an abstract longing for home" (Allen, "Promised Land," n.p.)—who will encourage these women to leave their stories behind and (re)create themselves anew. Like the people of Ruby, the Convent women must learn that the suffering that defines their past cannot be allowed to reign in the present.

## The Curse of a "Scattered" People

Morrison's claim that "all paradises, all utopias are designed by who is not there, by the people who are not allowed in," is substantiated by the presence of the Convent women, who exist physically, spiritually, socially, and culturally on the margins of Ruby (Morrison interview by Farnsworth). Yet Ruby is not entirely homogeneous in its understanding of the town's unique mission. The character Patricia Best Cato offers one of the best examples of this dissension from within. Patricia is among the first in the narrative to scrutinize what is at stake in Ruby's unspoken "law of continuance and multiplication" (279). She is uniquely situated to critique "the father's law," as she terms it, and to offer an alternative interpretation of the town's publicly sanctioned creation story. As the descendant of one of the founding families whose father, Roger Best, married "a wife of racial tampering" (197), Patricia also lives on the edge of a paradise that can never fully be her own. And too, as a schoolteacher and family historian, she is somewhat alienated and regarded with suspicion by her neighbors for asking difficult personal questions.

After attempting with great difficulty to compile "objective" genealogies of Ruby's fifteen families, Patricia becomes more fascinated with the persistent silences and inconsistencies that she records in "supplementary notes" (187). She compiles her own version of the town's history by reading between the lines of the family records kept in old Bibles (in which names are sometimes blotted out), in student composition assignments, church records, and personal letters as well as stories exchanged piecemeal from one generation to the next. Because of the town's intense secrecy, she keeps the charts of family trees and pages of notes completely private. Patricia's eventual dissatisfaction with the persistence of so many unanswered questions, however, leads her to burn the folders of her work. And while it is true that, as Page notes, Patricia failed in seeking "the kind of deterministic answers that Morrison withholds," her interpretation reveals several pivotal ideas that shape the town's spiritual self-image ("Furrowing," 641).

It is Patricia who raises the issue of "scattering" as a biblical concept that substantiates the social and religious values of Haven's founders. She speculates that the ex-slave Zechariah Morgan may have replaced his former name—Coffee—with that of the Old Testament prophet, in part because Zechariah's visions revealed to the people of Israel that "the punishment for not showing mercy or compassion was a scattering among all nations, and pleasant land made desolate" (192). How might enslaved people in America, historically known to regard the Hebrew Scriptures as a guide for surviving their "modern Egyptians," interpret the notion of scattering in relation to their own experience? (Wheatley, "To Samson Occum," 203). Of Zechariah, Patricia theorizes:

The scattering would have frightened him. The breakup of the group or tribe or consortium of families or, in Coffee's case, the splitting up of a contingent of families who had lived with or near each other since before Bunker Hill. He would not have had trouble imagining the scariness of having everybody he knew thrown apart, thrown into different places in a foreign land and becoming alien to each other. He would have been frightened of not knowing a jawline that signified one family, a cast of eye or a walk that identified another. Of not being able to see yourself re-formed in a third- or fourth-generation grandchild. Of not knowing where the generations before him were buried or how to get in touch with them if you didn't know. That would be the Zechariah Coffee would have chosen for himself. (192)

Indeed, "scattering" is cited frequently in the Bible as one of God's most painful and demanding reprimands. To be condemned to roam aimlessly like "sheep without a shepherd" (Num. 27:17) is to be both physically and spiritually disconnected from life's greater purpose. It is the fear of being scattered that causes the prideful builders of Babel to attempt to build a tower to the heavens (Gen. 11:1–9). The Lord cautions the Israelites on numerous occasions about the penalty for unfaithfulness and idolatry: "And you I will scatter among the nations, and I will unsheathe the sword against you" (Lev. 26:33, Deut. 4:27). Likewise, the bones of the dead are sometimes scattered to signal their unrest in the afterlife (Ps. 53:5, Ezek. 6:5).

All of which might have led Zechariah to interpret anything that caused his people to separate as an ominous sign, a "test" of the highest importance since, as has been previously stated, "being alone was being dead" (16). At stake for the Morgan elder is the life and death of a corporate body, for each individual movement carries the threat of nonexistence into future generations. Of course, the risks go beyond physical depletion. Patricia notes that being "disvalued by the impure"—light-skinned blacks as well as whites—would have been "an even more dangerous level of evil" because of the way such prejudices weakened the social status and moral authority of a people who considered themselves "uncorruptible" (194). Over time, this concern for the community's cultural health and mortality is bequeathed to Haven's descendants. The scattering of so many young men after World War II causes the remaining families to become even more insular and reactionary, clinging to the belief that evil and death would be "blocked from entering Ruby" for as long as its inhabitants remained within the town and associated only with others who looked and acted as they did (199).

With the Oven's presence in Ruby as a reminder of what the Old Fathers of Haven built and valued, the relocated community creates a "new testament" with God. Their covenant is celebrated with an annual Nativity play that juxtaposes Ruby's founding with the birth of Jesus Christ. The benefits of this connection are validated by Ruby's lucrative businesses, by the presumption that it is only the residents who ventured outside of the town who have died (soldiers, for instance), and by the fact that Patricia's mother, the only woman besides Ruby Morgan to die in the town, had light skin. The New Fathers attempt to hold their community together at all costs—Deacon and Steward use profits and power to control Ruby's development, while the fire-and-brimstone theology of Reverends Pulliam and Cary keep careful watch over the conservative moral standards of its populace. These men are also the ones who observe the mounting signs of evil that encroach upon the Ruby's supposedly peaceful existence. Various "outrages," including sickly children, wayward brides, rebellious youth, and of course, the presence of the Convent women at the edge of town, threaten yet another scattering (11). Their mistake, as Lone DuPres notes, is that when confronted with change, "they did not think to fix it by extending a hand in fellowship or love. They mapped defense instead and honed evidence for its need, till each piece fit an already polished groove" (275).

Therefore, what makes scattering as described in Patricia's "supplementary notes" especially significant is the way it points to the dangers inherent in ascribing infallible truths to the subjective act of interpretation. It is not difficult to see why the provocative language of God's displeasure would have struck a chord with former slaves and their descendants when not carefully following "all the words of [God's] law" condemns the offender to wander the land with "a trembling heart, failing eyes, and a languishing spirit," only to be reenslaved and sent "back in ships to Egypt" (Deut 28:58, 65, 68). For a newly freed people, these are chilling words indeed. But Haven's inhabitants respond by committing themselves to an exceedingly narrow and selective interpretation of God's justice, believing that a strict adherence will guarantee their survival and secure their place in a heavenly paradise. Despite Zechariah's commendable aspirations for his people, his exegesis is called into question by its crippling effects: reactionary isolation, immobility, and the xenophobic ramifications of a single-minded belief in the "uncorruptible worthiness" of their heritage (194). Overlooked, perhaps, in the haste to circumvent the anguish of a scattering at any cost is the hope and promise inscribed in the New Testament prophesy "that Jesus would die for the Jewish nation, and not only for that nation but also for the scattered children of God, to bring them together and make them one" (John 11:51–52).

Of course, the Bible is not the only sacred text in the narrative to be subjected to manipulative and selective readings. The New Fathers organize Ruby around an understanding of their history—with its idealized cultural myths and miracles—that is contextually inattentive and cruel in its restrictive applications. The pretense of objectivity that conceals a carefully crafted historical narrative prompts Patricia to conclude that, "all that nonsense she had grown up with seemed to her like an excuse to be hateful" (214). She bitterly recalls, as a child, how furtively "the Cato line was cut" from the community's past as she watched lifelong neighbors enjoy an annual Christmastime reenactment of the town's founding that featured only eight of Ruby's nine "holy families." Her father's so-called offense against the blood rule meant that, in addition to the unspoken indignities and slights suffered on a daily basis, their family was "not good enough to be represented by eight-year-olds on a stage" (216). Similarly, Patricia becomes suspicious about how women are obscured by the "official story" of the town; she repeatedly encounters great difficulties in determining the identities of her female ancestors—last names are often missing, or replaced with the surnames of their husbands or generalized last names like Brown or Smith.

Such erasures in the community's sacred history—a "text" considered by many to be inviolable—is certainly not unfamiliar to African Americans who have historically suffered from narrow biblical interpretations that justify destructive and dehumanizing powers. This includes the idea that members of the black race are the spiritual "sons of Ham" (Gen. 9:22–24) as well as the commands of Paul's letter to the Ephesians ("Servants, be obedient to them that are your masters") (Eph. 6:5). Morrison's religious critique manages to engage these turbulent racial politics while incriminating all of humanity in the desperate, and often misguided, yearning for clear, unqualified assurances of God's plan. We see this yearning in Reverend Pulliam's unsettling insistence that people "do not deserve love" and must labor tirelessly to "earn" God's favor (141), and in Reverend Cary declaration that his congregation must define happiness by "what [they] have given up" (274).

## "A Cross Was No Better Than the Bearer": Sacred Symbols and Texts

An alternative approach to Ruby's religious prescriptions takes shape in the conflicts that punctuate the novel and disrupt the sanctimonious contentment of the town's elders. Familiar quarrels erupt amidst the seismic changes of the civil rights era that challenge Ruby's understanding of their past, their social and political progress, and the role that religion plays in shaping their collective destiny. Instead of siding with a particular view, however, Morrison's narrative observes the process, favoring concepts and characters that are unafraid of the vitalizing tension between different perspectives. Roger Best, already known for his transgressive marriage to Patricia's mother, embodies this sentiment by straddling the boundaries between life and death as the town's resident veterinarian *and* butcher, ambulance driver *and* mortician. As a result, *Paradise* advocates an interpretive freedom that thrives in spite of life's unshakable ambiguities or the fearful vigilance that too often defines "tradition." For even in a town like Ruby, one never knows when Roger will be called upon to use his van as an ambulance or as a hearse (69). Morrison highlights two of the town's most sacred symbols—the Oven and the Cross—to further elaborate upon the spiritual consequences of Ruby's choices.

To begin, the people of Ruby obsess over the mystifying words that Zechariah carved onto the Oven's hood (or "lip") in the 1890s. With time, the first letters of the motto have faded and what remains are the impression of the letter *B* and the final words of a divine decree: ". . . the Furrow of His Brow." By the 1970s, disagreement arises over the missing verb. The elders maintain that Zechariah advised his people to "*Beware* the Furrow of His Brow" and point, as evidence, to the recollections of Miss Esther, a woman who was raised in Haven and claimed to remember the letters she traced with her fingers as a child. The youth, on the other hand, insist that the message begins with the word "Be." For them, to "*Be* the Furrow of His Brow" is in keeping with a more assertive humanist belief system that is closely aligned with the revolutionary politics of the civil rights era. And like interpretive disputes over other sacred and civil "legal" writings such as the Bible or the Constitution, the conflict over "be" and "beware" belies larger questions of authority: What does the Oven's text reveal about the fundamental principles that define a society? How does context shape these concerns? Who has the power to authorize particular readings and reject others?

Between the two interpretations of the Oven's motto are two opposing worldviews, two visions of the future that, in the process, also reveal different ways of understanding God and the problem of evil. As the youth become increasingly aware of the changing world around them— influenced, in part, by Reverend Misner's encouragement to "step outside the wall"—they begin to venture beyond the town's precarious physical, social, and spiritual boundaries (145). "Being [God's] instrument, His justice," as Luther Beauchamp's son, Destry, states, is this restless generation's response to the call for equal rights and social liberation (87). Deacon and Steward Morgan, Harper Jury, Sargeant Person, Reverend Pulliam, and others interpret the young people's unusual activities, from bringing a radio to the Oven to participating in political demonstrations outside the town, as the dangerous intrusions of a wicked, predatory world. The youth are convinced that their reading of the Oven's motto is not as defiant and blasphemous as their parents believe, but is actually in accord with the values of their ancestors. During a church meeting to discuss the issue, one youth declares: "No ex-slave would tell us to be scared all the time. To 'beware' God. To always be ducking and diving, trying to look out every minute in case He's getting ready to throw something at us, keep us down" (84).

The scene revisits the fierce intergenerational debates depicted by Ernest Gaines in "The Sky Is Gray," Alice Walker in *Meridian,* and Carolyn Rodgers in her poem "JESUS WAS CRUCIFIED" as young black nationalists force a reevaluation of time-honored beliefs and traditions in an effort to disrupt the perceived complacency, fear, and self-loathing of their elders. The dissenting voices in Morrison's novel further critique the notion of blind, unquestioned faith by doubting the reliability of Miss Esther's "finger memory." We are told that "they howled at the notion of remembering invisible words you couldn't even read by tracing letters you couldn't pronounce" (83). In contrast to their elders' belief that the faithful must continually prove their worth through one "test" after another, the young people's interpretation of the motto asserts that God calls men and women to actively combat racism and other evils. A familiar exchange between old and young in *Paradise* conveys the nuances of their functional theodicy:

> "God's justice is His alone. How you going to be His instrument if you don't do what He says?" asked Reverend Pulliam. "You have to obey Him."
>
> "Yes, sir, but we *are* obeying Him," said Destry. "If we follow His commandments, we'll be His voice, His retribution. As a people—"
>
> Harper Jury silenced him. "It says 'Beware.' Not 'Be.'" Beware means 'Look out. The power is mine. Get used to it.'"
>
> "'Be' means you putting Him aside and you the power," said Sargeant.
>
> "We *are* the power if we just—"
>
> "See what I mean? See what I mean? Listen to that! You hear that, Reverend? That boy needs a strap. Blasphemy!" (87)

This response is easily reminiscent of the preacher's accusations in "The Sky Is Gray" or Richard Wright's elders in *Black Boy;* the adults in *Paradise* dispute the terms of the debate while expressing incredulity over the young people's "backtalk" (85). The youth are taken to task for failing to refer to their elders as "sir," for singling out Zechariah and identifying him only as an "ex-slave" rather than as a man who was part of a "whole group making their own way" (85). And after Royal Beauchamp interrupts Reverend Pulliam, we are told that "everybody was so stunned by the boy's brazenness, they hardly heard what he said" (85).

Clearly, then, the charge of blasphemy extends beyond religious dimensions to suggest a kind of cultural and historical apostasy that threatens the fundamental integrity of the Oven and, by extension, the town itself. The seriousness of this threat is indicated by how fiercely the New Fathers reiterate the inerrancy of Zechariah's words. Steward Morgan, who actually craves power more than religious fidelity, stubbornly thwarts Misner's influence on the youth by declaring: "If you, any one of you, ignore, change, take away, or add to the words in the mouth of that Oven, I will blow your head off just like you was a hood-eye snake" (87). The New Fathers, who have protected the town's controlling story for decades, behave as if their understanding of the Oven's words is self-evident, natural. But the narrative refuses to offer definitive answers to the riddle Zechariah left behind and the timeless spiritual quandary that it contains. Instead, Morrison's narrative underscores an inconclusiveness that points to more complex realities. Her narrative legitimizes views that are alert to their own subjectivity, cleverly giving the last word to perspectives that open paths of interconnection instead of coveting exclusive and exceptional favors. Such is the case when, in response to the murders that their fathers committed at the Convent, the young people write across the fractured Oven that "*We Are* the Furrow of His Brow" (298)—a collectivist declaration that lifts the *B* from "Beware" and reverses the first two letters. This new linguistic construct builds on the old, while offering both an accusation and a sobering reminder of the town's moral and ethical abdications.

Next, the image of the cross joins the Oven in awakening multiple significations over the nature of God and religion. But where the Oven's pristine value emerges from within the community, the cross—as a fundamental sign most commonly associated with the Christian tradition—comes to represent beliefs and principles that are introduced from without. Its appearance in the text follows Reverend Pulliam's aforementioned sermon on earning God's love during K.D. and Arnette's wedding. Pulliam's "difficult love" reinforces man's depravity and describes a wrathful God who necessitates suffering. In response, Reverend Misner, who "knew this lethal view of his chosen work was a deliberate assault on all he believed," takes down the cross from the church wall and silently holds it up above the heads of the wedding party (144). He believes that no words need accompany this act, for the cross conveys a universal message that resonates with humankind. Misner conveys the symbol's power by reflecting on Jesus Christ, the "solitary black man" who was crucified on the intersecting lines of that "parody of human embrace":

> The cross he held was abstract; the absent body real, but both combined to pull humans from backstage to spotlight, from muttering in the wings to the principal role in the story of their lives. This execution made it possible to respect—freely, not in fear—one's self and one another. Which was what love was: unmotivated respect. All of which testified not to a peevish Lord who was His own love but to one who enabled human love. Not for His own glory—never. God loved the way humans loved one another; loved the way humans loved themselves; loved the genius on the cross who managed to do both and die knowing it.
>
> But Richard Misner could not speak calmly of these things. So he stood there and let the minutes tick by as he held the crossed oak in his hands, urging it to say what he could not: that not only is God interested in you; He *is* you.
>
> Would they see? Would they? (146–47)

Misner's attitude mocks Ruby's claims of communal strength and harmony by aspiring to a deeper, more reverent human connection that extends beyond boundaries of time, space. His emphasis on the mobilizing power of sight, as we shall see, resonates with the spiritual intuitiveness of Lone DuPres and Consolata's reluctant gift of "in sight." Outside the text, his exposition also brings to mind the self-affirming spiritual freedom of Alice Walker's Shug Avery in *The Color Purple*.

Yet, as the disagreement over the Oven makes evident, no symbol can denote a single clear and unmediated message. The novel suggests that Misner's attempt to make the cross "speak" in this manner, while commendable, fails to have the intended effect on his audience. Evidence of this can be found in the way the narrative shifts during the wedding service from one perspective to another, reflecting the cross in a host of disassociated connotations—the groom's anger, the bride's dread, the attendant's exasperation. As Katherine Clay Bassard explains, "the congregation fails to see exactly what Misner sees; the cross cannot speak for itself, but because it is vacant, it becomes a projection screen for each viewer's preoccupations and predispositions" ("Race," 112–13). Each person surveys the sacred symbol through the lens of their own experience. And much like Bigger Thomas in *Native Son*, who angrily conflates the cross that Reverend Hammond's placed around his neck with the one in flames outside the jail, Misner's act does little to separate Steward Morgan from the fact that the same cross that inspires "awe and wonder" can also generate "fear and panic." Steward's comments suggest that any intrinsic goodness that might be attributed to the cross is contaminated by its association with hatred, degeneracy, and warfare: "He had seen crosses between the titties of whores; military crosses spread for miles; crosses on fire in Negroes' yards, crosses tattooed on the forearms of dedicated killers. He had seen a cross dangling from the rearview mirror of a car full of whites come to insult the little girls of Ruby. Whatever Reverend Misner was thinking, he was wrong. A cross was no better than the bearer" (154).

Like the work of Baldwin and Gaines, *Paradise* elaborates upon the interpretive process through which African Americans evaluate the sacred signs and stories that give shape to their existence. Much of the narrative's creative energy is devoted to refuting absolute values and clarifying the aforementioned distinction between "cross" and "bearer," but it would be a mistake to conclude that Morrison is advocating a glib notion of relativism that sanctions every deed or thought. Indeed, Misner readily acknowledges the debilitating effects of a peaceable symbol so cruelly abused—his experience as a civil rights activist bears this out—and yet he also clings to a hope inspired by Saint Augustine that, "God's message [is] not corrupted by the messenger" (145). It is for this reason that Morrison overwhelms us with protean signs in *Paradise*, only to caution in the novel's concluding pages against the danger of concentrating on them too exclusively—"focusing on the sign rather than the event; excited by the invitation rather than the party" (305).

## Three Prophets of *Paradise*

The last chapter of *Paradise* opens with a sermon by Reverend Misner at a child's funeral that poignantly returns us to the spiritual and existential considerations of the problem of evil. Nearly a century after W. E. B. Du Bois wrote of the anguish of his own first-born son's passing,[8] Morrison's novel revisits the question of *why?* within an African American community in ways that speak to the inexplicable suffering of humanity:

This is why we are here: in this single moment of aching sadness—in contemplating the short life and the unacceptable, incomprehensible death of a child—we confirm, defer or lose our faith. Here in the tick tock of this moment, in this place all our questions, all our fear, our outrage, confusion, desolation seem to merge, snatch away the earth and we feel as though we are falling. Here, we might say, it is time to halt, to linger this one time and reject platitudes about sparrows falling under His eye; about the good dying young (this child didn't have a choice about being good); or about death being the only democracy. This is the time to ask the questions that are really on our minds. Who could do this to a child? Who could permit this for a child? And why? (295)

The child whose "short life" is being contemplated in the aforementioned passage is one of Sweetie Fleetwood's sickly infants named Save-Marie, but Misner and those gathered before him might as well be grieving the "unacceptable, incomprehensible death" of the black Oklahoma community they call home. For what is also being interred in this moment are the illusions that have shaped Ruby's way of life until now: a sense of unity that is based on exclusion, a goodness that is defined only in relation to immorality and wickedness, and an understanding of peace that requires heavily guarded borders.

Save-Marie's death follows the chilling decisions of nine men from Ruby to raid the Convent outside of town and blot out the "new and obscene breed of female" (279) that has taken up residence there. As Deacon would later reflect, the men had become "what the Old Fathers cursed: the kind of man who set himself up to judge, rout and even destroy the needy, the defenseless, the different" (302). The presence of Gigi, Mavis, and the others are said to have disrupted Ruby's "peaceable kingdom" and are blamed for "drawing folks out there [to the Convent] like flies to shit and everybody who goes near them is maimed somehow and the mess is seeping back into *our* homes, *our* families" (276). Gigi's brief affair with K.D. is included as part of this "mess," but most of the calamities that are falsely attributed to the women merely reflect the town's discontent: "A mother was knocked down the stairs by her cold-eyed daughter. Four damaged infants born in one family. Daughters refused to get out of bed. Brides disappeared on their honeymoons. Two brothers shot each other on New Year's Day. Trips to Demby for VD shots common" (11). We have seen how Ruby's response to suffering is informed by a history determined by strictly conservative religious dogma and the reactionary politics of racial purity and isolation. In the wake of the Convent murders, these convictions collapse—or shift off their foundation as the Oven does—and the town's inhabitants are forced to reckon with their own mortal existence in an ever-changing world.

Mourning parents, infertile couples, and absent children recur throughout *Paradise*, but it is this final loss that forces a deeper evaluation of the town's future. Misner uses the traumatic death of the Fleetwood child not only to be a voice for "the questions that are really on our minds," but to provide an answer of sorts, one that emerges from the inexhaustible possibilities of rebirth. His funeral sermon appeals to New Testament concepts of resurrection and redemption to demonstrate just how forgiving is the boundary between life and death. At the same time, Lone DuPres and Consolata Sosa draw on spiritual folk wisdom and healing to reawaken the "creative" impulse that maintains universal balance. The young minister, the midwife, and the "holy women" of the Convent all share an understanding of God as the source of a defiant optimism that locates "the 'trick' of life and its 'reason'" in that interminable urge to return home and start again (272).

We begin with Lone DuPres. At the heart of her belief system is a finely tuned sense of balance that, like the Doublemint gum she regularly chews, reflects her awareness of the world's dual nature. Lone intuits God's presence in moments of organic symmetry and synthesis, and seeks to maintain this same equilibrium in her own life. It comes as no surprise that this "disheveled woman in thong slippers" (242) acts as the novel's mediating figure (she is well-acquainted with the people of Haven, Ruby, and the Convent) or that her chosen profession is midwifery, as she attends to the possibility of life *and* death through the fickle birthing process. Lone is also a conjurer, or "hoodoo" woman, who combines her Christian faith with age-old folk beliefs and practices. She inhabits the margins of Ruby—much like Patricia, Anna Flood, and Reverend Misner—not only because of her uncommon talents, but because in a town so committed to blood ties, she is the adopted child of one of Haven's founding families. As a result, her stance as participant-observer allows her the freedom to ignore the rigidly manufactured laws and boundaries of Ruby, preferring instead to trust the moral compass that emerges from her own innate connection with God. Lone's attitude is perhaps best conveyed through an exchange with Consolata, her reluctant apprentice at the Convent:

> Consolata complained that she did not believe in magic; that the church and everything forbade its claims to knowingness and its practice. Lone wasn't aggressive. She simply said, "Sometimes folks need more."
>
> "Never," said Consolata. "In my faith, faith is all I need."

"You need what we all need: earth, air, water. Don't separate God from His elements. He created it all. You stuck on dividing Him from His works. Don't unbalance his world." (244)

It can be argued that Lone joins Baby Suggs and Pilate as one of Morrison's highly regarded "ancestor figures" because her prophetic wisdom and experience serves as a guiding (and grounding) force for those who are culturally and spiritually lost. The kind of self-loathing that dominates Consolata's early years in Oklahoma, for example, finds its antidote in Lone's assertion that "He created it all." Though she does not deny the existence of evil, Lone puts forth an inclusive message that treats the entire natural world, together with humanity's every attribute, as sacred, instead of praising only the qualities that are sanctioned by religious institutions and communities. Like the residents of the Bottom in *Sula*, Lone adheres to the belief that "the presence of evil was something to be first recognized, then dealt with, survived, outwitted, triumphed over" (*Sula*, 118). This is evident in the way Lone perceives Consolata's ability to restore life to the dying as a gift ("God don't make mistakes. Despising His gift, now, that is a mistake" [246]) and in her belief that even after the Convent murders, "God had given Ruby a second chance" (297). Lone is also endowed with the gift of reading minds, but she insists that the ability to see and understand God's "signs" is granted to everyone—everyone, that is, who "[pays] attention to His world" (273).

The signs of Ruby's downfall catch the midwife's attention one evening as she searches by the stream behind the Oven for mandrake root. There on the Oven's hallowed ground where the nine men are gathered, Lone senses "the devilment they were cooking" in their plot against the Convent women (269). Her hiding place behind the Oven affords the reader yet another glimpse into the town's tragic climax. It is also here that Lone reflects on the signs of encroaching malevolence that she missed—the buzzards that circled the town during the spring thaw, for instance. And as she chastises herself for "playing blind" and "ignoring what was going on and letting evil have its way" (273), her comments offer an instructive theological counterpoint to the diatribes of Ruby's more conservative ministers:

Playing blind was to avoid the language God spoke in. He did not thunder instructions or whisper messages into ears. Oh, no. He was a liberating God. A teacher who taught you how to learn, to see for yourself. His signs were clear, abundantly so, if you stopped steeping in vanity's sour juice and paid attention to His world. He wanted her to hear the men gathered at the Oven to decide and figure out how to run the Convent women off, and if He wanted her to witness that, he must also want her to do something about it. (273–74)

On the surface, Lone's concept of God as a "teacher" appears to be in line with Reverend Pulliam's earlier sermon about goodness as a "learned application" that humanity is obligated to earn and accept. Although true believers may never know if or when they have "graduated," the minister insists that all that need concern his congregation is that they are "human and therefore educable, and therefore capable of learning how to learn, and therefore interesting to God" (141–42). Indeed, the minister and the midwife arguably share a belief in the pedagogical aspects of God's nature with each necessitating particular kinds of acquired knowledge and conditioning to fulfill his purpose—for Lone, this means "paying attention" to God's signs, while Pulliam speaks of "practice and careful contemplation." It is clear, however, that a dynamic reciprocity thrives in Lone's evangelical understanding of the relationship between God and his creation that marks the difference. Her personal, liberating God strongly contrasts Pulliam's aloof one. The minister's allegation that "if you think [love] is natural you are blind" (141) itself would be regarded by Lone as a form of blindness and willful ignorance.

In addition, Pulliam's notion that, regardless of any human deed or thought, God "is interested only in Himself" (142) is undercut by the connection Lone establishes between being called by God to "witness" a situation and deciding to "do something about it." The spiritual attentiveness that the midwife cultivates is not merely capable of producing material effects; it is *intended* for this very purpose to bring about positive and lasting change. Lone's is not a faith that stands still. As she navigates her shabby Oldsmobile up and down muddy roads to notify others about the men's murderous plans, we may be reminded of young James's blues-inflected admonition to "just keep on going, keep on going" in "The Sky Is Gray" (107). She searches from family to family for someone who will listen and heed her warning. And in keeping with misunderstood prophets of ancient times, Lone has great difficulty finding "somebody who didn't talk to her as if she were a child unable to wake from a nightmare" (281); many are skeptical, and, in the days to come, others will find ways to discredit her version of events. By the time Lone is able to locate a sympathetic ear among the DuPres family, they are too late to stop the killing at the Convent. The significance of Lone's role as a prophet and witness cannot be overlooked, however, as it contributes to how the town of Ruby views itself and begins to come to terms with a new vision of God in the midst of this tragedy. Without her "version" of the story, the narratives states, "the whole thing might have been sanitized out of existence" (298).

Lone's gift as a "seer" is also significant, for it conveys yet another means of comprehending God's meaning and purpose for humanity. Convinced that signs are "the language that God spoke in," Lone places great emphasis on sight and hearing, vision, the costs of blindness, and as previously stated, the need to "pay attention" to God's efforts to communicate. It is important to note that this finely tuned sense can be easily distorted, even for Lone, who admits to ignoring and misunderstanding the signs on occasion. Other instances remind us how imprecise this mode of "reading" can be. On the road, for instance, she remarks that "if this mission was truly God's intention, nothing could stop her," but shortly afterward, her car breaks down on the side of the road (282). Later, surveying the women's bodies at the Convent, Lone wrongly predicts that "the dead don't move" (292). Yet she manages to see and hear enough—"to divine the thoughts behind [the words]" (277)—to understand the crux of the situation. A different kind of sensory perception is demanded here, one that returns us to that careful distinction between "sign" and "event," and recalls Reverend Misner's admonition during K.D. and Arnette's wedding as he holds up the cross: "Would they see?" (147).

Consolata, who is also endowed with a kind of special sight, ministers to the women of the Convent in similar fashion. She initially refuses to consider her ability to "see" into the sick and dying as anything more than "evil craft" (246). Having turned from the "living God" (spirit) to the "living man" (flesh) in her affair with Deacon Morgan, Consolata is already convinced of her sinfulness (225). Further, her craving for flesh—a "gobble-gobble love" (240)—is compounded when out of fear and helplessness she uses her hidden talent to keep alive the body of the Reverend Mother, Mary Magna. Over time, Consolata attempts to come to terms with the gift by reframing it as "seeing in" or "in sight"—a facility she argues that "God made free to anyone who wanted to develop it" (247). Nevertheless, with Mary Magna, Consolata is rendered nearly blind by frequent attempts to rescue the older woman's sacred light from the otherworld. We are told that, "the dimmer the visible world, the more dazzling her 'in sight' became (247). She is forced to wear sunglasses at all times, and after Mary Magna's death, she retreats into the darkness of the Convent's wine cellar.

The gaze of Ruby's citizens seems always to be focused on "what lay Out There," but Consolata, who struggles to understand the purpose of a life so filled with personal disappointment and suffering, can only see within. Having failed to devote her life and her body completely to Mary Magna's God, she finds herself, as Misner predicted, "ripped of light and thrown into the perpetual dark of choicelessness" (146). In Consolata, Morrison reveals once again the mercurial line between blessing and curse:

> "God don't make mistakes," Lone had shouted at her. Perhaps not, but He was sometimes overgenerous. Like giving satanic gifts to a drunken, ignorant, penniless woman living in darkness unable to rise from a cot to do something useful or die on it and rid the world of her stench. Gray-haired, her eyes drained of what eyes were made for, she imagined how she must appear. Her colorless eyes saw nothing clearly except what took place in the minds of others. (246)

It is through the fugitive women who arrive at the Convent that Consolata finds a more fulfilling use for her gift of "pure sight" (247). She once listened patiently to their stories of flight and lost desire, saying nothing as they confused their evasive meanderings for liberation, but over time Consolata bitterly senses that the journeys of these "broken girls, frightened girls" (222) have stalled inside the protective walls of the old embezzler's mansion. Emboldened by visions of a spiritual ancestor, Consolata shares with the women her own story about Mary Magna and the church who taught that "[her] body is nothing [her] spirit everything" (263). She departs from this philosophy, however, and offers the wisdom born from her own experience, saying: "Hear me, listen. Never break them in two. Never put one over the other. Eve is Mary's mother. Mary is the daughter of Eve" (263). In keeping with this matrifocal lineage, Consolata gives voice to a new utopian vision led by Piedade, an enchanted woman "who sang but never said a word" (264). The stories of Piedade's maternal solace and companionship stand in contrast to the patriarchal law of Ruby's leaders. Piedade's song, potent and forgiving, suggests "the unambivalent bliss of going home to be at home—the ease of coming back to love begun" (318).

Consolata's teachings recall the power of the creation story and its cultural signs, and draws on Lone's ideas of universal balance to foster an acceptance of both the "sweet" and the "bitter" qualities of life (263). She directs Mavis, Gigi, Seneca, and Pallas to the stone floor of the Convent's cellar where their spiritual journeys can continue within. Their rebirthing "began to begin," we are told, with "templates"—outlines of their body silhouettes etched on the floor and later filled in with chalk images, painted features, cloth, and personal objects that will later be misread by their murderers as devil worship. In the cellar, each projects their fears and longing onto these symbolic new bodies and shares their struggle through a mode of storytelling "half-tales and the never-dreamed" that they refer to as "loud dreaming" (264). The exchange can be compared to the musical dialogue in Baldwin's "Sonny's Blues" as the Greenwich Village jazz players encourage Sonny to share his pain through his piano in the closing scene. The Convent women also purge their sufferings collectively, revealing their vulnerabilities until they are "no longer haunted" by misery and self-loathing (266). In the process, each welcomes a kind of paradise into their waking life that cannot be invaded or corrupted or stolen away.[9]

After Lone drives away from the Convent, frustrated that her warning appears to have gone unheeded, an unexpected rainfall heralds the women's transformation. The scene recalls the nostalgia Soane Morgan once expressed for the communal "sweet water" baptisms at the stream near the Oven. Surely the dancing women symbolize a return to the open and unconditional absolution that Soane cherished in Ruby's past, where white-robed daughters waded from the water "hand in hand, heads on supporting shoulders" (103). At the Convent, the cathartic baptisms are made all the more poignant by the reader's awareness of the impending arrival of the New Fathers, intent on ousting women who, they are convinced, "don't need men and they don't need God" (276). Yet the slaughter that opens the novel is given new life in its final pages, for now we see how the women refused to become the hunters' prey and fought back before being shot (286–87). What we do not see, however, are their bodies after the attack. Roger Best discovers after his search of the empty Convent that the women (and Mavis's Cadillac) have disappeared—a startling reminder of Consolata's insistence that body and spirit cannot be broken in two.

Afterward, Morrison encourages us, in the words of Lone Dupres, to "let [our] mind grow long" and consider one last glimpse of the women—consoling and inspiring loved ones, welcoming contentment and readying for war—as their journeys carry on. These parting vignettes are both comforting and murky, forcing the reader to consider how the interpretive dexterity that has been brought to bear on the written and oral narratives within the text should now be applied to the novel itself. Have these holy women returned to the world of the living? Perhaps they exist only as spirits in the memories of people like Billie Delia who find hope in these "lively, free, unarmed females" or in the conscience of Deacon Morgan, who, in taking responsibility for his role in their expulsion, is able to see himself clearly (apart from his unrepentant twin) for the first time.

In Shirley A. Stave's engaging analysis of *Paradise*, Consolata plays a more prominent role as a Christ figure whose ability to exhort and resuscitate the dead is ultimately "subversive of the Christian tradition" ("Master's Tools," 220). She argues that the former nun's matrifocal power and guidance is affirmed through Morrison's redeeming image of the Mother Goddess. In Stave's view, Consolata reaches a higher state of enlightenment than the socially progressive Reverend Misner; for my purposes, however, the minister offers a critical reconsideration of goodness and evil that reawakens one of the most difficult theological conversations about God within traditional black Christian communities. It is Misner's hope that a renewed understanding of mortality (and morality) can make a positive difference in the lives of Ruby's citizens—black people for whom divine love is barbed with preconditions and laws that, when not meticulously followed, lead to a "scattering" into nonexistence. Misner encourages the community to see their crisis of faith as an opportunity for growth and attempts to assuage their fears and frustrations in his concluding remarks about Save-Marie's life.

> "Wait. Wait." He was shouting. "Do you think this was a short pitiful life bereft of worth because it did not parallel your own? Let me tell you something. The love she received was wide and deep, and the care given her was gentle and unrelenting, and that love and care enveloped her so completely that the dreams, the visions she had, the journeys she took made her life as compelling, as rich, as valuable as any of ours and probably more blessed. It is our own misfortune if we do not know in our long life what she knew every day of her short one: that although life in life is terminal and life after life is everlasting, He is with us always, in life, after it and especially in between, lying in wait for us to know the splendor." He stopped, disturbed by what he had said and how. Then, as if to apologize to the little girl, he spoke softly, directly to her.
>
> "Oh, Save-Marie, your name always sounded like 'Save me.' 'Save me.' Any other messages hiding in your name? I know one that shines out for all to see: there never was a time when you were not saved, Marie. Amen." (307)

Here Misner underscores the *quality* of human existence in a town where most of the inhabitants value only its length and the ease with which it can span generations. He emphasizes the unconditional love that attended Save-Marie's every breath and nurtured an unfettered creative imagination that allowed her to "journey" without ever leaving her sickbed. And so for those who may see divine malevolence or impotence in God's apparent inability to ease the infant's suffering, Misner responds, in keeping with

Anthony Pinn's appraisal of the problem, by *rethinking* the nature of evil (and of good). Morrison's minister suggests that God's benevolence cannot be measured in human terms, particularly when such evaluations are based on a one-sided "parallel" of human limitation. He goes on to declare that all are endowed with grace, dignity, and peace—gifts that the people of Ruby labor so hard to "earn" and guard like stolen treasure. Misner's most profound and succinct iteration of this idea, that "there never was a time when you were not saved," is intended not only for the little girl known as Save-Marie, but also for Save-Marie as the black community in its most vulnerable incarnation.

Reverend Misner believes that the love—or what he calls the "unmotivated respect"—of God awaits any and all seekers "in life, after it and especially in between." He joins Consolata and Lone DuPres, however, in stressing the need for attentiveness and active involvement in cultivating a fulfilling spiritual life. So in addition to rethinking evil's nature, it should be clear that Misner's burial sermon also puts forth a subtle reevaluation of God that harkens back to the debate over the Oven's imperative to *be* or *beware*. Inexplicable calamity and chaos may be personified in God's twin visage or even in his "fourth face," but moral evil is ultimately attributed to human deeds in the narrative. This interpretation leads Misner to suggest that what is commonly understood as divine justice—the power to alleviate suffering and annihilate moral evils—can only be achieved in collaboration with humanity.

For Misner, then, God guides human action through persuasive means. The minister's counsel is in keeping with the theologian Howard Burkle's explanation of how such persuasion is brought about: "God communicates, solicits, and tries by rational means to affect our choices. We are always responding to influences which are encouraging us to think, weigh and choose. Whenever a man seizes the possibilities of freedom and acts from within his own being, he is certifying the persuasive activity of God."[10]

Human freedom, when reasoned in this manner, does not eclipse God's omnipotence, but is a "consequence of God's will" (W. Jones, *White Racist?* 187)—a belief that is reiterated in Misner's claim that God "has given us Mind to know His subtlety. To know His elegance. His purity'" (*Paradise*, 307). Indeed, the nuanced distinctions that maintain the authority of *both* God and man ultimately guide Morrison's wisest and most perceptive characters. Burkle's declaration about the way God "communicates" recalls Lone's attempts to heed the signs of the Teacher "who taught you how to learn, to see for yourself" (273). Even the young people of Ruby who long to be His voice in cultural and political matters are answering the call of a God that encourages them to "think, weigh and choose."

How will this new message be received among the people of Ruby? Is a humanocentric theism enough to mitigate the beleaguered survival strategies of a wounded people who insist that "God justice is His alone" (*Paradise*, 87)? The full impact of Misner's closing words are unknown for the most part, and it is clear that he will have to continue to work hard to persuade his neighbors of their truth (the fact that Misner must *shout* above the crowd's "musings" to be heard is only one indication of this). But his eagerness to accept the challenge is an extension of his deeper religious and philosophical views. Misner remains confident that there will be others as reflective as Deacon Morgan that are willing to acknowledge that they, too, have "a long way to go" (303). Still others may find hope in the transformation of Consolata and her followers at the Convent, for their womanist affirmations of wholeness and goodness can also be viewed as the result of concerted efforts to, in Burkle's words, "act from within [their] own being."

Ultimately Morrison compels us, as individual and collective bodies, to reevaluate goodness and relocate paradise to our present reality, outrageous flaws and all. Her conclusions recall John Hick's response to what he believes is the presumptive claim that God "might have done better." Drawing from the beliefs of St. Irenaeus, Hick's analysis turns from the potential pitfalls of a so-called utopian existence to argue that our current world is already "rather well adapted" to a higher purpose—that of activating humanity's free will and fostering the kind of meaningful spiritual growth that can bring men and women closer to God (*Religion*, 47).

> For it is by grappling with the real problems of a real environment, in which a person is one form of life among many, and which is not designed to minister exclusively to one's own well-being, that one can develop in intelligence and in such qualities as courage and determination. And it is in the relationship of human beings with one another, in the context of this struggle to survive and flourish, that they can develop the higher values of mutual love and care, of self-sacrifice for others, and of commitment to a common good.[11]

*Paradise* gestures toward a similar stance in its response to the "real problems of a real environment" as Morrison illustrates the potential of Hick's "soul-making process" through the suffering, growth, and prophetic wisdom of her people's lived experience. Her novel plainly validates—in ways that are admittedly less systematic and not as explicitly grounded in Christianity as Hick's—questing individuals who aspire to true self-fulfillment by facing the inexplicable with bravery and intrepid optimism, rather than being cloistered by the fear of "what lay Out There."

The novel also supports Hick's insistence that the ultimate fulfillment of human struggle lies in otherworldly bliss. Morrison closes the story with a mystical image of Piedade patiently awaiting one of many ships sailing to a shore. Of the unidentified "disconsolate" travelers on board, the narrative assures us that "now they will rest before shouldering the endless work they were created to do down here in paradise" (318). These words point to Morrison's insistence that humanity's boundless purpose lies in our capacity to discern and deliberate among the stories we share, to be fearless in our decisions, self-correcting when necessary, and merciful with those still unwilling to accept the divine challenge of "endless work."

THE QUESTIONS that trouble the mourners at Save-Marie's funeral about the meaning of human suffering have been a source of misery and strife in the works of an overwhelming number of twentieth-century African American writers. Each narrative I have investigated in this study creates a discursive structure "to halt, to linger" in pivotal moments of religious crisis—at gravesides and sickbeds, through angry tears on the mourner's bench, while uttering sacred vows or even singing the blues. My analysis argues the literary value, philosophical consequence, and aesthetic distinction of these approaches to the problem of evil, particularly as it concerns the arbitrary and inexplicable existence of racial suffering and shapes the governing belief systems of black communities. So in light of the larger black cultural tradition epitomized by the questions invoked at the burial ("Who could permit this . . . ? And why?"), it can be somewhat surprising to hear one of Morrison's characters conclude: "May I suggest those are not the important questions. Or rather those are the questions of anguish but not of intelligence. And God, being intelligence itself, generosity itself, has given us Mind to know His subtlety" (306–7). What Richard Misner tentatively refers to here as "anguish," the religious philosopher Michael Peterson identifies as the existential dimension of the problem of evil that emerges from the painful immediacy of "real-life" suffering. This is also what John G. Stackhouse Jr. characterizes as a religious problem on "the 'three-in-the-morning' level that involves our hearts as well as our heads."[12] We have seen how such spiritual struggles can be used in literature as a creative space from which to process incomprehensible realities. The writers in this study reflect and reason critically on the world they have inherited with its seemingly unshakable legacies of oppression, and they, too, declare that "this is the time to ask the questions that are really on our minds."

Yet the quality of spiritual and existential wakefulness that is characterized in the above passage as "intelligence" poses an immense new challenge to the mourners in Morrison's novel. Far from dismissing their pain, Misner asserts that this sorrow is only the first step in a longer, more arduous life journey. His push to move his community beyond what are "not the important questions"[13] recalls a similar cautioning by Hick in the chapter epigraph against "incomplete" ones. Certainly Morrison's mythic excavation in *Paradise* complicates the riddle of whether or not, as Hick states, "an omnipotent Creator might have done better" to address the underlying concern: "Better for what?" In spite of (and, perhaps, because of) the enormity of evil and human suffering, Misner does not hesitate in his plea for deeper self-awareness to recognize the inherent worth of every human being and acknowledging all of creation as home. Such sentiments remind readers that the urge to question God's justice and explore the problem of evil—in *Paradise* and in every text investigated in this book—is not wholly driven by despair. The struggle also emanates from a fierce longing for more goodness, more compassion and ingenuity, more hope.

# "Something as Inexplicable as Water"

For her son who understood, as he climbed onto the roof
by the help of two trembling hands, that his father, only
a man and not a god, could not save his mother's life
from something as inexplicable as water.

—RACHEL ELIZA GRIFFITHS, "Hymn to a Hurricane"

ONE YEAR after the catastrophic storms and flooding from Hurricane Katrina resulted in the deaths of more than 1,500 people on the U.S. Gulf coast in 2005, the African Diaspora literary journal *Callaloo* published a special issue of fiction, essays, interviews, and photographs titled "American Tragedy: New Orleans under Water." In contributions such as Rachel Eliza Griffiths's poem "Hymn to a Hurricane," we see creative minds grappling with deep loss and the incomprehensible suffering of a twenty-first-century natural disaster. The "two trembling hands" in her verse evoke a dialectic of human vulnerability and endurance that is the collection's philosophical subtext, whether the focus is on the hurricane's social, cultural, and economic costs, on its systemic political failures, or on individual stories of survival. Abandonment is another common theme to which Griffiths and others return, often by emphasizing the disproportionate number of poor and African American people stranded, displaced, and killed by the storm. In her poem, the dead are discarded carelessly, "their lives devoured by neglect" (line 19), children wander lost, and "storefronts [are] shattered" (25) out of desperation and anger.

Spiritual desertion is contemplated, too, as Griffiths's hymn pays tribute to a family's painful choice:

For a husband who could not save his entire family
because he only had two hands. For their house split
in half by water. For his wife's last words: *you can't hold on*

> *and hold me.* For the absence of God as she dropped his hands
> and gave herself like a petal to the gulf.
>
> (29–33)

A forthright, penetrating concern with divine justice and the problem of evil will persist, if this issue of *Callaloo* is any indication, as new generations of writers experience and reflect upon new generations of suffering. The spiritual bearing of the journal's contributions are clear from the outset; in his editor's notes, Charles Rowell characterizes the issue as both a "threnody" and a "praise song" for the vibrant, multicultural city in mourning ("My Byzantium," 1029). Rowell quotes the author Louis Edwards, who, when asked about the effect of the disaster on the New Orleans writing community, explains: "We're now forced to think of things spiritually, and we're now forced to think about God—and that's not necessarily a bad thing. I think that our writing may somehow become more profound because we're responding to something profound" (1306).

Present throughout the journal's literary selections are images of church steeples, rosary beads, and invocations of prayer, protection, and rescue that merge material and spiritual needs. In his poem "After Katrina," Kevin Simmonds envisions the recovery effort as a new Sabbath day "and work we do, prayer" (line 26). Three poems by Peter Cooley speak of renewal and incorporate biblical figures such as Adam, Eve, and St. Paul. The speaker in James Nolan's poem "Acts of God," who was born during a New Orleans hurricane, contemplates Katrina's laboring winds outside his home and notes, "This year August ends / with God banging on the door like the police" (lines 7–8). Significantly, Nolan's verse seems to personalize God in a hostile image of the police rather than in a protective or defensive role. If the metaphorical irony of this verse is interpreted as a criticism of law enforcement, it also raises concerns about the way God's justice operates among those hardest hit by tragedy.

Artistic communities have begun to confront the muddied waters of Hurricane Katrina in a variety of ways, particularly through visual media and song. The guitarist Bryan Lee follows the long blues tradition of the Gulf Coast in his song "Katrina Was Her Name," while the jazz musician Terence Blanchard memorializes the inexplicable loss in his CD *A Tale of God's Will.* The literary responses revisit in meaningful ways the philosophical and theological scrutiny of Ernest Gaines, James Baldwin, and other writers under investigation in this study. While not all the contributors to "American Tragedy: New Orleans under Water" are African American, the collection highlights survivors who are overwhelmed by the moral evils of racism and poverty that are brought to the surface by the natural disaster. Implicit in these literary representations are profound meditations on the questions raised by the black cultural critic Michael Eric Dyson:

> Did God cause the wind to roar and the waters of New Orleans to rage? Did God cause the destruction and death and mayhem we see? Is it ever God's will for black people to suffer? Can good come from black suffering, as even Martin Luther King, Jr., argued? Does that mean that black suffering, then, is God's way to redeem black people or the nation? Is that a sadomasochistic theology that black people should give up? Or is such an explanation a way for blacks to steel themselves against the meaninglessness of events so as not to suffer psychic and literal death? Some critics have claimed that God saved Africans from their savagery and their heathenism through slavery. Is the same true for catastrophes like Katrina? Is this a punishment from God—as one black Katrina survivor was heard to ask, "What did we do wrong for God to do this to us?" (Dyson 193)

In his analysis of race, poverty, and the hurricane, Dyson acknowledges the existential dimensions of the problem of evil, and, in a manner not unlike the fictitious Reverend Misner from Morrison's *Paradise*, he uses its familiar questions to encourage a personal accounting of the moral and spiritual self, as well as a critical evaluation of collective beliefs.[1] Dyson views the disaster as part of a larger narrative of African American encounters with evil that reaches back to slavery and provokes a range of attitudes toward suffering as redemptive, compensatory, punitive, and indifferent. Water instantiates these tensions in Dyson's account; he juxtaposes liberating biblical images of river crossings with the "watery grave" of the Middle Passage and the "foul spray of white supremacy and Jim Crow" during segregation (194). The connection lends cultural resonance to Griffiths's literary portrayal of hurricane victims lost to "something as inexplicable as water" and locates her text within the same tradition as "slaveships"—the Lucille Clifton poem that opens this study.

For a more explicit engagement with the problem of evil, perhaps none of the *Callaloo* selections are as uninhibited or as fiercely provocative as Bill Lavender's antitheistic critique in his poem "The Reason." The text turns the vacant consumerism and self-interest of the Christmas holiday against Christians who blame the disaster victims for their own misery, or claim that the hurricane was God's punishment for the so-called "sins" of New Orleans—rampant sexual immorality and crime, abortion clinics, and environmental negligence.[2] Lavender's speaker cross-examines the followers of the lowercased "savior / of the american retail outlet" with variations of a platitudinous Christmas refrain, asking: "is jesus the reason/for this flood and this drought?" (lines 36–37) and "is jesus the reason/for these jam-packed malls/and last minute sales?" (47–49). In later stanzas, the speaker responds bitterly to what he believes is a duplicitous logic of divine retribution, suggesting that "if jesus is the reason/for this season/maybe we ought to kill him again" (80–82).

The satirical tone, style, and social critique of Lavender's verse invite useful intertextual comparisons with Amiri Baraka's poem "When We'll Worship Jesus." Published in 1975, Baraka's text also uses "jesus" as a metonym for the misguided ideological conceits of Christianity in times of crisis. "We'll worship jesus," the poem begins, "when jesus do/somethin/when jesus blow up/the white house/or blast nixon down" (lines 1–6). Once the 1970s revolutionary in Baraka's poem associates institutionalized religion with pimps, materialistic preachers, corrupt politicians, and greedy industrialists, he argues "jesus need to be thrown down and whipped" (line 44). Similarly, Lavender's poem depicts vivid images of a crucifixion that relocates Jesus to the flooded streets and abandoned houses of New Orleans, where believers leave him to die as the sacrificial reason for this "hurricane season."

> if jesus is the reason
> for this season
> drown him in his attic
> tie the carcass to a street sign
> lay him in the ninth ward mud
> with his feet sticking out from under a barge
> put him on the danzinger bridge
> with nineteen police-issue bullets in his back
> put him in the superdome
> and let him shit in the hallway
> with 65,000 believers
> put him on bourbon street
> and have the people he asks for help
> beat him to a pulp
>
> (lines 93–106)

This stanza vividly imagines the Christian savior in one of the most devastated poor, black neighborhoods of New Orleans, the Lower Ninth Ward. It subsequently casts him as homeless and humiliated, an evacuee stranded without adequate aid in the city's Superdome. "The Reason" relies on these embittered sentiments to break through the hyperreal media images of Hurricane Katrina and juxtapose the startling surplus of need against a scarcity of compassion. Like Baraka, Lavender flaunts a transgressive tone in his poem that thwarts moral and ethical complacency; his verses use astonishing images of corporal desecration to force a reorientation of view.

Perhaps, then, we cannot proclaim of these contemporary writers, as Benjamin Mays once stated in 1938, that "we move now into new territory," given the extent to which questions about God, religion, and the problem of evil continue to frequent our literary landscape. On the pages of American literature, black sufferers continue to seek redemption and retribution for their misery, and with remarkable consistency, they defy charges of blasphemy to demand spiritual explanations for wrongs committed against the race. This is not to say that distinctive trends are not emerging. Black inspirational fiction has become increasingly popular, with authors such as Victoria Christopher Murray and Jacquelin Thomas publishing stories that focus on the everyday struggles of black women and their families within Christian communities. On the other hand, recent African American literary fiction remains mesmerized by Dostoevsky's "eternal questions," yet it tends to minimize the pivotal role that religion has traditionally played in shaping and legitimizing cultural blackness. In texts by Edward P. Jones, Colson Whitehead, Martha Southgate, and others, the resistance of the skeptic and the unbeliever is less pronounced, even though the consequences are not necessarily less severe.

This subtle shift may indicate an effort on the part of contemporary black writers to represent questions of faith as constituting merely one formative aspect of multifaceted social identities. Such texts also echo the findings of a recent survey by the Pew Forum on Religion and Public Life that substantiates the increasing fluidity of American religious experience and states that "more than a quarter of American adults (28%) have left the faith in which they were raised in favor of another religion—or no religion at all."[3] It is clear, then, that the bold creativity with which African Americans writers approach the inevitability of pain and suffering will continue to evolve as the processes of our diverse religious life come under scrutiny. Their work bears witness to a kaleidoscopic spiritual inheritance, shaped by what Toni Morrison calls "circles and circles of sorrow" (*Sula*, 174), where shouts of praise and deliverance converge with the aggrieved's cry for justice.

# NOTES

## Preface

1. In 1953, Senator Joseph McCarthy was chairman of this committee, whose highly publicized hearings were intended to expose Communists and other subversives among government employees, labor activists, liberal educators, and artists; his accusations, while often based on thin evidence, managed to end many careers and tarnish many reputations (see Rampersad, *Hughes*, 2: 211).

2. Rampersad states that one of Hughes's associates, a contributing editor of the *Negro Worker* named Otto Huiswood, submitted the poem to the journal "apparently without Hughes's knowledge" (*Hughes*, 1: 253).

3. Though Hughes was subject to criticism and protest regarding the poem during a book tour in North Carolina, he eagerly continued his speaking engagements and spoke out against the miscarriage of justice in Scottsboro, stating: "I believe that anything which makes people think of existing evil conditions is worth while. Sometimes in order to attract attention somebody must embody these ideas in sensational forms. I meant my poem to be a protest against the domination of all stronger peoples over weaker ones" (quoted in Rampersad, *Hughes*, 1: 226).

4. See Daniel, "Langston Hughes versus the Black Preachers"; and Emanuel, "Christ in Alabama."

5. In 2004, Senator John Kerry attempted to use Hughes's poem "Let America Be America Again" as one of the slogans of his presidential campaign. Soon afterward, conservative spokesmen such as William F. Buckley Jr. and Rush Limbaugh questioned Kerry's association with a "communist" poet whose vision of America was best represented by "Goodbye, Christ." Suddenly new and improved versions of the misinterpretations that Hughes once lamented appeared in the media and on Internet blogs.

## Introduction

1. J. Sella Martin quoted in Raboteau, *Fire*, 42.

2. See Andrews, *Sisters of the Spirit* and *To Tell a Free Story*; Bassard, *Spiritual Interrogations*; Felder, *Stony the Road We Trod*; Hopkins and Cummings, *Cut Loose Your Stammering Tongue*; Moody, *Sentimental Confessions*; C. Peterson, *"Doers of the Word"*; Pierce, *Hell without Fires*; and Raboteau, *Slave Religion*.

3. As John Hick states: "Philosophy of religion, then, is not an organ of religious teaching. Indeed, it need not be undertaken from a religious standpoint at all. The atheist, the agnostic, and the person of faith all can and do philosophize about religion. . . . It studies the concepts and belief systems of the religions as well as the prior phenomena of religious experience and the activities of worship and meditation on which these belief systems rest and out of which they have arisen" (*Religion*, 1).

4. Unless stated otherwise, I have chosen to use the King James Version throughout this book because of its preferred use in the texts I am investigating. This reality is in keeping with James Weldon Johnson's insistence that the earliest black preachers and their communities were "saturated with the sublime phraseology of the Hebrew prophets and steeped in the idioms of King James English"—a preference that continues well into the twentieth century (*God's Trombones*, 9). On occasion, in the interest of clarity, verses are quoted from the New Revised Standard Version.

5. Cornel West and Eddie S. Glaude Jr. locate African American religious studies from 1969 to the present in a kind of "Golden Age." More focused attention on issues of class, gender, and religious culture begins to take place during this time, along with substantial research into the history of African American religious traditions by Albert Raboteau, Evelyn Brooks Higginbotham, and others. Additionally, "theological interests stand alongside other approaches to the subject, and African American religious studies begins to emerge from under the rubric of black theology and a singular Christian preoccupation" (*African American Religious Thought: An Anthology*, xv).

6. In later chapters, Jones directly addresses the shortcomings of the work of the black theologians Joseph Washington, James Cone, Albert Cleage, Major Jones, and J. Deotis Roberts.

7. According to Jones, his book "challenged as flawed the twin claims that 'though blacks accepted the white man's religion,' they recreated and remolded it to fit their 'own particular needs,' and that 'the black man's pilgrimage in America was made less onerous because of his religion" (*White Racist?* xv).

8. See the following works by Pinn: *By These Hands; Varieties of African-American Religious Experience; African-American Humanist Principles;* and *Moral Evil.*

9. It should also be noted that, in making his claims, Pinn often draws support from cultural sources such as black folklore and song as well as fiction. He is among a substantial number of contemporary religious scholars such as Albert Raboteau, Delores Williams, Victor Anderson, and Katie Canon who follow Benjamin Mays's lead by affirming the legitimacy of oral and literary narratives in elaborating upon black theological and philosophical concepts.

10. In his discussion of slave conversion experiences, the anthropologist Paul Radin has surmised that, "In the Christian God [the Negro] found a fixed point, and he needed a fixed point, for both within and outside of himself he could see

only vacillation and endless shifting. All that this God demanded was an unqualified faith and a throwing away of doubt" ("Status," ix).

11. Prolific writers such as Frances E. W. Harper offer a significant departure from this claim, as her work continued to draw meaningfully and positively from biblical sources in the late nineteenth century. In Katherine Clay Bassard's analysis of Harper's late poetry, she notes that collections such as *Idylls of the Bible* (1901) generate a "liberationist Christian subjectivity" that runs counter to the "predominant view of declining biblical influence in American literature" ("Private Interpretations," 110). Bassard argues that Harper's frequent depictions of Jesus Christ do not refashion biblical discourse to suit a political agenda, but rather, the poet foregrounds "the subversiveness inherent in [the Bible's] textuality" (139).

12. Wallace D. Best's extensive research on religion in Chicago between the world wars expounds upon the social and theological transformations of urban churches as more religious leaders insisted that "black Protestant churches must strive for comprehensiveness and be attentive to the 'every day problems' of people as well, no longer fashioning themselves as suitable only for 'paying, praying, and preaching'" (*Passionately Human*, 18).

13. The full title of Roark Bradford's collection is *Ol' Man Adam an' His Chillun: Being the Tales They Tell about the Time When the Lord Walked the Earth Like a Natural Man.*

14. Fauset, in *Black Gods of the Metropolis*, labors against similar assumptions by Robert E. Park and Melville Herskovits that "there is something in the Negro amounting to an inner compulsion which drives him into religious channels." Despite evidence of a sizable "non-church going population" among African Americans in the 1930s and 1940s, Faust states that "the opinion of universality of religious attitudes among Negroes, as contrasted to whites, persists" (96–97).

15. Citing Jenny Franchot, Roger Lundin speculates that American literary criticism's reluctance to regard religion as a legitimate and complex field of investigation ultimately neglects a significant aspect of American cultural identity (xi–xii).

16. Significantly, Matthews's study is most convincing when his spiritual hermeneutic is coupled with a discussion of the blues, which he characterizes as "ethical laments on a world gone mad" (125). I would argue that this kind of ethical confrontation with the absurd dominates twentieth-century African American literary representations of religion, particularly when we consider how black fiction is inundated by moments when, as Matthews describes, "the blues person cries to the Lord over the injustice of love gone wrong or over the pain of social injustice" (126).

17. As one reviewer of Coleman's work states, "One comes to the end of this argument feeling that Coleman believes that to be authentically black—for the discourses throughout are the discourses of racial and cultural authenticity—one must be Christian, or at least influenced by Christianity, or perhaps at least committed in some way, shape, or form to a supernaturalist view of the world that articulates itself in relationship to Christianity" (Powers, "Elephants in the Room," 357).

18. The work of Richard Wright poses a formidable challenge for many literary critics concerned with religion and spirituality. Kimberly Rae Connor, in *Imagining Grace: Liberating Theologies in the Slave Narrative Tradition*, expertly unpacks the push and pull of Wright's stance as expressed in his autobiography, yet her analysis ultimately casts his ambivalence in terms of a collective religious consciousness that recapitulates the aims of liberation theology. For Connor, Wright's commitment to his art as an inspiration to others further demonstrates how his "religious spirit endured" and so "Wright functions like a liberation theologian but in the guise of a secular artist and social critic" (109). Another example of this can be found in James H. Evans Jr.'s efforts, in *Spiritual Empowerment in Afro-American Literature*, to place the black literary quest for cultural renewal in concert with a kind of religious awakening that recognizes "the timeliness of God" to resolve "the hard contradictions of present reality" (17). He supports his claims by framing Bigger's responses in *Native Son* as part of a larger journey toward his mother's Christian faith. And while he does acknowledge the inconclusive nature of Wright's "critical-reflexive self-examination," Evans's approach also leads to incongruent observations such as the idea that Wright's representation of a basement church is meant to signify its "subversive" qualities (129 n. 15). I argue differently in chapter 2 that the Christian church *is* the established authority that many of Wright's characters are attempting to subvert.

19. In addition to Hardy and Harris, other studies that have served for models for my approach include: T. Smith, *Conjuring Culture*; Caron, *Struggles over the Word*; Hubbard, *The Sermon and the African American Literary Imagination*; and Montgomery, *The Apocalypse in African American Fiction*.

## 1. "In My Flesh Shall I See God"

1. Sundquist, *To Wake the Nations*, 593; Redding, *To Make A Poet Black*, 112. Cullen's contemporaries also remarked that *The Black Christ and Other Poems* seemed to fall short of his previous achievements (see C. Wood, "Black Pegasus," 93).

2. Smylie, "Countée Cullen's 'The Black Christ'"; W. Jones, *Is God a White Racist?* 28–34.

3. Written and composed by Abel Meeropol, "Strange Fruit" was first sung by Billie Holiday in 1939 at the Café Society. Whether or not the white Christians who revived the extralegal practice of lynching during Reconstruction singled out public hanging on trees and poles as a matter of expediency or as a part of a religious imperative is not clear. Nevertheless, the dishonoring of the black sufferer is further exacerbated by the way in which corpses were often left unburied and were harvested for souvenirs. It should also be noted that there are traditional African religions that feature cross symbols as well. According to Kelly Brown Douglas, "the intimate relationship between the living and the dead, which the African cross

pointed to, more than likely influenced the slaves' development of a special relationship with Jesus, the crucified one" (*Black Christ*, 23).

4. Many African Americans, especially during the nineteenth century, read the redeeming potential of Africa in Psalm 68:31, which states, in the King James Version: "Princes shall come out of Egypt; Ethiopia shall soon stretch out her hands unto God" (see Raboteau, *Fire*, 41–42).

5. Jim's actions in these scenes have been compared to the title character of Herman Melville's *Billy Budd*, which was published five years before "The Black Christ" in 1924 (see Smylie, "Countée Cullen's 'The Black Christ,'" 170).

6. Hughes makes this statement in the first line of his 1926 essay "The Negro Artist and the Racial Mountain" (27). Nathan Huggins attributes Hughes's comment to Cullen in *Harlem Renaissance* (208). Cullen's literary editorials in *Opportunity* frequently expressed his concern that African American poets were unduly pressured to limit the subject matter of their work to racial issues. In the introduction to *Caroling Dust*, he further maintained his wish that "any merit that may be in his work to flow from it solely as the expression of a poet—with no racial consideration to bolster it up" (quoted in Turner, *Minor Chord*, 71).

7. By characterizing the poem as a conversion narrative, I hope to expand upon a similar claim made by Houston Baker in his 1974 monograph *A Many-Colored Coat of Dreams*. In his brief discussion of Cullen's poem, Baker remarks: "If the poem is seen in this light, some of its apparent flaws turn out to be necessities, e.g., the long retelling of incidents and the sense of suspense and wonder the narrator attempts to create toward the conclusion" (48). Where Baker connects Cullen's agenda to the cultural forms and techniques common to conversion stories, my analysis uses the poem's engagement with Job to evaluate the quality of the conversion and the use of racial violence as its catalyst.

8. Religious scholars have identified parallels between Job and Babylonian, Sumerian, and other wisdom literature of the Ancient Near East (see Rodd, *The Book of Job*, 128–33). In the nineteenth and twentieth century, allusions to the story's theme can be seen in Goethe's prologue to the first part of *Faust* (1808) and in Fyodor Dostoevsky's *The Brothers Karamazov* (1879–80). More explicit references appear in works such as H. G. Wells's novel *The Undying Fire* (1919) and Robert Frost's drama *A Masque of Reason* (1945).

9. Shackelford, "To Dr. William A. Creditt," in *My Country and Other Poems*, 19–20.

10. It is for this reason that Cullen's contemporaries compared the narrator in "The Black Christ" to the redeemed sinner of John Masefield's poem "The Everlasting Mercy" (1911) (see Shillito, review of *The Black Christ and Other Poems*, by Cullen, 92–93; and Ferguson, *Countee Cullen*, 115).

11. Weems explains that, "Five human relationships are used as metaphors repeatedly in prophetic speeches to describe the relationship between Israel and

Yahweh: (1) judge and litigant, (2) parent and child, (3) master and slave, (4) king and vassal, and (5) husband and wife" (*Battered Love*, 16).

12. For lynching statistics, see Zangrando, *The NAACP Crusades against Lynching*.

13. For more information on the conversion narratives of black American slaves, see C. Johnson, *God Struck Me Dead*.

14. In her discussion of "literary lynchings," Trudier Harris notes the way in which representations of ritual violence are often manipulated to fit the author's agenda: "Indeed, lynching and burning scenes sometimes become accessory devices, embellishments to suggest the innate character of white society, its destructive nature and brutality" (*Exorcising Blackness*, 69).

15. According to Fyall, the Hebrew translation reads: "And after my skin they have stripped off—this." The word "they" was replaced with "worms" in the King James Version of the Bible (*My Eyes*, 51).

16. "And the King shall answer and say unto them, Verily I say unto you, Inasmuch as ye have done it unto one of the least of these my brethren, ye have done it unto me" (KJV, Matt. 25:40).

17. For more information, see P. Smith and Cobbs, *Long Time Coming*.

## 2. "Wrastl' On Jacob"

1. Wright, *Black Boy*, 151; Wright, "Memories," 5.

2. When asked in 1946 to account for the overwhelming number of black Baptists and Methodists in America, Wright asserted that "[The American Negro's] motivation springs, not from religious faith, but from the shared feeling of victimization. Such altruism and benevolence as he may exhibit are the results of need, a part of the imposed technique of survival" (Schmid, "An Interview with Richard Wright," 108).

3. Critical examples include: Hayes, "Double Vision"; Lynch, "Haunted by Innocence"; Tate, "Christian Existentialism in *The Outsider*"; Adell, "Richard Wright's *The Outsider* and the Kierkegaardian Concept of Dread"; and Hakutani, "Richard Wright's *The Outsider* and Albert Camus's *The Stranger*."

4. In this regard, I am mindful of Lewis Gordon's distinction between the European historical phenomenon known as "existentialism" and the term "philosophy of existence," or "existential philosophy," which connotes the experiencing of "philosophical questions premised upon concerns of freedom, anguish, responsibility, embodied agency, sociality, and liberation" (*Existence in Black*, 3).

5. John Mbiti provides a more detailed discussion of African initiation and puberty rites in *African Religions and Philosophy*, 118–29.

6. Although "moaning" refers to the singing of spirituals or laments *on* the special bench, the words "moaner" and "mourner" are typically used interchangeably in former slave interviews.

7. My use of the term "metanoia" is influenced by Raboteau's description as "a change of heart, a transformation in consciousness—a radical reorientation of personality, exemplified in the stories of St. Paul the Apostle and St. Augustine of Hippo as a life-changing event brought about by the direct intervention of God" (*Fire*, 152–53).

8. In referencing "tribalism," Johnson takes his cue from Wright's discussion of traditional African religions in his book *Black Power*. Particularly troubling for Johnson is the manner in which Wright approaches his understanding of African peoples through problematic observations that are "impossible to distinguish from the paternalistic notions of inferiority with which white colonizers have long regarded the people of Africa" (180). Such attitudes, Johnson suggests, are indicative of how limited Wright's interpretations of African American religious traditions are, even as his work provides "a compelling assessment of American Christian identity among poor black Southerners" (185).

9. According to the biographer Michel Fabre, *Tarbaby's Dawn* was written sometimes between 1934 and 1935 (*Unfinished Quest*, 135). More recently, Hazel Rowley states that the novel was begun in 1936 (*Richard Wright*, 112–13). Originally titled *Tarbaby's Sunrise: A Folk-Saga*, the novel was rejected by numerous publishers, and in 1940, Wright turned the final chapters into the short story "Almos' a Man" for *Harper's Bazaar*.

10. Indeed, Tarbaby will be baptized later alongside both men and women, but it is noteworthy that here only black "boys" are called to join. Such formal rites of passage do not exist for the black female characters in Wright's work; they do not require the kind of persuasion that Elder Hargrove features in his sermon. Tarbaby's mother, sister, and girlfriend are depicted as born believers.

11. Book 1 of *The Outsider*, "Dread," begins with an epigraph from Søren Kierkegaard: "Dread is an alien power which lays hold of an individual, and yet one cannot tear oneself away, nor has a will to do so, for one fears what one desires" (1).

12. The manuscript of *Tarbaby's Dawn* concludes soon after Tarbaby's baptism with a scene Wright later adapted into the 1940 short story "Almos' a Man."

13. My approach to *Black Boy* is in keeping with Timothy Dow Adams's generic assessment of the text as a "collective autobiography" that "should not be read as historical truth which strives to report those incontrovertible facts that can be somehow corroborated, but as narrative truth" ("I Do Believe," 314).

14. Wright, "Bright and Morning Star," in *Uncle Tom's Children* 225; Wright, *The Outsider*, 553.

15. Significantly, Sylvester Johnson characterizes the relentless threats that Wright incurred over his *refusal* to join the church as "intimate violence" in which "these individuals, despite loving him, reject him in absolute, ultimate terms" (185). I would extend the designation to include Wright's painful acquiescence and submission as further evidence of how he viewed their love as "violence."

16. Loeb and Leopold, both from affluent families, were captured after attempting to exact a $10,000 kidnapping ransom from the victim's father, who, unaware of his son's death, had initially agreed to pay. Wright would later use the incident, which occurred in 1924, to inspire Bigger's ransom note to Mary Dalton's family in *Native Son* (136).

17. Robert L. Douglas suggests that Wright uses the song "Steal Away to Jesus" to act as a metaphor for Bigger "as he is attempting his own flight to freedom" ("Religious Orthodoxy," 87). However, the revulsion Bigger expresses upon hearing the folk song suggests the opposite. The memories of his mother's submissive nature that the song evokes indicate that stealing away to Jesus is tantamount to spiritual *and* physical acquiescence. The song encourages Bigger, at this pivotal moment in the narrative, to forfeit his life. In this context, the spiritual might be better characterized as a metaphor for *choice* and its life-threatening repercussions, or, as the narrative states: "It was dangerous to stay here, but it was also dangerous to go out" (254).

18. Margolies, *The Art of Richard Wright*, 113; Wright, "Bigger," 458.

19. When Cross Damon's mother makes a similar request for her son to pray in *The Outsider*, he dodges "the fountain of emotion that made him feel guilty" by fleeing her home (29).

20. Tate notes that Wright often placed such instances of racism and white betrayal alongside the image of the "bad mother." She theorizes that "Wright could vent his outrage at both by means of his characters' violent responses, without exposing his guilty feelings and thereby inviting public censure" (*Psychoanalysis*, 111–12).

21. S. Wright, *This Child's Gonna Live*, 73–85; Walker, *The Third Life of Grange Copeland*, 188; Gaines, *The Autobiography of Miss Jane Pittman*, 211.

22. In his written accompaniment to the photo documentary *12 Million Black Voices*, Wright describes the institution as "the door through which we first walked into Western civilization" (131). The essay "Blueprint for Negro Writing" portrays the church as a "portal" (47).

## 3. "A Loveless, Barren, Hopeless Western Marriage"

1. Nearly all of the contributors to *A Troubling in My Soul* have published book-length studies of their own, yet the Townes collection is invaluable for its in-depth focus on theodicy and the problem of evil in relation to the theological structures of womanism. See also Cannon, *Katie's Canon*; Grant, *White Woman's Christ*; Townes, *Embracing the Spirit*; and Williams, *Sisters in the Wilderness*.

2. Importantly, Weems reminds us that Hebrew men, "who set the nation's moral and political course," were the intended audience for these prophetic metaphors of marriage and infidelity (*Battered Love*, 42). In fact, "there is rarely any mention by the prophets of the actual lives of women" (69). Modern applications of the marital rhetoric may overlook these contextual details, yet Weems argues

that this metaphor continues to shape our assumptions and expectations of the human-divine relationship in new social contexts—a claim further substantiated by the works of Larsen, Walker, and other African American writers.

3. Walker, "Beyond the Peacock: The Reconstruction of Flannery O'Connor," in *Gardens*, 43.

4. In *Sisters in the Wilderness*, Grant further explores this conflict through the notion of "social-role surrogacy" and the historical exploitation of black women. Emilie M. Townes offers a similar critique of servanthood and states that "loss, denial, and sacrifice, if used, must be reinterpreted and reimagined if the vision of society and the nature of the Black church are to provide more than impotent security" ("Living in the New Jerusalem," 90).

5. Walker made these remarks in her speech as "Humanist of the Year" to the American Humanist Association in 1997 ("The Only Reason," 297).

6. Carby, *Reconstructing*. See also Tate, "Death and Desire"; and Sollors, *Neither Black nor White*.

7. Although Larsen's critiques of the conservative practices and philosophies of black colleges were common concerns during the 1920s and 1930s, few fictional writers explored their racial complexities so incisively. Two decades later, Ralph Ellison's profound interpretation of the institution in *Invisible Man* would visit many of Larsen's critical characterizations.

8. Larsen's own experience as a student at Tennessee's Fisk University and as a nurse at Tuskegee University in Alabama offer additional insight into her fictional character's attitude. In her biography of Larsen, Thadious Davis notes that the *Quicksand* author was an adequate student who "found a measure of happiness in her life at Fisk" (*Nella Larsen*, 65). But coming from Chicago, where "her family life had failed to instill a healthy appreciation for Christian devotion to the uplifting of the Negro race," Larsen bristled at the religious obligations of her school. Everything from the campus missionary societies to the daily demands of devotional service seemed to reinforce for Larsen "the negative stereotypes of the needy, backward, downtrodden race" (Davis, *Nella Larsen*, 59). Fifteen years later, Larsen worked as a head nurse at Tuskegee's John Andrew Memorial Hospital, where she encountered more restraints as part of the staff.

9. I am indebted to Lawrence Rodgers for his incorporation of Van Wyck Brooks and Lewis Mumford's term "usable past" to scrutinize the experience of black migrants. In his reading of *Quicksand*, Rodgers notes, "with neither real nor surrogate family to sustain and guide [Helga], she is unable to imbed herself within a stabilizing, unified, progressive community" (*Canaan Bound*, 90; see also 190 n. 21).

10. Hazel Carby observes that Helga "was brought to a recognition of her exchange value which denied her humanity while cementing her fragile dependence on money" (*Reconstructing*, 173).

11. Significantly, the early twentieth-century proliferation of the urban storefront church is generally attributed to the influx of southerners during the World

War I era, when Larsen's novel takes place. According to Milton Sernett, many newcomers "resisted total assimilation into the cultural traditions of the Old Settlers and set up their religious safe places in a hostile urban environment" (*Promised Land*, 180). These smaller congregations typically met in an abandoned house, apartment, or storefront. Sernett goes on to note the characteristics of these religious enclaves, such as "independence from mainline denominations, institutional instability over time, the lack of formal theological training for clergy, the preponderance of women among members, and a proclivity for Pentecostal ritual and Holiness doctrine" (188). Larsen incorporates each of these components in her depiction of the "impoverished meeting-house" where Helga seeks asylum (*Quicksand*, 110).

12. In "Nella Larsen and the Intertextual Geography of *Quicksand*," Anna Brickhouse also offers a compelling reading of the revival scene in *Quicksand* alongside William Dean Howells's novella *An Imperial Duty* (1892).

13. Walker utilizes similar images of the buried mother in her novel *Meridian* through the mummified Marilene O'Shay and the title character's mother, Mrs. Hill, and in *The Color Purple* through Celie's spiritually suffocating marriage of convenience.

14. Considering the southwest location of the mountains, one might speculate that the African people in "The Diary of an African Nun" are based on one of the many Bantu kingdoms.

15. "Her Sweet Jerome," another short story from Walker's *In Love & Trouble*, also uses accusations of infidelity to explore the interpersonal and political implications of male/female relationships. In the early 1970s tale, an uneducated southern black hairdresser, described as a "big awkward woman, with big bones and hard rubbery flesh," suspects that she is being cheated on by her abusive husband, a young, handsome schoolteacher (25). Once she realizes that Jerome has forsaken her for a political and intellectual commitment to black nationalist "revolution," she burns his books. But she fails to escape before the flames consume her own body. "Her Sweet Jerome" does not explicitly engage religious themes, but the self-destructive actions of the protagonist have much in common with the women in the unfulfilling couplings of "Roselily" and "The Diary of an African Nun."

16. McDowell's influential analysis of "public and private narrative fiction" also traces the role of audience as a measure of the black heroine's development from Frances E. W. Harper's novel *Iola Leroy* (1892) to Walker's text.

17. Walker's phrasing also recalls the accusation that Mrs. Hill directed toward her daughter in *Meridian*: "I always thought you were a *good* girl. And all the time you were fast" (87).

18. Peter Kerry Powers also takes note of Celie's ambiguous use of the pronoun "he" that conflates her stepfather with God. Later, Celie makes a similar reference to her husband in the statement: "Well, sometimes Mr. ____ git on me pretty hard. I have to talk to Old Maker. But he my husband. I shrug my shoulders. This life soon be over, I say. Heaven lasts all ways" (47) (see Powers, *Recalling Religions*, 46–47).

19. This is the second of only two instances in which Celie speaks (writes) directly to God in the novel. The first instance occurs in the opening letter when she inquires: "Maybe you can give me a sign letting me know what is happening to me" (11).

20. hooks, *Talking Back*, 6; also quoted in Glenn, *Unspoken*, 27.

21. See Townes, "Living in the New Jerusalem," 78; and Pinn, *Why Lord?* 157.

22. It should be noted that Nettie, too, struggles with what God "looks like" as she works as a Christian missionary to convert the Olinka people. Nettie is astonished by the description of Jesus' features, with his hair like "lamb's wool," and, she is comforted by the presence of Africa in the Bible. Later, in Liberia, Nettie also takes a great interest in the indigenous customs and religions there, remarking upon the Olinka's worship of the "Roofleaf" that protects the villagers. She writes of her efforts to closely examine her faith and concludes that, "most people think he has to look like something or someone—a roofleaf or Christ—but we don't. And not being tied to what God looks like, frees us" (227). As a result, Nettie's new concept of God has much in common with the divine spirit that Celie and Shug honor together on the other side of the Atlantic.

23. For example, hooks argues that Celie's new worldview is rewarded by blessings of economic prosperity, but it is not associated with any "collective effort to effect radical social change" ("Writing the Subject," 221, 224).

24. Similar theological critiques are entwined throughout Walker's writing, including recent fiction not discussed in this chapter such as *By the Light of My Father's Smile* (1998); *The Way Forward Is with a Broken Heart* (2001); and *Now Is the Time to Open Your Heart* (2004). Along with these works, the recent poetry collection *Absolute Trust in the Goodness of the Earth: New Poems* maintains her spiritual celebration of nature. Also of interest in the collection is the poem "They Made Love" about a bride and groom making love on a church altar. When discovered by an old woman, the bride remarks: "It is an honest/Way/To become/Married/To/The church" (lines 41–46).

## 4. "There Is No Way Not to Suffer"

1. The story was published in *Negro Digest* in August 1963 before appearing in the short-story collection *Bloodline*.

2. Echoes of the "lady" can be found in the maternal wisdom of aunts, grandmothers, and godmothers of works such as *Catherine Carmier* (1964), *The Autobiography of Miss Jane Pittman* (1971), *In My Father's House* (1978), and *A Lesson before Dying* (1993). The self-righteous voice of the "preacher" also emerges in each narrative as evidenced, respectively, by Reverend Armstrong, Deacon Just, Reverend Martin, and Reverend Ambrose, while the young male characters Jackson Bradley, Jimmy Aaron, Robert X, and Grant Wiggins all reflect the skeptical antagonism of the "boy."

3. "Sonny's Blues" was originally published in the *Partisan Review* in 1957. Marlene Mosher indicates that the story was written nearly a decade earlier in 1948.

4. Pinn uses the terms "usable religion" and "productive religiosity" to refer to belief systems that do not "place abstraction and neat theological categories above human experience." According to Pinn, "productive religiosity is fluidlike in that its dynamics alter with the existential situation; in this way, it avoids applicability dilemmas resulting from the rigid demands and dictates of tradition" (*Why Lord?* 120).

5. Likewise, Donald C. Murray notes a connection between teaching algebra and the brother's "desire for standard procedures and elegant, clear-cut solutions" ("Complicated," 353–57).

6. Baldwin, "Sonny's Blues," 63; Margolies, "The Negro Church," 63.

7. In his provocative reading, Keith Byerman uses the narrator's difficulties with language to raise questions about his reliability and trustworthiness in articulating the power of music. He states: "In the very act of telling his story, the narrator falsifies (as do all storytellers) because he must use words to express what is beyond words ("Words and Music," 203).

8. The poule d'eau, or water chicken, is a common slate-gray American coot that frequents lakes such as the False River in southern Louisiana's Pointe Coupee Parish, where Ernest Gaines was raised. See George H. Lowery Jr., *Louisiana Birds* (1974) http://losbird.org/labirds/amco.htm.

9. Considering Ty's complaint about their bread and syrup breakfast, it could also be argued that the family's eating conditions, brought about by poor and adverse labor opportunities and lack of federal aid, inevitably led to James's health problems.

10. See Margolies, "The Negro Church"; Byerman, "Words and Music"; and Klein, "James Baldwin: A Question of Identity." Marlene Mosher's study is one of the few that acknowledges Grace's possible relevance to the narrator's development in the story ("James Baldwin's Blues," 112). Donald C. Murray also remarks on the connection between Grace's death, Sonny's trouble, and his uncle's murder ("Complicated," 355).

11. Baldwin revisits this dilemma in *The Amen Corner* as Luke and Maggie argue over who is responsible for the stillborn death of their daughter. Where Maggie, now a preacher, sees her child's death as punishment for her faithlessness, Luke refuses to accept this notion, declaring: "All we'd done to be cursed was to be *poor*, that's all. That's why little Margaret was laid in the churchyard. . . . Don't you come on with me about no judgment, Maggie" (60).

12. Similar connections can be made between Snead's formulations and Henry Louis Gates's linguistic analysis of "Signifyin'" in black literature, which emphasizes the vernacular processes of revision and repetition "with a signal difference" (Gates, *Signifying Monkey*, xxiv).

13. In her discussion of the distinctive elements of African American writing, Toni Morrison remarks on the presence of the "ancestor," which she describes as

"not just parents, they are sort of timeless people whose relationships to the characters are benevolent, instructive, and protective, and they provide a certain kind of wisdom" ("Ancestor as Foundation," 343).

14. Buddhist tradition also refers to the material world as a "sea of suffering," suggesting a possible non-Christian connection to Baldwin's representations of water here as well.

15. Baldwin expresses a similar sentiment in his play *The Amen Corner* through the wayward jazz musician Luke. Once Luke, who is suffering from a terminal illness, learns that his son is also an aspiring musician, he reminds him that "music don't come out of the air, baby. It comes out of the man who's blowing it" (44).

16. The cup of trembling is a usage common to the King James Version of the Bible, while other versions refer to the cup of "wrath," "anger," and "fury" instead.

17. Ryken, Wilhoit, and Longman, *Dictionary of Biblical Imagery*, "Cup," 186.

18. I am grateful to Kevin Kyzer for calling this particular connection to my attention.

19. One may be inclined to compare James's distinctive voice in "The Sky Is Gray" to Gaines's other child protagonists including Sonny from the story "A Long Day in November"; Chuckkie and Ben O. from "Just Like a Tree" in *Bloodline* (1968); Jane as a young girl in *The Autobiography of Miss Jane Pittman* (1971); or Snookum from *A Gathering of Old Men* (1983). Yet as a nascent bluesman, James's narration actually has more in common with Jim Kelly, the aging guitar player and tractor driver in Gaines's second novel, *Of Love and Dust* (1967).

## 5. "But God Is Not a Mystery. We Are."

1. A number of critical sources on Toni Morrison's work emphasize the role of religion and spirituality in her representations of black life (see Stave, *Toni Morrison and the Bible*; Higgins, *Religiosity, Cosmology, and Folklore*; Alexander, "The Fourth Face"; Pessoni, "She Was Laughing at Their God"; C. Jones, "*Sula* and *Beloved*"; Morey, "Margaret Atwood and Toni Morrison"; Mitchell, "I Love to Tell the Story"; Bryant, "The Orderliness of Disorder"; and Edelberg, "Morrison's Voices").

2. *American Heritage Dictionary*, 4th ed. (2000), "Paradise."

3. *Sula*, 6; *Paradise*, 318 (my emphasis).

4. *Sula*, 115; *Paradise*, 276.

5. Similarly, Beverley Foulks argues that "Instead of using experiences such as the suffering or death of children as a springboard for fairly abstract theological musing, the people at the Bottom use those experiences to understand the human side of suffering" ("Trial by Fire," 16).

6. For Morrison's description of the "ancestor," see chap. 4, n. 13.

7. While my interpretation pays special attention to biblical allusions, this is not by any means the only possible reading of Haven's creation. Therese E. Higgins,

for instance, in emphasizing the Africanist perspective of Morrison's work, asserts that this sacred history is "rich in African tradition and [involves] a god-like figure and mystical signs" (*Religiosity*, 120).

8. Du Bois, "On the Passing of the First-Born," in *Souls of Black Folk*, 127–32.

9. Similarly, Page asserts that "ordinary methods of knowing and interpreting—exemplified by Patricia's charts and notes—will not suffice, but instead deeper, more transcendent, more holistic kinds of knowing and interpreting, as modeled by Lone and Consolata, are required" ("Furrowing," 646).

10. Quoted in W. Jones, *White Racist?* 192.

11. Hick, "An Irenaean Theodicy," quoted in Mesle, *John Hick's Theodicy*, xxxi; Hick's theory is not without its critics, of course, and it should be noted that William Jones, whom I have cited frequently throughout this study, takes issue with Hick's failure to address the specifics of ethnic suffering. Jones maintains that the idea of suffering as "spiritual pedagogy" is tantamount to labeling blacks and others "who suffer most in this world" as "slower learners" (*White Racist?* 197–200). Likewise, Mesle offers a book-length response to Hick, posited on his belief that "people are shattered by suffering as often as they are strengthened, and harmed far more than healed. So while it is one thing to see the good which *can* arise from our suffering, it is quite another to be grateful for our griefs" (*Hick's Theodicy*, 5). I believe that Morrison would concur with Mesle's distinction, though it is clear that a full range of responses is represented in *Paradise*.

12. M. Peterson, *Evil*, 7; Stackhouse, *Can God Be Trusted?* 27.

13. It is worth noting that Misner does not say that these questions are "unimportant," but rather that they are "not the important questions." It is a subtle distinction, to be sure, but one that stops short of dismissing the mourners' concerns completely, which is more in keeping with the minister's compassionate and thoughtful approach to those in pain throughout the novel.

## Conclusion

1. Ultimately, Dyson builds upon the black liberation theology of the post–civil rights era to advocate "black prophetic religion" as the most effectual form of spiritual sustenance in the aftermath of Hurricane Katrina. He encourages black churches to reject punitive theodicies, respond thoughtfully to the questions of sufferers, and to "recapture their prophetic anger and to transform that passion into social action" (Dyson 198).

2. The evangelical Christian pastor John Hagee was one of the most prominent religious figures to express a belief that "Hurricane Katrina was, in fact, the judgment of God against the city of New Orleans" (Hagee, interview by Gross).

3. "U.S. Religious Landscape Survey," Pew Forum on Religion and Public Life (Washington, D.C.: Pew Research Center, 2008), 5.

# BIBLIOGRAPHY

## Primary Sources

Baldwin, James. *The Amen Corner*. New York: Vintage, 1968.

———. "Down at the Cross: Letter from a Region in My Mind." In *The Fire Next Time*, by Baldwin, 13–105. 1963. New York: Modern Library, 1995.

———. *Go Tell It on the Mountain*. New York: Random House, 1952.

———. *Just Above My Head*. New York: Dial Press, 1979.

———. "Sonny's Blues." In *Vintage Baldwin*, 26–77. 1957. New York: Vintage, 2004.

———. *Tell Me How Long the Train's Been Gone*. New York: Dial Press, 1968.

Baraka, Amiri. "When We'll Worship Jesus." 1975. In *The LeRoi Jones/Amiri Baraka Reader*, 251–54. New York: Thunder's Mouth Press, 2000.

Bechet, Sidney. *Treat It Gentle: An Autobiography*. Cambridge: De Capo Press, 2002.

Bradford, Roark. *Ol' Man Adam an' His Chillun: Being the Tales They Tell about the Time When the Lord Walked the Earth Like a Natural Man*. New York: Harper and Brothers, 1928.

Brown, William Wells. *Clotel*. 1853. New York: Carol Publishing Group, 1969.

Christian, Barbara. "The Race for Theory." In *African American Literary Theory*, edited by Winston Napier, 280–89. New York: New York University Press, 2000.

Clifton, Lucille. *The Terrible Stories*. Brockport, N.Y.: BOA Editions, 1996.

Connelly, Marc. *The Green Pastures: A Fable*. New York: Farrar and Rinehart, 1929.

Cullen, Countée. *The Black Christ and Other Poems*. New York: Harper and Brothers, 1929.

———. "Christ Recrucified." 1922. In *Black Poets of the United States: From Paul Laurence Dunbar to Langston Hughes*, edited by Jean Wagner, 335. Urbana: University of Illinois Press, 1973.

Delany, Martin R. *Blake; or, The Huts of America*. 1861–62. Boston: Beacon Press, 1970.

Dostoevsky, Fyodor. *The Brothers Karamazov*. 1879–80. New York: Barnes and Noble, 2004.

Douglass, Frederick. *Narrative of the Life of Frederick Douglass*. 1845. In *The Oxford Frederick Douglass Reader*, edited by William L. Andrews. New York: Oxford University Press, 1996.

Du Bois, W. E. B. *Darkwater: Voices within the Veil*. 1920. New York: AMS Press, 1969.

———. "A Litany of Atlanta." 1906. In *Book of American Negro Poetry*, edited by James Weldon Johnson, 90–94. New York: Harcourt, Brace, 1922.

———. *Souls of Black Folk.* 1903. New York: Dover, 1994.

Ellison, Ralph. *Shadow and Act.* New York: Vintage, 1964.

Gaines, Ernest. *The Autobiography of Miss Jane Pittman.* New York: Bantam, 1971.

———. *A Lesson before Dying.* New York: Vintage, 1993.

———. *Bloodline.* New York: Vintage, 1968.

———. *Catherine Carmier.* New York: Vintage, 1964.

———. *Mozart and Leadbelly: Stories and Essays.* New York: Knopf, 2005.

———. *Of Love and Dust.* New York: Vintage, 1967.

———. "The Sky Is Gray." In *Bloodline*, by Gaines. New York: Vintage, 1964.

Griffiths, Rachel Eliza. "Hymn to a Hurricane." *Callaloo* 29, no. 4 (2007): 1307–8.

Hughes, Langston. *The Big Sea.* New York: Hill and Wang, 1940.

———. "Christ in Alabama." *Contempo* 1 (December 1931): I.

———. "Concerning 'Goodbye, Christ.'" January 1, 1941. In *The Collected Works of Langston Hughes*, edited by Arnold Rampersad, 9: 207–9. Columbia: University of Missouri Press, 2001.

———. "Goodbye, Christ." *Negro Worker* 2 (November/December 1932): 32.

———. "My Adventures as a Social Poet." *Phylon* 8, no. 3 (1947). In *The Collected Works of Langston Hughes*, edited by Arnold Rampersad, 9: 269–77. Columbia: University of Missouri Press, 2001.

———. "The Negro Artist and the Racial Mountain." In *African American Literary Theory*, edited by Winston Napier. New York: NYU Press, 2000.

———. "Personal." 1933. In *The Collected Works of Langston Hughes*, edited by Arnold Rampersad, 2: 140. Columbia: University of Missouri Press, 2001.

———. *Scottsboro, Limited.* New York: Golden Stair Press, 1932.

Hurston, Zora Neale. *Dust Tracks on a Road.* 1942. New York: Harper Collins, 1996.

Johnson, Georgia Douglas. *A Sunday Morning in the South.* In *Black Theater, U.S.A.: Forty-Five Plays by Black Americans, 1847–1974*, edited by James V. Hatch. New York: Free Press, 1974.

Johnson, James Weldon. *God's Trombones: Seven Negro Sermons in Verse.* New York: Penguin, 1927.

Johnson, Robert. "Hellhound on My Trail." *The Complete Recordings.* Sony Records, B000002757-CD.

Larsen, Nella. *Quicksand.* 1928. New Brunswick, N.J.: Rutgers University Press, 1986.

Lavender, Bill. "The Reason." *Callaloo* 29, no. 4 (2007): 1486–89.

McKay, Claude. "The Lynching." 1920. In *African American Literature: A Brief Introduction*, edited by Al Young, 378. New York: HarperCollins College, 1996.

Morrison, Toni. *Paradise.* New York: Plume, 1998.

———. *Sula.* New York: Plume, 1973.

Nolan, James. "Acts of God." *Callaloo* 29, no. 4 (2007): 1253.

Rodgers, Carolyn. *how i got ovah*. Garden City, N.Y.: Anchor, 1975.

Rowell, Charles. "My Byzantium: The Editor's Notes." *Callaloo* 29, no. 4 (2007): 1028–31.

Shackelford, Theodore Henry. *My Country and Other Poems*. Philadelphia: I. W. Klopp, 1916–18.

Simmonds, Kevin. "After Katrina." *Callaloo* 29, no. 4 (2007): 1116–17.

Stewart, Maria. "Lecture Delivered at the Franklin Hall." Boston, September 21, 1832. In *The Norton Anthology of African-American Literature*, 2nd ed., edited by Henry Louis Gates Jr., 252–55. New York: Norton, 2004.

Toomer, Jean. *Cane*. New York: Liveright, 1923.

Walker, Alice. *Absolute Trust in the Goodness of the Earth: New Poems*. New York: Random House, 2003.

———. *The Color Purple*. New York: Washington Square Press, 1982.

———. "The Diary of an African Nun." In *In Love & Trouble: Stories of Black Women*. San Diego: Harcourt Brace, 1973.

———. *In Love & Trouble: Stories of Black Women*. San Diego: Harcourt Brace, 1973.

———. *In Search of Our Mother's Gardens: Womanist Prose*. San Diego: Harcourt Brace, 1983.

———. "Janie Crawford." In *Good Night Willie Lee, I'll See You in the Morning: Poems*, by Walker, 18. New York: Dial Press, 1979.

———. "The Only Reason You Want to Go to Heaven Is That You Have Been Driven Out of Your Mind." In *By These Hands: A Documentary History of African American Humanism*, edited by Anthony Pinn. New York: New York University Press, 2001.

———. "Roselily." In *In Love & Trouble: Stories of Black Women*. San Diego: Harcourt Brace, 1973.

———. *The Third Life of Grange Copeland*. New York: Washington Square Press, 1970.

Walker, David. *David Walker's Appeal to the Colored Citizens of the World*. 1829. State College: Pennsylvania State University Press, 2000.

Wheatley, Phillis. "To Samson Occum, February 11, 1774." In *The Poems of Phillis Wheatley*, 203. Chapel Hill: University of North Carolina Press, 1989.

White, Walter. *The Fire in the Flint*. 1924. Athens: University of Georgia Press, 1996.

Whitehead, Colson. *Apex Hides the Hurt*. New York: Doubleday, 2006.

Wilson, August. *Joe Turner's Come and Gone*. New York: Penguin, 1988.

Wilson, Harriet E. *Our Nig, or Sketches from the Life of a Free Black*. Boston, 1859.

Wright, Richard. *Black Boy*. 1945. New York: HarperCollins, 1998.

———. "How 'Bigger' Was Born." In *Native Son*. 1940. New York: HarperCollins, 1993.

———. "Memories of My Grandmother." Richard Wright Papers. Yale Collection of American Literature, Beinecke Rare Book and Manuscript Library.

———. *Native Son.* 1940. New York: HarperCollins, 1993.

———. *Tarbaby's Dawn.* Richard Wright Papers. Yale Collection of American Literature, Beinecke Rare Book and Manuscript Library.

———. "The Man Who Was Almost a Man." In *Eight Men: Short Stories.* 1961. New York: HarperCollins, 1996.

———. *The Outsider.* 1953. New York: HarperCollins, 1993.

———. *Uncle Tom's Children.* New York: HarperCollins, 1938.

Wright, Sarah E. *This Child's Gonna Live.* New York: Feminist Press, 1969.


## Secondary Sources

Adams, Timothy Dow. "I Do Believe Him Though I Know He Lies: Lying as Genre and Metaphor in Richard Wright's *Black Boy.*" In *Richard Wright: Critical Perspectives Past and Present*, edited by Henry Louis Gates Jr. and K. A. Appiah, 302–15. New York: Amistad Press, 1993.

Adell, Sandra. "Richard Wright's *The Outsider* and the Kierkegaardian Concept of Dread." *Comparative Literature Studies* 28, no. 4 (1991): 379–94.

Alexander, Allen. "The Fourth Face: The Image of God in Toni Morrison's *The Bluest Eye.*" *African American Review* 32, no. 2 (1998): 293–303.

Allen, Brooke. "The Promised Land," *New York Times*, January 11, 1998. http://www.nytimes.com/books/98/01/11/reviews/980111.11allent.html.

Anderson, Victor. *Beyond Ontological Blackness: An Essay on African American Religious and Cultural Criticism.* New York: Continuum, 1995.

Andrews, William. *Sisters of the Spirit: Three Black Women's Autobiographies of the Nineteenth Century.* Bloomington: Indiana University Press, 1986.

———. *To Tell a Free Story: The First Century of Afro-American Autobiography, 1760–1865.* Urbana: University of Illinois, 1986.

Bair, Barbara. "Though Justice Sleeps: 1880–1900." In *To Make Our World Anew*, edited by Robin D. G. Kelley and Earl Lewis, 3–66. Oxford: Oxford University Press, 2000.

Baker, Houston A., Jr. *Blues, Ideology, and Afro-American Literature: A Vernacular Theory.* Chicago: University of Chicago Press, 1974.

———. *A Many-Colored Coat of Dreams: The Poetry of Countée Cullen.* Detroit: Broadside Press, 1974.

Baldwin, James. "The Uses of the Blues: How a Uniquely American Art Form Relates to the Negro's Fight for His Rights." Reprinted in *Voices of Concern: The Playboy College Reader*, edited by the editors of *Playboy*, 89–97, New York: Harcourt Brace Jovanovich, 1971.

Bassard, Katherine Clay. "Private Interpretations: The Defense of Slavery, Nineteenth-Century Hermeneutics, and the Poetry of Frances E. W. Harper." In *There Before Us: Religion, Literature, and Culture from Emerson to Wendell Berry*, edited by Roger Lundin, 110–40. Grand Rapids, Mich.: William Eerdmans, 2007.

———. "The Race for Faith: Justice, Mercy, and the Sign of the Cross in African American Literature." *Religion & Literature.* 38, no. 1 (spring 2006): 95–113.

———. *Spiritual Interrogations: Culture, Gender, and Community in Early African American Women's Writing.* Princeton: Princeton University Press, 1999.

Best, Wallace D. *Passionately Human, No Less Divine: Religion and Culture in Black Chicago, 1915–1952.* Princeton: Princeton University Press, 2005.

Blanchard, Terence. *A Tale of God's Will: A Requiem for Katrina.* Blue Note Records compact disc. 2007.

Brickhouse, Anna. "Nella Larsen and the Intertextual Geography of *Quicksand.*" *African American Review* 35, no. 4 (2001): 533–60.

Bryant, Cedric Gael. "The Orderliness of Disorder: Madness and Evil in Toni Morrison's *Sula.*" *Black American Literature Forum* 24, no. 4 (1990): 731–45.

Byerman, Keith E. "Words and Music: Narrative Ambiguity in "Sonny's Blues." In *Critical Essays on James Baldwin,* edited by Fred L. Standley and Nancy V. Burt. Boston: G. K. Hall, 1988.

Callahan, John F. "Hearing Is Believing: The Landscape of Voice in Ernest J. Gaines' *Bloodline.*" *Callaloo,* no. 20 (winter 1985): 86–112.

Cannon, Katie Geneva. *Katie's Canon: Womanism and the Soul of the Black Community.* New York: Continuum, 1995.

Carby, Hazel V. *Reconstructing Womanhood: The Emergence of the Afro-American Woman Novelist.* New York: Oxford University Press, 1987.

Caron, Timothy P. *Struggles over the Word: Race and Religion in O'Connor, Faulkner, Hurston, and Wright.* Macon, Ga.: Mercer University Press, 2000.

Clarke, Cheryl. *"After Mecca": Women Poets and the Black Arts Movement.* New Brunswick, N.J.: Rutgers University Press, 2005.

Coleman, James W. *Faithful Vision: Treatments of the Sacred, Spiritual, and Supernatural in Twentieth-Century African American Fiction.* Baton Rouge: Louisiana State University Press, 2006.

Cone, James. *For My People: Black Theology and the Black Church.* Maryknoll, N.Y.: Orbis, 1984.

———. *Risks of Faith: The Emergence of a Black Theology of Liberation, 1968–1998.* Boston: Beacon Press, 1999.

Connor, Kimberly Rae. *Conversions and Visions in the Writings of African-American Women.* Knoxville: University of Tennessee Press, 1994.

———. *Imagining Grace: Liberating Theologies in the Slave Narrative Tradition.* Urbana: University of Illinois Press, 2000.

Dalsgard, Katrine. "The One All-Black Town Worth the Pain: (African) American Exceptionalism, Historical Narration, and the Critique of Nationhood in Toni Morrison's *Paradise.*" *African American Review* 35, no. 2 (2001).

Daniel, Walter C. "Langston Hughes versus the Black Preachers in the *Pittsburgh Courier* in the 1930s." In *Critical Essays on Langston Hughes,* edited by Edward J. Mullen, 129–35. Boston: G. K. Hall, 1986.

Davis, Thadious. *Nella Larsen, Novelist of the Harlem Renaissance: A Woman's Life Unveiled*. Baton Rouge: Louisiana State University Press, 1994.

Dawahare, Anthony. *Nationalism, Marxism, and African-American Literature between the Wars: A New Pandora's Box*. Jackson: University Press of Mississippi, 2003.

Douglas, Kelly Brown. *The Black Christ*. Maryknoll, N.Y.: Orbis Books, 1994.

Douglas, Robert L. "Religious Orthodoxy and Skepticism in Richard Wright's *Uncle Tom's Children* and *Native Son*." In *Richard Wright: Myths and Realities*, edited by C. James Trotman, 79–88. New York: Garland, 1988.

Doyle, Mary Ellen. *Voices from the Quarters: The Fiction of Ernest J. Gaines*. Baton Rouge: Louisiana State University Press, 2002.

Dray, Philip. *At the Hands of Persons Unknown: The Lynching of Black America*. New York: Modern Library, 2002.

duCille, Ann. *The Coupling Convention: Sex, Text, and Tradition in Black Women's Fiction*. New York: Oxford University Press, 1993.

Dyson, Michael Eric. *Come Hell or High Water: Hurricane Katrina and the Color of Disaster*. New York: Civitas, 2006.

Early, Gerald. Introduction to *My Soul's High Song: The Collected Writings of Countee Cullen*. New York: Anchor, 1991.

Edelberg, Cynthia Dubin. "Morrison's Voices: Formal Education, the Work Ethic, and the Bible." *American Literature* 58, no. 2 (May 1986): 217–37.

Eliade, Mircea. *The Sacred and the Profane: The Nature of Religion*. New York: Harper and Row, 1957.

Emanuel, James A. "Christ in Alabama: Religion in the Poetry of Langston Hughes." In *Modern Black Poets: A Collection of Critical Essays*, edited by Donald B. Gibson, 57–68. Englewood Cliffs, N.J.: Prentice-Hall, 1973.

Evans, James H. *Spiritual Empowerment in Afro-American Literature*. Lewiston, N.Y.: Edwin Mellen Press, 1987.

Fabre, Michel. *The Unfinished Quest of Richard Wright*. 2nd ed. Urbana: University of Illinois Press, 1993.

Fauset, Arthur Huff. *Black Gods of the Metropolis: Negro Religious Cults of the Urban North*. Philadelphia: University of Pennsylvania Press, 1944.

Felder, Cain Hope, ed. *Stony the Road We Trod: African-American Biblical Interpretation*. Minneapolis: Augsburg Fortress, 1991.

Ferguson, Blanche E. *Countee Cullen and the Negro Renaissance*. New York: Dodd, Mead, 1966.

Fishel, Leslie, Jr., and Benjamin Quarles. "In the New Deal's Wake." In *The Segregation Era 1863–1954: A Modern Reader*, edited by Allen Weinstein and Frank Otto Gatell, 218–32. New York: Oxford University Press, 1970.

Fisk University. *Unwritten History of Slavery: Autobiographical Accounts of Ex-Slaves*. Nashville: Fisk University Social Science Institute, 1945. In *The American Slave: A Composite Autobiography*, vol. 18, edited by George P. Rawick. Westport, Ct.: Greenwood, 1972.

Foulks, Beverly. "Trial by Fire: The Theodicy of Toni Morrison in *Sula*." In *Toni Morrison and the Bible: Contested Intertextualities*, edited by Shirley A. Stave, 8–25. New York: Peter Lang, 2006.

Fyall, Robert. *Now My Eyes Have Seen You: Images of Creation and Evil in the Book of Job*. Downers Grove, Ill.: InterVarsity Press, 2002.

Gates, Henry Louis, Jr. *The Signifying Monkey: A Theory of African-American Literary Criticism*. New York: Oxford University Press, 1988.

Gilkes, Cheryl Townsend. "The 'Loves' and 'Troubles' of African-American Women's Bodies: The Womanist Challenge to Cultural Humiliation and Community Ambivalence." In *A Troubling in My Soul: Womanist Perspectives on Evil and Suffering*, edited by Emilie M. Townes, 232–49. Maryknoll, N.Y.: Orbis, 1993.

Glenn, Cheryl. *Unspoken: A Rhetoric of Silence*. Carbondale: Southern Illinois University Press, 2004.

Gordon, Lewis. *Existence in Black: An Anthology of Black Existential Philosophy*. New York: Routledge, 1997.

Grant, Jacquelyn. "The Sin of Servanthood: And the Deliverance of Discipleship." In *A Troubling in My Soul: Womanist Perspectives on Evil and Suffering*, edited by Emilie M. Townes, 199–218. Maryknoll, N.Y.: Orbis, 1993.

———. *White Woman's Christ and Black Woman's Jesus: Feminist Christology and Womanist Response*. New York: Oxford University Press, 1990.

Griffin, Farah Jasmine. *Who Set You Flowin': The African-American Migration Narrative*. New York: Oxford University Press, 1995.

Hagee, John. Interview by Terry Gross. *Fresh Air*. National Public Radio, WHYY, Philadelphia, September 18, 2006.

Hakutani, Yoshinobu. "Richard Wright's *The Outsider* and Albert Camus's *The Stranger*." *Mississippi Quarterly: The Journal of Southern Culture* 42, no. 4 (1989): 365–78.

Hardy, Clarence. *James Baldwin's God: Sex, Hope, and Crisis in Black Holiness Culture*. Knoxville: University of Tennessee, 2003.

Harris, Trudier. *Black Women in the Fiction of James Baldwin*. Knoxville: University of Tennessee Press, 1985.

———. *Exorcising Blackness: Historical and Literary Lynchings and Burning Rituals*. Bloomington: Indiana University Press, 1984.

———. "Failed, Forgotten, Forsaken: Christianity in Contemporary African American Literature." E. Maynard Adams Lecture, University of North Carolina in Chapel Hill. October 7, 2007.

———. "Lynching." In *The Companion to Southern Literature: Themes, Genres, Places, People, Movements and Motifs*, edited by Joseph M. Flora and Lucinda MacKethan, 464. Baton Rouge: Louisiana State University Press, 2002.

———. *Saints, Sinners, Saviors: Strong Black Women in African American Literature*. New York: Palgrave, 2001.

———. "Three Black Women Writers and Humanism: A Folk Perspective." In *Black American Literature and Humanism*, edited by R. Baxter Miller, 50–74. Lexington: University Press of Kentucky, 1981.

Hayes, Floyd W., III. "The Concept of Double Vision in Richard Wright's *The Outsider:* Fragmented Blackness in the Age of Nihilism." In *Existence in Black: An Anthology of Black Existential Philosophy*, edited by Lewis Gordon, 173–83. New York: Routledge, 1997.

Hengel, Martin. *Crucifixion in the Ancient World and the Folly of the Message of the Cross*. Philadelphia: Fortress Press, 1977.

Herskovits, Melville J. *The Myth of the Negro Past*. 1941. Boston: Beacon Press, 1990.

Hewitt, Glenn A. *Regeneration and Morality: A Study of Charles Finney, Charles Hodge, John W. Nevin, and Horace Bushnell*. New York: Carlson, 1991.

Hick, John. *Evil and the God of Love*. New York: Harper and Row, 1966.

———. *Philosophy of Religion*. 4th ed. New Jersey: Prentice Hall, 1990.

———. "The World as a Vale of Soul-Making." In *The Problem of Evil: Selected Readings*, edited by Michael L. Peterson. Notre Dame: University of Notre Dame Press, 1992.

Higginbotham, Evelyn Brooks. *Righteous Discontent: The Woman's Movement in the Black Baptist Church 1880–1920*. Cambridge: Harvard University Press, 1993.

Higgins, Therese E. *Religiosity, Cosmology, and Folklore: The African Influence in the Novels of Toni Morrison*. New York: Routledge, 2001.

Honko, Lauri. "The Problem of Defining Myth." In *Sacred Narrative: Readings in the Theory of Myth*, edited by Alan Dundes, 41–52. Berkeley and Los Angeles: University of California Press, 1984.

hooks, bell. *Talking Back: thinking feminist, thinking black*. Boston: South End Press, 1989.

———. "Writing the Subject: Reading *The Color Purple*." In *Alice Walker: Modern Critical Views*, edited by Harold Bloom, 215–28. New York: Chelsea House, 1989.

Hopkins, Dwight N., and George C. L. Cummings, eds. *Cut Loose Your Stammering Tongue: Black Theology in the Slave Narratives*. Louisville: Westminster John Knox Press, 2003.

Hubbard, Dolan. *The Sermon and the African American Literary Imagination*. Columbia: University of Missouri Press, 1994.

Huggins, Nathan. *Harlem Renaissance*. London: Oxford University Press, 1981.

Hume, David. *Dialogues Concerning Natural Religion*. 1779. In *Ten Essential Texts in the Philosophy of Religion*, edited by Steven M. Cahn. New York: Oxford University Press, 2005.

Hunter, Patricia L. "Women's Power—Women's Passion: And God Said, "That's Good." In *A Troubling in My Soul: Womanist Perspectives on Evil and Suffering*, edited by Emilie M. Townes, 189–98. Maryknoll, N.Y.: Orbis, 1993.

Johnson, Clifton H., ed. *God Struck Me Dead: Voices of Ex-Slaves* 1969. Cleveland: Pilgrim Press, 1993.

Johnson, Sylvester. "Tribalism and Religious Identity in the Work of Richard Wright." *Literature & Theology* 20, no. 2 (June 2006): 171–88.

Jones, Carolyn M. "*Sula* and *Beloved:* Images of Cain in the Novels of Toni Morrison." *African American Review* 27, no. 4 (1993): 615–26.

Jones, William R. *Is God a White Racist? A Preamble to Black Theology.* Boston: Beacon Press, 1973.

Katz, Tamar. "Didacticism and Epistolary Form in *The Color Purple.*" In *Alice Walker: Modern Critical Views*, edited by Harold Bloom, 185–94. New York: Chelsea House, 1989.

Klein, Marcus. "James Baldwin: A Question of Identity." In *James Baldwin: Modern Critical Views*, edited by Harold Bloom, 17–36. New York: Chelsea House, 1986.

Larson, Charles. *Invisible Darkness: Jean Toomer & Nella Larsen.* Iowa City: University of Iowa Press, 1993.

Lauret, Marie. *Alice Walker.* New York: St. Martin's Press, 2000.

Lee, Bryan. *Katrina Was Her Name.* Justin Time Records. Compact disc. 2007.

Lincoln, C. Eric, and Lawrence H. Mamiya. *The Black Church in the African American Experience.* Durham: Duke University Press, 1990.

Lundin, Roger. Introduction to *There Before Us: Religion, Literature, and Culture from Emerson to Wendell Berry*, x–xxii. Grand Rapids, Mich.: William Eerdmans, 2007.

Lynch, Michael. "Haunted by Innocence: The Debate with Dostoevsky in Wright's 'Other Novel,' *The Outsider.*" *African American Review* 30, no. 2 (1996): 255–66.

Margolies, Edward. *The Art of Richard Wright.* Carbondale: Southern Illinois University Press, 1969.

———. "The Negro Church: James Baldwin and the Christian Vision." In *James Baldwin: Modern Critical Views*, edited by Harold Bloom, 59–76. New York: Chelsea House, 1986.

Matthews, Donald H. *Honoring the Ancestors: An African Cultural Interpretation of Black Religion and Literature.* New York: Oxford University Press, 1998.

Mays, Benjamin E. *The Negro's God as Reflected in His Literature.* 1938. New York: Russell and Russell, 1968.

Mbiti, John. *African Religions and Philosophy.* 2nd ed. Oxford: Heinemann, 1969.

McDowell, Deborah E. "'The Changing Same': Generational Connections and Black Woman Novelists." In *Reading Black, Reading Feminist: A Critical Anthology*, edited by Henry Louis Gates Jr., 91–115. New York: Meridian, 1990.

McLoughlin, William G. *Modern Revivalism: Charles Grandison Finney to Billy Graham.* New York: Roland Press, 1959.

Mesle, C. Robert. *John Hick's Theodicy: A Process Humanist Critique.* New York: St. Martin's Press: 1991.

Mill, John Stuart. *Three Essays on Religion.* New York: H. Holt, 1884.

Mitchell, Carolyn A. "'I Love to Tell the Story': Biblical Revisions in *Beloved.*" *Religion and Literature* 23, no. 2 (1991).

Mitchem, Stephanie. *Introducing Womanist Theology.* Maryknoll, N.Y.: Orbis, 2002.

Montgomery, Maxine Lavon. *The Apocalypse in African American Fiction.* Gainesville: University Press of Florida, 1996.

Moody, Joycelyn. *Sentimental Confessions: Spiritual Narratives of Nineteenth-Century African-American Women.* Athens: University of Georgia Press, 2001.

Morey, Ann-Janine "Margaret Atwood and Toni Morrison: Reflections on Postmodernism and the Study of Religion and Literature." *Journal of the American Academy of Religion* 60, no. 3 (1992): 493–513.

Morrison, Toni. "The Ancestor as Foundation." In *Black Women Writers (1950–1980): A Critical Evaluation,* edited by Mari Evans, 339–45. New York: Anchor, 1984.

————. Interview by Elizabeth Farnsworth. *The NewsHour with Jim Lehrer,* March 9, 1998. www.pbs.org/newshour/bb/entertainment/jan-june98/morrison_3-9.html.

Mosher, Marlene. "James Baldwin's Blues." In *James Baldwin: Modern Critical Views,* edited by Harold Bloom, 111–20. New York: Chelsea House, 1986.

Murray, Donald C. "James Baldwin's 'Sonny's Blues': Complicated and Simple." *Studies in Short Fiction* 14 (1977): 353–57.

Myrdal, Gunner. *An American Dilemma: The Negro Problem and Modern Democracy.* New York: Harper and Row, 1944.

Neiman, Susan. *Evil in Modern Thought: An Alternative History of Philosophy.* Princeton: Princeton University Press, 2002.

Nolan, Paul T. *Marc Connelly.* New York: Twayne, 1969.

O'Neale, Sondra A. "Fathers, Gods, and Religion: Perceptions of Christianity and Ethnic Faith in James Baldwin." In *Critical Essays on James Baldwin,* edited by Fred L. Standley and Nancy V. Burt, 125–43. Boston: G. K. Hall, 1988.

Ortlund, Raymond C., Jr. *God's Unfaithful Wife: A Biblical Theology of Spiritual Adultery.* Downers Grove, Ill.: InterVarsity Press, 2002.

Oyelade, E. O. "Evil in Yoruba Religion and Culture." In *Evil and the Response of World Religion,* edited by William Cenkner, 157–69. St. Paul, Minn.: Paragon House, 1997.

Page, Philip. "Furrowing All the Brows: Interpretation and the Transcendent in Toni Morrison's *Paradise.*" *African American Review* 35, no. 4 (2001): 637–49.

Papa, Lee. "'His Feet on Your Neck': The New Religion in the Works of Ernest J. Gaines." *African American Review* 27, no. 2 (summer 1993).

Patterson, Orlando. *Slavery and Social Death.* Cambridge: Harvard University Press, 1982.

Pessoni, Michele. "'She Was Laughing at Their God': Discovering the Goddess within in *Sula.*" *African American Review* 29, no. 3 (1995): 439–51.

Peterson, Carla L. *"Doers of the Word": African-American Women Speakers and Writers in the North (1830–1880)*. New York: Oxford University Press, 1995.

Peterson, Michael L. *The Problem of Evil: Selected Readings*. Notre Dame: University of Notre Dame Press, 1992.

Pierce, Yolanda. *Hell without Fires: Slavery, Christianity, and the Antebellum Slave Narrative*. Gainesville: University Press of Florida, 2005.

Pinn, Anthony. *African-American Humanist Principles: Living and Thinking Like the Children of Nimrod*. New York: Palgrave, 2004.

———, ed. *By These Hands: A Documentary History of African-American Humanism*. New York: New York University Press, 2001.

———, ed. *Moral Evil and Redemptive Suffering: A History of Theodicy in African-American Religious Thought*. Gainesville: University Press of Florida, 2002.

———. *Varieties of African-American Religious Experience*. Minneapolis: Augsburg Fortress, 1998.

———. *Why Lord? Suffering and Evil in Black Theology*. New York: Continuum, 1995.

Powers, Peter Kerry. "Elephants in the Room." Review of *Faithful Vision: Treatments of the Sacred, Spiritual, and Supernatural in Twentieth-Century African American Fiction*, by James W. Coleman. *Twentieth-Century Literature* 52, no. 3 (fall 2006): 352–59.

———. *Recalling Religions: Resistance, Memory, and Cultural Revision in Ethnic Women's Literature*. Knoxville: University of Tennessee Press, 2001.

Raboteau, Albert J. *A Fire in the Bones: Reflections on African-American Religious History*. Boston: Beacon Press, 1995.

———. *Slave Religion: The "Invisible Institution" in the Antebellum South*. New York: Oxford University Press, 1978.

Radin, Paul. "Status, Fantasy, and the Christian Dogma." In *God Struck Me Dead: Voices of Ex-Slaves*, edited by Clifton H. Johnson, vii–xii. Ohio: Pilgrim Press, 1969.

Rampersad, Arnold. *The Life of Langston Hughes*. Vol. 1, *1902–1941: I, Too, Sing America*. New York: Oxford University Press, 1986.

———. *The Life of Langston Hughes*. Vol. 2, *1941–1967: I Dream a World*. New York: Oxford University Press, 1988.

Redding, J. Saunders. *To Make a Poet Black*. 1939. Ithaca: Cornell University Press, 1998.

Roberts, J. Deotis. "Faith in God Confronts Collective Evils." In *Moral Evil and Redemptive Suffering: A History of Theodicy in African-American Thought*, edited by Anthony Pinn, 302–14. Gainesville: University Press of Florida, 2002.

Roberts, John W. "The Individual and the Community in Two Short Stories by Ernest J. Gaines." *Black American Literature Forum* 18, no. 3 (autumn 1984): 110–13.

Rodd, C. S. *The Book of Job*. Philadelphia: Trinity Press International, 1990.

Rodgers, Lawrence. *Canaan Bound: The African American Great Migration Novel.* Urbana: University of Illinois Press, 1997.

Rowley, Hazel. *Richard Wright: The Life and Times.* New York: Henry Holt, 2001.

Ryken, Leland, James C. Wilhoit, and Tremper Longman III, eds. *Dictionary of Biblical Imagery.* Downers Grove, Ill.: InterVarsity Press, 1998.

Sartre, Jean-Paul. "Existentialism Is a Humanism." 1946. In *Existentialism from Dostoevsky to Sartre,* edited by Walter Kaufmann. Cleveland: Meridian, 1956.

Schmid, Peter. "An Interview with Richard Wright." 1946. In *Conversations with Richard Wright,* edited by Kenneth Kinnamon and Michel Fabre, 106–10. Jackson: University Press of Mississippi, 1993.

Sernett, Milton C. *Bound for the Promised Land: African American Religion and the Great Migration.* Durham: Duke University Press, 1997.

Shillito, Edward. Review of *The Black Christ and Other Poems,* by Countée Cullen. *Southern Workman* 59, no. 2 (February 1930): 92–93.

Smith, Petric, and Elizabeth Cobbs. *Long Time Coming: An Insider's Story of the Birmingham Church Bombing That Rocked the World.* Birmingham: Crane Hills, 1994.

Smith, Theophus H. *Conjuring Culture: Biblical Formations of Black America.* New York: Oxford University Press, 1994.

Smylie, James H. "Countée Cullen's 'The Black Christ.'" *Theology Today* 38, no. 2 (July 1981): 160–73.

Snead, James A. "Repetition as a Figure of Black Culture." In *The Jazz Cadence of American Culture,* edited by Robert G. O'Meally, 62–81. New York: Columbia University Press, 1998.

Sobel, Mechal. *Trabelin' On: The Slave Journey to an Afro-Baptist Faith.* Westport, Conn.: Greenwood Press, 1979.

Sollors, Werner. *Neither Black nor White Yet Both: Thematic Explorations of Interracial Literature.* New York: Oxford University Press, 1997.

Stackhouse, John G. *Can God Be Trusted? Faith and the Challenge of Evil.* New York: Oxford University Press, 1998.

Stave, Shirley A. "The Master's Tools: Morrison's *Paradise* and the Problem of Christianity." In *Toni Morrison and the Bible: Contested Intertextualities,* edited by Stave, 215–31. New York: Peter Lang, 2006.

———, ed. *Toni Morrison and the Bible: Contested Intertexualities.* New York: Peter Lang, 2006.

Stepto, Robert B. "'Intimate Things in Place': A Conversation with Toni Morrison." In *Toni Morrison: Critical Perspectives Past and Present,* edited by Henry Louis Gates Jr. and K. A. Appiah, 378–95. New York: Amistad, 1993.

Sundquist, Eric. *To Wake the Nations: Race in the Making of American Literature.* Cambridge: Harvard University Press, 1993.

Tate, Claudia. "Christian Existentialism in *The Outsider.*" In *Richard Wright: Critical Perspectives Past and Present,* edited by Henry Louis Gates Jr. and K. A. Appiah, 369–87. New York: Amistad, 1993.

———. "Death and Desire in *Quicksand,* by Nella Larsen." *American Literary History* 7, no. 2 (1995): 234–60.

———. *Psychoanalysis and Black Novels: Desire and the Protocols of Race.* New York: Oxford University Press, 1998.

Thurman, Howard. "Suffering." In *Moral Evil and Redemptive Suffering: A History of Theodicy in African-American Thought,* edited by Anthony Pinn, 227–45. Gainesville: University Press of Florida, 2002.

Townes, Emilie M., ed. *Embracing the Spirit: Womanist Perspectives on Hope, Salvation, and Transformation.* Maryknoll, N.Y.: Orbis, 1997.

———. "Living in the New Jerusalem: The Rhetoric and Movement of Liberation in the House of Evil." In *A Troubling in My Soul: Womanist Perspectives on Evil and Suffering,* edited by Townes, 78–91. Maryknoll, N.Y.: Orbis, 1993.

Turner, Darwin. *In a Minor Chord: Three Afro-American Writers and Their Search for Identity.* Carbondale: Southern Illinois University Press, 1971.

United States Senate. Executive Sessions of the Senate Permanent Subcommittee on Investigations of the Committee on Government Operations. Vol. 2, *Testimony of Samuel Dashiell Hammett; Helen Goldfrank; Jerre G. Mangione; and James Langston Hughes.* 83rd Cong., 1st sess., 1953, 945–98. Washington: GPO, 2003.

Wall, Cheryl A. *Women of the Harlem Renaissance.* Bloomington: Indiana University Press, 1995.

Wall, Wendy. "Lettered Bodies and Corporeal Texts." In *Alice Walker: Critical Perspectives Past and Present,* edited by Henry Louis Gates Jr. and K. A. Appiah, 261–74. New York: Amistad Press, 1993.

Weems, Renita J. *Battered Love: Marriage, Sex, and Violence in the Hebrew Prophets.* Minneapolis: Fortress Press, 1995.

West, Cornel. "American Africans in Conflict: Alienation in an Insecure Culture." In *African American Religious Thought: An Anthology,* edited by Cornel West and Eddie S. Glaude Jr., 77–98. Louisville: Westminster John Knox Press, 2003.

West, Cornel, and Eddie S. Glaude Jr., eds. *African American Religious Thought: An Anthology.* Louisville: Westminster John Knox Press, 2003.

———. "Black Strivings in a Twilight Civilization." In *The Cornel West Reader,* 87–118. New York: Basic Civitas Books, 1999.

Whitted, Qiana J. "Using My Grandmother's Life as a Model": Richard Wright and the Gendered Politics of Religious Representation." *Southern Literary Journal* 36, no. 2 (2004): 13–30.

Williams, Delores S. *Sisters in the Wilderness: The Challenge of Womanist God-Talk.* Maryknoll, N.Y.: Orbis, 1993.

Wood, Clement. "The Black Pegasus." *Opportunity* 8, no. 3 (March 1930): 93.

Wood, Frances E. "'Take My Yoke upon You': The Role of the Church in the Oppression of African-American Women." In *A Troubling in My Soul: Womanist Perspectives on Evil and Suffering,* edited by Emilie M. Townes. Maryknoll, N.Y.: Orbis, 1993.

Wright, Richard. "Blueprint for Negro Writing." 1937. In *African American Literary Theory: A Reader,* edited by Winston Napier, 45–53. New York: New York University Press, 2000.

———. *12 Million Black Voices.* New York: Thunder's Mouth Press, 1941.

Zangrando, Robert L. *The NAACP Crusades against Lynching, 1909–1950.* Philadelphia: Temple University Press, 1980.

# INDEX

Larsen, Nella: biographical information, 197n8; and post–World War I religious representation, 3. See also *Quicksand*
Larson, Charles, 88
Lauret, Maria, 101
Lavender, Bill, 185–87
Lee, Bryan (musician), 184
*Lesson Before Dying, A* (Gaines), 199n2
lynching: and crucifixion, 38–41; historical background, 34, 39; and the law, 46–47; as represented in literature, 32–33, 35. *See also* violence, racial

manhood, and religious identity, 55, 112, 135–36, 142, 145, 195n10. *See also* paternalism, religious
Margolies, Edward, 196n18, 200n6
marriage, 77–79, 82–83, 89–90, 92–96, 102, 159
Matthews, Donald H., 2, 19
Mays, Benjamin E. See *Negro's God, as Reflected in His Literature*
Mbiti, John S., 73, 194n5
McDowell, Deborah E., 99, 104
McKay, Claude, 36
"Memories of My Grandmother" (Wright), 62, 65, 70–71
*Meridian* (Walker), 166, 198n13, 198n17
Mesle, C. Robert, 197–98n11
Mill, John Stuart, 124, 125
Mitchem, Stephanie, 10–11
Morrison, Toni, 100–201n13. *See also specific titles*
Moses and Hebrew Deliverance. *See* Exodus
Mosher, Marlene, 200n10
motherhood: as "church mother" figure, 44, 71–72, 81–82, 112; and sin, 73, 89–90; and spiritual guidance, 57, 60–61, 63–65, 91, 128, 141–43, 174–76
mourner's bench, 54, 56–60, 67, 69–70, 72–73. *See also* conversion experiences, spiritual
*Mozart and Leadbelly: Stories and Essays* (Gaines), 112, 146
Murray, Donald C., 115, 135–36, 200n10
Murray, Victoria Christopher, 187
Myrdal, Gunnar, 75

*Native Son* (Wright), 19–20, 64, 71–73
*Negro's God, as Reflected in His Literature, The*, 2–4, 16–18, 83, 187
Neiman, Susan, 4, 5, 9, 49, 120–21

New Negro (Harlem Renaissance), xiv, 3, 16, 36, 83–86
New Testament. *See under* Christ, Jesus; cups, biblical significance of
Nolan, James, 184

*Of Love and Dust* (Gaines), 201n19
Old Testament, prophecy, 14, 78–79, 107, 139, 161–62, 165–66. *See also* Deuteronomy; Exodus; Job
O'Neale, Sondra, 22, 115
Ortlund, Raymond C., Jr., 78, 80, 107
otherworldly belief: criticisms of, 24, 50, 67, 71, 90; promotion of, 3, 17, 50, 64, 80, 94–95, 100
*Outsider, The* (Wright), 61, 68, 196n19

paganism, as distinct from Christianity, 33, 38, 78–79, 81
Page, Philip, 155, 161, 202n9
Papa, Lee, 123
*Parable of the Sower, The* (Butler), 21–22
*Paradise* (Morrison), 148–81
paternalism, religious, 20–21, 60, 78–79, 89, 155, 157, 161–64. *See also* manhood, and religious identity
Patterson, Orlando, 36
Payne, Daniel Alexander, 16
Peterson, Michael L., 1, 5–6, 9, 27, 180
Pierce, Yolanda, 14–15
Pinn, Anthony, 7, 11, 34, 49, 91–92, 113, 177–78, 200n4
Powers, Peter Kerry, 191n17, 198n18
preachers and preaching, 59–60, 72, 84, 93–94, 122–24, 153–54, 167–71, 177–79
problem of evil: definitions of, 1–2, 4, 5–11, 16, 27, 114–15; and philosophy of religion, 5, 20, 127–28, 147–49, 177–81. *See also* evil, moral and natural distinctions

*Quicksand* (Larsen), 3, 64, 82–92, 98, 100

Raboteau, Albert, 54, 57–58, 156
Radin, Paul, 190–91n10
*Raisin in the Sun, A* (Hansberry), 21
Rampersad, Arnold, xii–xvi
Reconstruction, era of, and post-Emancipation: literary representations of, 15–16, 155–57; religious history during, 4–5
Roberts, J. Deotis, 8, 35
Roberts, John, 143